falling in
love again

falling in love again

Romantic Comedy in Contemporary Cinema

Edited by
**Stacey Abbott &
Deborah Jermyn**

I.B. TAURIS
LONDON · NEW YORK

Published in 2009 by I.B.Tauris & Co Ltd
6 Salem Road, London W2 4BU
175 Fifth Avenue, New York NY 10010
www.ibtauris.com

In the United States of America and Canada
distributed by Palgrave Macmillan, a division of St Martin's Press
175 Fifth Avenue, New York NY 10010

ISBN 978 1 84511 771 9

A full CIP record for this book is available from the British Library
A full CIP record is available from the Library of Congress

Library of Congress Catalog Card Number: available

Typeset by JCS Publishing Services Ltd, www.jcs-publishing.co.uk
Printed and bound in India by Thomson Press India Ltd

~

Deborah dedicates this book to Matt –
More Marlon than Hugh, but always my leading man
– you had me at 'Cello'.

~

Stacey dedicates this book to Simon –
♫ *'And that smile that wrinkles your nose,*
Touches my foolish heart.' ♫

~

Contents

~ *Illustrations*

~ *Contributors*

Stacey Abbott is Senior Lecturer in Film and TV at Roehampton University. She is the author of *Celluloid Vampires* (University of Texas Press, 2007) and *Angel* (Wayne State University Press, forthcoming). She has also edited and co-edited collections on the television series *Angel* and *Alias.*

Karen Bowdre received her doctorate in film and television studies at the University of Southern California's School of Cinema-Television. She is currently an Assistant Professor of Media Studies at Indiana University. Her research interests include race and representation, gender, adaptation, romantic comedies and telenovelas.

Alan Dodd is a PhD candidate at Aberdeen University. His research focuses on the relationship between traditional Hollywood stardom and present celebrity culture. Conference papers include 'From Hollywood to *heat*: J.Lo and Synergy' (2005) and 'The War of the "Roses": Kate Winslet and Contemporary Hollywood Stardom' (SCMS, 2007).

Martin Fradley teaches American Studies at the University of Manchester. He has published variously on topics such as the films of Oliver Stone, masculinity in *Gladiator* and on the contemporary American horror genre.

Lesley Harbidge is Lecturer in Film Studies at the University of Glamorgan. Her broad research interests lie in contemporary American cinema and comedy, and she is particularly interested in the work of Steve Martin, the tradition of comedian comedy, stand-up, audiences and laughter.

Claire Hines is Senior Lecturer in Film and Television Studies at Southampton Solent University. She is the co-editor of *Hard to Swallow* (Wallflower, forthcoming), a collection of articles on hardcore screen pornography. She has published articles on James Bond, gender representation and queerness in contemporary film and TV.

Annabelle Honess Roe is a doctoral candidate in the critical studies PhD programme at the University of Southern California's School of Cinematic Arts in Los Angeles.

Tamar Jeffers McDonald is Lecturer in Film Studies at the University of Kent. She is the author of *Romantic Comedy: Boy Meets Girl Meets Genre* (Wallflower, 2007) and *Hollywood Catwalk: Exploring Costume in Mainstream Film* (I.B.Tauris, forthcoming). She is currently researching film costume, male-focused rom-coms, and Doris Day.

Deborah Jermyn is Senior Lecturer in Film and TV at Roehampton University. She is the author of *Crime Watching: Investigating Real Crime TV* (I.B.Tauris, 2007) and *Sex and the City* (Wayne State University Press, 2009) and happily admits to having been teary-eyed in *Notting Hill.*

Janet McCabe is Research Fellow (TV Drama) at Manchester Metropolitan University. She is author of *Feminist Film Studies: Writing the Woman into Cinema* (Wallflower, 2004), and co-editor of several collections on contemporary American TV, including *Sex and the City* and *Desperate Housewives.*

Hilary Radner holds the Foundation Chair of Film and Media Studies at the University of Otago. Her publications include: *Shopping Around: Feminine Culture and the Pursuit of Pleasure* (Routledge, 1995), as co-editor, *Swinging Single: Representing Sexuality in the 1960s* (University of Minnesota Press, 1999), *Jane Campion: Cinema, Nation, Identity* (Wayne State University Press, forthcoming).

Sean Redmond is Senior Lecturer in Film Studies at the University of Victoria, Wellington. He is the co-editor of *Framing Celebrity: New Directions in Celebrity Culture* (Routledge, 2006) and *Stardom and Celebrity: A Reader* (Sage, 2007). He has published in journals such as the *Journal of Consumer Culture, Scope* and *Screening the Past.*

Brigitte Rollet is Senior Lecturer in French at the University of London Institute in Paris, author of *Coline Serreau* (Manchester University Press, 1998), and co-author of *Cinema and the Second Sex: Women's Filmmaking in France 1980s–1990s* (Continuum, 2001). Her book

Télévision et Homosexualité: 10 ans de fictions françaises 1995-2005 (L'Harmattan, Paris) was published in 2007.

Kyle Stevens is a doctoral candidate at the University of Pittsburgh. He is currently writing his dissertation, which examines how cinematic characters make claims upon the spectator in the films of Mike Nichols.

Robynn J. Stilwell is Associate Professor in Performing Arts at Georgetown University. Her research interests primarily centre on the meaning of music as cultural work. Topics in her publications on film and television music include constructions of gender and class, the aestheticisation of violence, musical numbers across genres and figure skating competitions.

Paul Sutton is Principal Lecturer in Film Studies at Roehampton University. He has published articles on cinematic spectatorship, French and Italian cinema and the cinematic remake. He is currently preparing *Remaking Film: In History, in Theory* (Blackwell, forthcoming).

Acknowledgements

WHILE HAVING LONGSTANDING interests in genre, we came to this book from very different backgrounds. After years of writing about the darker side of popular culture (vampires for Stacey; TV crime shows for Deborah) it has been a delight to immerse ourselves in the world of the rom-com. While we would resist the familiar presumption that rom-coms are always or necessarily 'light', they are, more often than not, *bright*. Part of this project's 'feel-good factor' has come, too, from working with such an enthusiastic team of scholars, who shared our sense of the significance and neglect of the genre and who came to it with a diversity of fresh perspectives. We thank them for all of the creativity and commitment they brought to this book. We are also grateful to Philippa Brewster and her colleagues at I.B.Tauris, particularly Jessica Cuthbert-Smith, for wholeheartedly supporting the idea for this book and its development. Special thanks, finally, to Simon Brown and Matt Wagner, for watching rom-coms beyond the call of duty, and hardly ever complaining.

Introduction – A Lot Like Love

The Romantic Comedy in Contemporary Cinema

~ Stacey Abbott and Deborah Jermyn ~

[It contains] brilliant insights into human nature; it is visually breathtaking . . . It has been on my list of the five best movies ever made ever since I saw it in 1979, chiefly for its realistic dialogue and probing commentary on the desperate nature of human beings in search of love . . . It captures the times perfectly . . . And as a hilarious commentary on the human instinct to find someone to love no matter what the consequences, there is nothing finer.

IN THIS REVIEW, posted in 1999 on the user comments board of the Internet Movie Database (imdb.com), 'suze 12' expresses how the film in question moved her. She describes the way it has stayed with her for two decades and how, in a sense, it touched something in her, opening her mind to contemplate the human condition more closely. She speaks too of its command of the language of cinema ('it is visually breathtaking'), of its skill in rendering the zeitgeist of its age ('it captures the times perfectly') and elevates it to the status of high art by suggesting that it reveals something about the fundamental desires that lie at the very heart of our being ('as a commentary on the human instinct to find someone to love . . . there is nothing finer'). And yet, surprisingly it could be argued, the film being championed is a romantic comedy or 'rom-com', a genre that in the hierarchy of most worthwhile, most thought-provoking or most culturally incisive film movements lurks somewhere down around the action or exploitation movie. Admittedly, the rom-com in question here has more serious credentials than most; 'suze 12' is referring to auteur and independent filmmaker Woody Allen's critically acclaimed *Manhattan* (1979). Yet we open with this quote from an 'ordinary' viewer (albeit one who posts on the IMDb) since it encapsulates a great deal about the tensions that surround the rom-com, tensions that this book in part seeks to address.

While rom-coms in recent years have often struggled to be taken seriously – to win awards or critical enthusiasm or academic attention – they have remained beloved of fans and a virtually constant presence in popular cinema in some shape or form since the 1930s. Allen's *Manhattan*, like its 'nervous romance' predecessor *Annie Hall* (1977), succeeded in attracting all these forms of attention precisely because it was seen in many ways at this time as *reinventing* a tired and predictable genre. It returned to and reimagined New York during a period of urban and economic decline, embracing it, not as the antithesis but as the epitome of romance; it placed an unlikely neurotic and narcissistic male in the lead (anti-)hero role, a figure far removed from the dashing romantic norm; and it dared to end equivocally, without a happy ending or a romantic future evidently in place. To win critical approbation within the broad arena of the rom-com by the late 1970s, it seemed, one had to *undo* the popular image of it.

The low critical esteem that typically meets the rom-com in contemporary cinema derives from a number of arenas. First, its audience is enduringly presumed to be predominantly female and 'chick flicks' in all their incarnations are frequently critically constructed as inherently trite or lightweight. Second, romantic fiction generally is thought to be essentially calculating in its execution, cynically manipulating an emotional and sentimental response from the viewer (witness the merciless teasing that Suzy (Rita Wilson) endures in *Sleepless in Seattle* (1993) from Sam (Tom Hanks) and Greg (Victor Garber) when she tearfully describes her affection for *An Affair To Remember* (1957)). Furthermore, the genre is widely depicted as slavishly formulaic, adhering to well-worn and obvious conventions (boy meets girl; boy and girl face obstacles to their romantic union; boy and girl conquer obstacles to find true love). Finally, the perception of comedy per se as inherently frivolous and anti-intellectual has resulted in its critical and cultural marginalisation, where it is presumed that eliciting laughs from the audience is antithetical to 'serious' reflection.

This popular account of the rom-com, which, like the critique it formulates, might itself be described as 'well-worn', fails to recognise adequately a number of significant qualities within and issues raised by the genre which are addressed in the essays that follow here. First, it is important both to acknowledge and seek to understand how the genre facilitates the kind of powerful emotional and personal investment often described by viewers such as 'suze 12'. Second, the presumption that rom-coms constitute a self-evident category belies the fact that this is an often contested and somewhat elusive 'genre', marked by numerous different inflections rather than clearly defined generic boundaries. Third, and linked to this, while the rom-com frequently maintains certain of its traditions and conventions it is nevertheless a *living* genre. While many other genres, such as the Western and horror, have been widely explored with a recognition of their capacity to evolve, the contemporary rom-com has less often been understood as one that continues to negotiate and respond dynamically to the issues and preoccupations of its time.

Hence *Falling in Love Again: Romantic Comedy in Contemporary Cinema* comes at what is arguably a critical moment in the history of the genre. Hollywood rom-coms in particular have enjoyed a massive revival since the 1990s, with *When Harry Met Sally* in 1989 marking a pivotal moment in the renewed visibility of the genre. The rom-com has enjoyed such momentous box-office success of late that it has become a parody-able commodity, demonstrating the manner in which its conventions are part of a shared cultural landscape. For example, the genre has enjoyed the dubious distinction of being lampooned in *Date Movie* (2006), a film that apes famous rom-com dialogue and moments drawn from this period such as *Jerry Maguire*'s 'You had me at hello,' and *Notting Hill*'s 'I'm just a girl standing in front of a boy asking him to love her.' While the fact that it can be parodied in this manner suggests at one level the homogeneity of the rom-com, at the same time, the genre has been marked throughout this period by an unprecedented and rich diversification of interests that the essays here reflect. From the emergence of rom-coms 'for boys' such as *The 40-Year-Old Virgin* (2005), to different national inflections beyond Hollywood, to the growing prominence of queer or gay romances in both popular and independent cinema and the figure of the older woman as a viable romantic heroine (see *Something's Gotta Give* (2003)), the romantic comedy continues to regenerate.

This state of affairs is also reflected in the tentative but burgeoning new critical work in the field. For example, William Paul discusses the evolution and 'radical reorientation' of the genre through 'the rise of animal comedy' and the emergence of new leading comedians within the genre (2002: 117), while Frank Krutnik considers the diversification of the rom-com in his 'diagnostic' analysis of the recent 'dominant trends within [the genre's] production and reception' (2002: 130). Elsewhere, Celestino Deleyto has argued that where the genre once privileged heterosexual union, in a number of contemporary films heterosexual love has instead been increasingly 'challenged, and occasionally replaced, by friendship' (2003: 168). In addition, Tamar Jeffers McDonald has published *Romantic Comedy: Boy Meets Girls Meet Genre* (2007), providing a useful introductory and historical overview of the genre. The inclusion of her book within a series of study guides dedicated to exploring key concepts within Film Studies is testament to the growing acknowledgement of the significance of the rom-com and its previous neglect. Further publications on the genre include Kelly McWilliam's *When Carrie Met Sally* (2008), the first book-length study to examine the 'lesbian romantic comedy', which McWilliam suggests is contemporary cinema's predominant form of mainstream lesbian feature filmmaking. Alongside these and other recent interventions, *Falling in Love Again* aims to revisit and reinvigorate discussion of this most enduring of genres.

We commence with a number of essays that examine elements common to the rom-com across many of its different inflections, but which have nevertheless received only rather fleeting critical attention to date. Deborah Jermyn's essay examines why it is that time and again the Hollywood rom-com returns to New York, asking what it is about the city 'that has embedded it so firmly within popular consciousness as cinema's romantic playground'. She explores how its prevalence in the genre speaks to the enduring fascination New York holds for audiences and argues that its 'romanticism' can in part be linked to the city having fostered the figure of the 'independent woman' and mass immigration in the late nineteenth to mid-twentieth century.

Robynn J. Stilwell's essay examines another of the most expressive features at the heart of the rom-com: its use of music. Looking particularly at the work of Woody Allen and his 'acolyte/heir' Ed Burns, she contends that they share an approach to music that 'creates disruptions of affective and structural norms in the genre'. She argues that both filmmakers moved away from the use of an illustrative underscore or collection of pop tunes commonly found elsewhere in the rom-com, and suggests that Burns in particular uses his dynamic soundtracks to 'emphasise his allegiance to an "independent" aesthetic, both cinematically and musically'. Next, Paul Sutton initiates a discussion of the theme which forms the cornerstone of the whole genre; love. 'Love' is arguably a subject that scholars of the rom-com have generally shied away from conceptualising in detail, no doubt in part because it remains so elusive and intangible despite being so revered and sought after in so many cultures. Using *Groundhog Day* (1993) as a case study and drawing on a psychoanalytic Laplanchian model, Sutton particularly examines how the formation and resonance of 'love at first sight' is in fact structured by the temporality of 'afterwardsness'.

While 'love at first sight' has long constituted a familiar narrative trope across popular culture, since the 1980s Hollywood has seen the continued development of the 'teen comedy', films devoted to exploring some of the more amusing (though still frequently painful) experiences of adolescence. In her essay, Stacey Abbott notes that the search for love 'is a key structuring element' in the genre and is conceived of as integral to the search for social acceptance, hence the prevalence of the high-school prom as a particularly evocative setting within it. Looking at films such as *Never Been Kissed* (1999) and *13 Going on 30* (2004), Abbott argues that these 'prom-coms' appeal to youth and adult audiences alike, playing out 'an ambivalent exploration of the pleasures and horrors' of adolescence and high-school romance.

Romance is, of course, a theme that continues to preoccupy many different modes of cinema that lie outside mainstream Hollywood and the USA and across other national and cultural contexts, hence the next essays in the collection consider the ramifications and uses of the genre within some of these different contexts. Focusing on *Raja Hindustani* (1996), Sean Redmond's essay explores the way 'Indian romantic comedies attempt to come to terms with what are imagined to be the divisive footprints of globalization, (post)modernity, and social and gender inequality' in contemporary Indian society. He argues that the genre and its evocation of romantic love is used as a means of 'healing' social divisions and negating the potentially disruptive and divisive experience of diaspora distance 'to take their audiences home again'. Annabelle Honess Roe's essay examines how Working Title's rom-coms, which took off with the success of *Four Weddings and a Funeral* in 1994, can similarly be understood as in some ways exploring the 'special relationship' that has existed between the UK and USA since the Second World War. She argues that through the constant return to a central couple formed through the union of a charming but hapless British male with a feisty but irresistible American woman, the films explore both the tensions and attractions that exist between the two nations and 'can be read as symptomatic of the time of uncertain national identity' in which they were made.

Brigitte Rollet finds that despite love being a 'key element' across numerous genres and movements within French cinema, 'romantic comedy' is not one of its narrative traditions. Examining some of the cultural reasons that may account for this, she reflects on whether a sea change may nevertheless be occurring with the rise of recent French filmmakers who play with generic boundaries and the growing fondness of many French audiences for 'Hollywood-like films'. Her case study of *Décalage horaire* (*Jet Lag*) (2002) argues that the film simultaneously embraced and self-consciously critiqued the conventions of the genre in order to appeal both to critics and the general cinema-going public. In the following essay, Karen Bowdre argues that within Hollywood cinema, significant differences exist in the genre when mainstream conventions and white casts are replaced by black stars in films made more specifically for black audiences. She argues that the pre-eminence of the transformative power of love is exchanged instead for an emphasis on comedy and sex, the result of 'the highly sexualised and comical meanings placed on African-American bodies' within US culture.

While the rom-com has long been held to be the purview of hetero-sexual romance, Claire Hines posits an alternative interpretation by offering a queer reading of *Miss Congeniality* (2000) and its sequel *Miss Congeniality 2: Armed and Fabulous* (2005). Through close analysis of both films, Hines demonstrates the transgressive potential of the genre by reinterpreting these films' status as rom-coms and buddy films respectively, reading them instead as queer romances. Here she shows the genre's potential for providing alternative pleasures simultaneously for both straight and gay audiences. Kyle Stevens follows Hines' queer reading with an examination of the recurring figure of the gay best friend in the genre since the 1990s, a character that is increasingly a part of the landscape of the contemporary rom-com and yet one who remains rather neglected in critical work on it. By looking at films such as *My Best Friend's Wedding* (1997) and *As Good As It Gets* (1997), Stevens places this figure centre stage and considers the significance of this character within a genre that often privileges the heterosexual institution of marriage, at a time when gay partnership legislation 'emerged as a highly volatile issue with viable potential to impact on traditional definitions of marriage'.

Along with its traditional emphasis upon heterosexual relationships, the romantic comedy has typically been perceived as a genre for and about women. Tamar Jeffers McDonald, however, points to the emergence of a new type of romantic comedy that focuses on a male central protagonist and is seemingly aimed at male audiences, as exemplified by *Along Came Polly* (2004) and *Wedding Crashers* (2005). Designating this sub-genre the 'homme-com', Jeffers McDonald sees this new hybrid genre as the male answer to the 'chick flick'. Incorporating the eruption of scatological and sexual humour more often associated with the gross-out comedy or the sex-quest film, it undercuts some of the sentimentalism associated with what she describes as the 'Ephronesque' form of the genre. While she welcomes the re-infusion of the subject and depiction of sex, she raises the question, is sex within comedy 'a generally or exclusively male concern'?

Similarly focusing upon men within the genre, Janet McCabe next examines the star persona of comic romantic lead Bill Murray. Here McCabe considers how Murray's iconic deadpan delivery has come to represent a catatonic masculinity in crisis, facing changing attitudes to gender and romance in a post-feminist world. Additionally, by focusing upon a series of independent romantic-comedies, such as *Lost in Translation* (2003) and *Broken Flowers* (2005), McCabe highlights how the indie sector evokes the conventions of the rom-com while consciously subverting its more traditional elements. Lesley Harbidge also turns her attention to indie films by focusing on two 'comedian comedies', *Punch-Drunk Love* (2002) and *Eternal Sunshine of the Spotless Mind* (2004), starring the comedians Adam Sandler and Jim Carrey respectively. In this chapter, she considers how these films create a hybrid form, conjoining the rom-com with the comedian comedy, in which Sandler's and Carrey's comedic personas are consciously manipulated and constricted in order to offer new reflections upon the state of romance and relationships.

While the growing prominence of male stars within the genre demonstrates how it contains greater diversity than is often presumed, the contemporary rom-com is, however, still enduringly associated with women's stories and female stars. Alan Dodd and Martin Fradley offer a new spin on rom-com stardom by focusing their attention on Jennifer Lopez, a movie star and multimedia celebrity with strong ties to the genre. They consider how Lopez's media career and personal life, and in particular a highly publicised series of relationships, has had an impact upon the evolution of her screen persona within such films as *Maid in Manhattan* (2002) and *Monster-in-Law* (2005). Finally, if Jeffers McDonald has signalled the presence of a sub-genre of rom-coms aimed at – and comically structured to appeal to – 'boys', Hilary Radner identifies a sub-group of films aimed quite consciously at women. Using a case study of *Le Divorce* (2003), she describes how these 'girly films' are hybrids formed from the romantic comedy and melodrama. Here she returns to the woman-centred nature of the genre but considers the way in which these films chronicle how women, in a post-feminist world, are instructed in the ways of femininity.

The title of this book – *Falling in Love Again: Romantic Comedy in Contemporary Cinema* – was chosen in part since it highlights our intention to return to the genre and offer an array of original and wide-ranging insights into its various guises at this time. It recognises how, just as love itself is a dynamic condition that develops and transforms throughout the different stages and milestones of a relationship, so too is the romantic comedy a living, breathing entity within cinema. More than this, our title evokes something of the way we experience rom-coms, the manner in which every time we watch a romantic comedy we fall in love again with falling in love. We hope as you read the essays contained here that they will provide moments of recognition while suggesting avenues for further critical exploration; that they will chime with the many pleasures and tensions offered by the genre; and speak, too, to the hopeless romantic in all of us.

Stacey Abbott and Deborah Jermyn

1   *I* ♥ *NY*

The Rom-Com's Love Affair with New York City

~ Deborah Jermyn ~

I began to like New York, the racy adventurous feel of it at night, and the satisfaction that the constant flicker of men and women and machines gives to the restless eye. I liked to walk up Fifth Avenue and pick out romantic women from the crowd and imagine that in a few minutes I was going to enter into their lives, and no one would ever know or disapprove. Sometimes, in my mind, I followed them to their apartments on the corners of hidden streets, and they turned and smiled back at me before they faded through a door into warm darkness. At the enchanted metropolitan twilight I felt a haunting loneliness sometimes, and felt it in others. (Nick Carraway in F. Scott Fitzgerald, *The Great Gatsby*, 1950: 57)

FIRST PUBLISHED IN 1926, *The Great Gatsby* is regarded as home to one of literature's most accomplished accounts of the allure of New York. Seen through the eyes of the provincial Nick Carraway, it invites the reader to share his wonder at all the promise the city holds. His description of the sensations that grip him as he drives into Manhattan over the Queensboro Bridge ('Anything can happen now we've slid over this bridge . . . anything at all . . .' (ibid.: 67)) has become a feted moment in the literary history of the city. Later, the vantage point he describes would become further immortalised in Woody Allen's celebrated cinematic paean to New York, *Manhattan* (1979), when Isaac (Allen) and Mary (Diane Keaton) sit by the bridge at sunrise looking out at the city in the film's classic poster shot and he remarks in awe-struck tones, 'Boy, this is really a great city.'

Returning to Fitzgerald's descriptions today, in a world where New York's status as global city and the familiarity of its iconic landscape is unquestionable, one of the characteristics that seems most striking about his prose in 1926 is its filmic quality. The 'constant flicker' of people and machines; the 'restless eye' with which he watches the city, the way his imagined lovers fade to black in his mind, the 'warm darkness' that envelops them: all evoke the conditions of the screen and the cinematic space. Fitzgerald lights New York like a set; its characters are enveloped by the darkness of 'hidden streets', while our protagonist wanders the urban space at twilight. So, too, do we see how the city prompts a fantasy life akin to that of the cinema: it enables Nick to escape into a 'racy adventurous' world, an 'enchanted' metropolis, where he can narcissistically possess any woman his eye falls on without fear of retribution ('I was going to enter into their lives, and no one would ever know or disapprove'). Equally, *The Great Gatsby* evokes the dark shadow of modern life that frequently underlies both the representation of the city and of the search for love; a fear of being alone. Yet Fitzgerald's description imagines New York, not despite its 'haunting loneliness' but because of it, as essentially a romantic space; the women he picks out of the crowd to be his fantasy lovers are not noted as beautiful, wealthy or charming; they are 'romantic women'.

Fitzgerald's account, then, seems to crystallise the rich and potent relationship that was already underway at this time between cinema and the representation of New York, a pervasiveness that, I will argue here, is nowhere more evident than in the romantic comedy. Surprisingly, rom-coms are featured few and far between in Murray Pomerance's collection, *City That Never Sleeps: New York and the Filmic Imagination* (2007), arguably indicating the enduringly low critical status of this generally highly populist, mainstream genre. Yet, beyond any other city, New York (and Manhattan more specifically) has evolved as the pre-eminent and most memorable location adopted by the Hollywood rom-com. At the time of writing in 2007 fledgling plans are underway (driven by the New York-based film and TV site bus-tour company, On Location Tours) to initiate a series of commemorative blue plaques around the city marking its most celebrated film locations; demonstrating the significance of the genre to the history of New York on screen, it is Katz's Deli, scene of Meg Ryan's unforgettable faked orgasm in *When Harry Met Sally* (1989) (see Fig. 1.1) – not one of the city's innumerable thriller or gangster movies, but a rom-com – that is proposed as the first site to be honoured in this way (Blau, 2007).[1] Moreover, the first film to be shot in New York following 9/11 (according to its DVD extras) was a rom-com – *Two Weeks Notice* (2002) – while the first New York-set film due to be released following 9/11 (and subsequently postponed as a result) was Ed Burns' indie rom-com, *Sidewalks of New York* (2001). Time and again the contemporary Hollywood rom-com evidences how the aerial view of 'the island', often seen from the skies or over the Hudson River, has become the genre's quintessential establishing shot. From *Down With Love* (2003) to *Guess Who?* (2005), from *Mickey Blue Eyes* (1999) to *Two Weeks Notice*, a spectacular aerial view or bravura panning shot across the New York skyline signals entry into rom-com territory and is used with remarkable ubiquity. The seeming compulsion to return to this landscape within the genre is underlined by films such as *The Wedding Date* (2005), where it is adopted in order to establish the story even though the film is set largely *outside* NY, as is the case too with *Sweet Home Alabama* (2002). In the latter film, the DVD back

1.1: Katz's Deli, Manhattan, scene of Meg Ryan's unforgettable faked orgasm in *When Harry Met Sally* and proposed site of the first commemorative plaque to recognise New York's most celebrated film locations.

cover is even graced with a picture of the Manhattan skyline, despite the premise of the film (the return of the heroine to her small-town first love) eulogising rural Alabama as offering a more sincere and authentic way of life than the big city.

~ *'Anything can happen now . . . anything at all'* ~

In this essay I want to look at this rich and hugely evocative relationship a little more closely. Why is it that the theme of romance is so vividly serviced by Manhattan as a backdrop, and what is it about New York City that has embedded it so firmly within popular consciousness as cinema's romantic playground, since in broader cultural terms (or European ones at least) it is Paris that is the 'city of lovers'? As Charlotte Brunsdon notes in her discussion of the 'poignancy of place' in representations of London on film, the instantly recognisable iconography of London 'like that of all capital cities, is an historically formed, multi-media iconography which is, at one level, always about location, but which is never just about location: it is always, of necessity, also *about national identity*, and increasingly about the marketing of unique tourist destinations' (2004: 64, my emphasis). While not formally the capital of the USA, New York nevertheless holds a uniquely visible and central place with US culture and history, attracting millions of overseas visitors every year in a massive tourist industry undeniably serviced by popular film and television, and, as Fenimore Cooper remarked in 1851, 'No-one thinks of the place as belonging to a particular state, but to the United States' (cited in Reitano, 2006: 5). Driven by the frenetic pace of an island that measures just over 23 square miles, yet is home to over 1.5 million people (www.nycvisit.com), Manhattan's population multiplies every day as it fills with workers and commuters from across New York City's other four boroughs and beyond. This melting pot of ambition, desire, hope and confusion, with its urban tapestry of class, age, race and sexuality, intrinsically has the potential to fuel a seemingly endless array of comic and dramatic mishaps and scenarios. It is this same dynamic context, I want to argue – facilitating fulfilment as well as disappointment, hopefulness as well as anxiety, happenstance as well as crisis – that also provides the genre with the perfect milieu to explore the most potent of modern Western culture's mores; the belief that somewhere, out there, is the someone who is 'the one'.

While any number of titles from the annals of the rom-com might serve to illustrate this contention, the role of Hollywood in popularising New York as the cinematic palimpsest of our collective romantic dreams is perhaps best demonstrated by the relationship between *An Affair To Remember* (1957) and *Sleepless in Seattle* (1993). In the latter film the heroine Annie (Meg Ryan) tearfully and nostalgically watches the old Hollywood classic with her girlfriend Becky (Rosie O'Donnell) before later seeking to recreate its romantic climax, travelling to New York to meet Sam (Tom Hanks), the man she's never met before but has fallen in love with, at the top of the Empire State Building. The culmination of their consuming but unconsummated affair, then, can only occur here, in New York, not in the eponymous city of the title, thereby endowing their relationship with all the transformative romanticism and wonder of the city's cinematic history.[2] However, in what follows I want to make particular reference to a handful of the genre's most successful films from the last two decades, chief among them *When Harry Met Sally* and *Hitch* (2005), all of which demonstrate in their own way that New York – as 'real' geographic location and as symbolically loaded imaginary landscape – continues to constitute the quintessence of faith in the possibility and attainability of romance.

Indeed, in *When Harry Met Sally*, the onset of the protagonists' personal journeys and the narrative trajectory towards finding romance is specifically signalled by the film's shift in location to New York. We are introduced to the newly graduated eponymous leads when they meet for the first time in 1977 as university ends and they embark on a road trip from Chicago to New York together. To pass the time Harry (Billy Crystal) invites Sally (Meg Ryan) to tell him 'the story of her life', to which Sally responds:

> Sally: The story of my life isn't even going to get us out of Chicago. I mean, nothing's happened to me yet. That's why I'm going to New York.
> Harry: So something can happen to you?
> Sally: Yes!

Here, Sally's wish to have 'something happen' to her can again only, it seems, be fulfilled in New York. Revealing his neurotic and cynical tendencies, however, Harry warns against the 'dark side' of the city, speculating that she might well end up '[dying] one of those New York deaths that nobody notices for two weeks until the smell drifts into the hall'. Here, Harry invokes another cinematic and cultural history of New York, connoting the menacing urban decay of the 1970s when New York became a place to be feared. Vividly captured to critical acclaim in Scorsese's *Mean Streets* (1973) and *Taxi Driver* (1976), these films and the city imagined by Scorsese would have been particularly germane to the protagonists at the time of this 'prologue' (1977). Nevertheless, Sally's optimistic spirit of adventure (she is 'Sally Albright', after all) instead echoes Nick Carraway's anticipation that 'anything can happen now' that Manhattan is in sight (Fitzgerald, 1929: 67).

Clearly, a detailed cultural history of New York and its relationship with cinema is beyond the scope of this essay, but there are a number of significant and interwoven themes worth noting here that would feature prominently in such a project and which inform the rom-com's penchant for the city. First, both New York and cinema are intricately

1.2: The aerial view of 'the island' seen from the skies has become the quintessential establishing shot of the Hollywood rom-com.

embedded in the history of modernity, since New York evolved in the nineteenth century as the urban capital of US modernity, while cinema came to constitute its quintessential art form. As Nezar AlSayaad has observed, 'No medium has ever captured the city and the experience of urban modernity better than film' (2006: 1) and this privileged relationship was sustained and captured by early and classical Hollywood cinema. Moreover, and linked to this, New York or 'Gotham' features prominently in the cultural history of the evolution of the single, independent, desiring/desirable, urban woman, a figure who forms an important cornerstone of popular cinema, both as protagonist within it and as consumer of it.

Connections have long existed between the popular image of New York, the urban woman and consumerism; by the second half of the nineteenth century the area extending from Union Square to Madison Square was home to a growing number of splendid department stores where respectable women could go out unescorted. The area became known as 'The Ladies' Mile', facilitating the rise of the *flâneuse* and indeed increasingly providing women with employment. James Sanders notes too how in the mid-1930s, a series of romantic comedies made at Paramount, RKO and Columbia featured women stars such as Claudette Colbert playing feisty strong-willed heroines who 'found their natural home in the vast urban arena of New York, where they could pursue romance and career, and seek to balance conventional social pressure toward matrimony with their own instinct for independence' (2004: 2.17). This theme would later be returned to time and again by films with varying degrees of connection to the romantic comedy from *Pillow Talk* (1959) to *An Unmarried Woman* (1978), and beyond. While it would be wrong not to acknowledge the real economic and cultural disadvantages many women continue to negotiate in the city, Joanne Reitano argues that historically, 'In the early and mid-nineteenth century, Gotham offered America a radical model of egalitarianism that applied beyond white men to include women, blacks and immigrants' (2006: 4). It is because New York permitted the rise of the 'savvy' or 'spunky' urban single woman that she became so readily available and focal to the genre (and its hero) within this location, flourishing into a dynamic character type with which to facilitate the romantic machinations of the rom-com plot. As Jonathan Forbes (Tony Randall) tells Jan (Doris Day) in *Pillow Talk*, pointing through the window of his Manhattan office to the frenetic world outside, 'Look at that! New York! People, jostling, shoving, struggling, milling, fighting for their lives. *And you're part of it'* (my emphasis).

~ *Immigration, romance and the rom-com's American Dream* ~

However, there is one particular aspect of New York's history that I want to argue forms the historical backbone of the city's privileged place specifically within the Hollywood rom-com (and which Reitano also touches on above); the fact that it is New York City – not Los Angeles and not Chicago, the USA's other foremost cultural and economic centres – that served as the gateway to expansive American immigration. Ever since the Dutch had arrived there, naming it New Amsterdam in 1624, the city had emerged as 'a uniquely polyglot society' (Reitano, 2006: 8-9) with over half of its population having been foreign born by 1860 (ibid.: 56). Between 1892 and 1954, more than 12 million immigrants passed through Ellis Island to be 'processed' at the end of their journey to America, entering the USA with hopes and dreams, romantic and otherwise, of future happiness.[3] The island's unique historical importance in this respect was formally recognised in 1965 when it was declared part of the Statue of Liberty National Monument (National Park Foundation, 2006-7: 2). Capturing the spirit of immigration alongside the moment of modernity, then, Hollywood skilfully crafted and disseminated the aura of adventure that the city continues to hold in the popular imagination, one bolstered too by literature and other media and television texts such as *Sex and the City* (HBO 1998-2004),[4] an aura that can be summed up in the belief that, again as Fitzgerald put it, 'anything can happen' here.

Crucially, Fitzgerald's sentiment is of course closely tied to the principles that inform the American Dream and its ethos of egalitarianism, enterprise and aspiration. As the official visitors' guide to Ellis Island puts it, the story of the monument is 'the story of immigrants' faith and courageous dedication in their pursuit of happiness: this is the saga of America' (National Park Foundation, 2006-7). The 'right' to seek romantic love as part of this 'saga' is indeed why, in his much lauded analysis of the 1930s and 1940s 'comedies of remarriage' (one of the earliest forms of rom-com), Stanley Cavell borrowed from the American constitution to call his book *Pursuits of Happiness* (1981). Elaborating on Fitzgerald's reflection a little further, then, as the American Dream and the mythos of New York would have it, anything can happen here *for anyone*; and it is this belief that ties the history of immigration, the optimism embodied within it, and the dreams of the romantic comedy, together in New York.

Today in New York, tourists can visit the Statue of Liberty on a short ferry ride, which goes on to stop at Ellis Island. Presented by the people of France to the USA in 1886 as a symbol of the friendship between the two nations and emerging as 'America's key symbol of freedom' (Reitano, 2006: 83), visitors can go to the museum housed in the statue's pedestal to view a small but moving display of personal letters written by immigrants recalling their arrival at the USA. In this exhibit, Olaf Holen describes the moment he set eyes on the landmark monument en route to Ellis Island in the early years of the twentieth century:

> I first saw you on the eve of May 4, 1909, from the deck of the immigrant ship that brought me from Norway. I was wondering, as I looked at you and the lights in all directions, 'What is going to happen to me in this vast, new land of America?' (Olaf Holen, Iowa, 21 January 1986)

Holen's poignant testimony is as evocative as any Hollywood moment in capturing the immigrant spirit valorised by the American Dream and the anticipation that was, and is still, felt on seeing the New York skyline for the first time. It is intriguing then, that one of the biggest box-office rom-coms of recent years,[5] *Hitch*, should choose to bring its two would-be lovers together in a memorable first date on Ellis Island. Starring Will Smith, one of the most celebrated black actors in Hollywood history, as the film's eponymous New York City dating-consultant hero and Eva Mendes as Sara, the sassy gossip columnist and object of his affections, the film traces how for all his dating 'know-how' Hitch has to work hard to win Sara over. Hoping to surprise and impress her with a mystery outing, Hitch persuades Sara to meet him at the waterfront early one weekend morning, where he has jet-skis and life-jackets awaiting them both. After an exhilarating (and slapstick) ride across the river, they arrive at their destination – Ellis Island. Hitch's gift to Sara is an exclusive visit to the museum, which has been opened early just for the two of them.

In a remarkable and strikingly reflective scene, played out with stillness amongst all the confusion, misunderstanding and comic chaos of the rom-com world, Larry, the security guard at the museum, escorts them around the displays, sharing a history lesson about Ellis Island with them as they wander. Here 'Over 100 million Americans can trace their ancestry back to a single man, woman or child,' we learn, as Larry's voiceover fades and the stirring soundtrack swells. Sara looks thoughtful, contemplating the black-and-white archive photos showing hundreds of unknown faces disembarking at the island, yet, as the camera cuts between her and these distant, evocative images, the scene remains flirtatious too. She and Hitch exchange smiles and circle each other before they meet at 'The Kissing Post' exhibit, while the music fades away and Larry explains that this display examines how different cultures kiss one another after a long absence. As they walk into the Great Hall where immigrants were processed, Sara tells Hitch and Larry that she had an ancestor pass through here; walking to a display of one of the Island's log-books, Hitch reveals the pièce de résistance of his date: he has arranged for the book to be opened at the page where her

1.3: The Great Hall at Ellis Island where over 12 million immigrants arriving in the USA were processed and where Hitch (Will Smith) woos Sara (Eva Mendes) in *Hitch* (2005).

great-great-grandfather actually signed his name, Juan Melas. Sara is overcome, but, it emerges, for all the wrong reasons. The scene returns to comedy mishap mode when we learn that her ancestor, the 'Butcher of Cadiz', was so called not because of his profession, but because of his penchant for murder.

What does it mean that a rom-com, a genre know for its lightness of tone, should take this diversion, should almost suspend time and action to reflect in such a contemplative way instead on the history of New York and the USA itself? To embark on a romance is to embrace life's possibilities, to take a leap of faith, just as these immigrants did in coming to the USA; for this reason, their stories form a seductive function for Hitch in his efforts to woo Sara. He tells her, 'You can't really know where you're going to till you know where you've been.' In this respect what is curious about this scene is what is left unsaid in it, the subtext that lies unspoken but hanging in the air: the fact that Hitch's story, like that of the black security guard, like most African Americans and indeed other immigrant groups is *not* written here at Ellis Island. This is a history they are excluded from. In this way *Hitch* both draws on the powerful narrative meanings of immigration to reinforce its romantic sensibility, yet evades an explicit engagement with race.

~ The 'real' and the 'reel' New York City in rom-com ~

In *When Harry Met Sally*, the drive to capture and collapse both the 'real' New York – the tangible spaces and experiences of a living city – and the 'reel' New York – the intangible site of romantic escapism – meet in a film that both invigorated the rom-com genre when released in 1989 and paid homage to Woody Allen's classic 1970s 'nervous romances' (consider its flamboyantly nostalgic soundtrack, its charmingly eccentric *Annie Hall*-style heroine, its neurotic and garrulous male protagonist and his climactic *Manhattan*-style race through the streets to reach the object of his affections on realising he loves her). Like *Hitch*, though less explicitly so, the film also invokes the city's history of immigration. Throughout the film, the conventional Hollywood narrative, which traces the peaks and troughs of Harry and Sally's relationship from initial antagonism through to friendship then estrangement and eventually romance, is interspersed by brief interviews with a variety of elderly couples who recount the story of how they met, tales that form a backdrop to the growing tentative romance between Harry and Sally. Listed in the end credits as the 'documentary couples', it is not immediately apparent to the spectator whether they have been watching a parallel series of fictions in these scenes or the testimonies of real-life partners. In the film's DVD extras ('The Making of *When Harry Met Sally*') and in director Rob Reiner's commentary, however, writer Nora Ephron and Reiner reveal that though these participants were actors, in Reiner's words, their 'testimonials' were 'all stories that are actual stories of real people'. In the first of these anecdotes (a story Reiner explains he took from a friend's father) an elderly man recalls, 'I was sitting with my friend Arthur Cornbloom in a restaurant and this beautiful girl walked in and I turned to Arthur and I said, "Arthur, you see that girl? I'm going to marry her." And two weeks later we were married. And it's over 50 years later and we're still married'.

What is interesting about these 'documentary' interviews is the manner in which they repeatedly suggest not merely the mythologies of romance (love at first sight, serendipity, destiny) but sometimes traces too of the experience of romance among New York's immigrant communities. The different stories are delivered in both 'foreign' and New York/US accents that, situated alongside the New York City setting of Harry and Sally's story, leads us to read them all as being citizens of New York, now. It is intriguing that the very first anecdote, described above, which places the couple's courtship as having taken place in the mid-1930s, is delivered by the husband in a thickly accented, possibly Eastern European enunciation (his wife remains silent and therefore 'unplaced') and hints at a time when whirlwind romances also served a pragmatic purpose among immigrant communities struggling to put down new roots and establish stability in part through forming families. In a later vignette, an elderly East Asian man tells how an arranged marriage had been set up between him and a girl in the next village. Anxious at this prospect, he went there secretly in order to spy on her and on liking what he saw decided he would indeed take her as his wife; 55 years later they are still together. Here, we must fill in the 'gaps' in their story and imagine the journey that brought them from this unspecified, faraway place of villages and arranged marriages, to live out their life together in modern-day New York.

In situating all these storytellers as contented lovers who found their soul-mate despite the odds, it is not merely romance that is idealised by

When Harry Met Sally's 'documentary couples'. So too is immigration[6] and, ultimately, the move to assimilation. In the final interview (and the final sequence of the film), Harry and Sally sit together and describe the story of how they met, condensing the story we have, of course, just witnessed. Evidently far younger than any of the other interviewees, they represent modern New York. This is a city idealised by Ephron and Reiner, not just through the loving cinematography of New York, but through the central relationship that hints at how the contemporary city has facilitated cultural integration (for some at least). Billy Crystal's performance as Harry draws on the caricature of the neurotic Jewish male (he is clearly coded as a Woody Allen 'type' even if not explicitly placed as Jewish, while in the DVD extras Ephron describes how the film draws on the 'Jewish tradition' of rom-com) but such is the liberal zeitgeist of New York here that he and the all-American girl-next-door can form a romantic couple.

Because their story unfolds against a vision of New York that evidences a proximity between the 'real' and the 'reel' New York, it takes on not merely the mythologies of the city and of romance, but a kind of plausibility; the rom-com demands of us that we believe that, however apparently insurmountable, obstacles can be overcome and true love found. As Ephron and Reiner emphasise on the DVD extras when they list the real spaces where filming took place, much of the film was made on location,[7] albeit often using a series of picture-postcard settings where the city becomes a playground for (would-be) lovers: an early morning summer's drive in golden light over the Hudson into the city; a walk through the autumnal leaves of Central Park; Christmas at the Rockefeller Center. Played out against these spaces that are both recognisably real and the stuff of fantasy, Harry and Sally's unlikely courtship becomes one which the audience, at one level, can imagine as really possible, here, in the most dynamic, most engaging, most exciting city in the world. At the same time, of course, *When Harry Met Sally* neatly sidesteps race-related issues, as *Hitch* did and as the genre does more generally. Despite its traces of immigrant histories, this is an overwhelmingly white vision of the city and, just as Harry's apparent Jewish-ness is sublimated, so too is this a New York in which racial diversity is largely absented.

More recently, *Maid in Manhattan* (2002) at one level arguably makes a more concerted effort to tackle this subject and to confront the division of New York into classed and raced ghettoes, although it still

1.4: Central Park, one of numerous recurrent spaces used in the genre where the city becomes a playground for (would-be) lovers.

indulges in the romantic escapism and iconography that its location affords, and ends in fairytale style. Here, a *Pretty Woman*-style fantasy – in which hotel maid and single mother Marisa Ventura (Jennifer Lopez) falls in love with Republican politician hotel guest Chris Marshall (Ralph Fiennes) after he mistakes her for a wealthy socialite – collides with an effort to reflect on some of the contemporary issues facing Latina women living and working in poorly paid service-industry jobs in the city. On discovering that Marshall plans to deliver a speech about housing conditions in the Bronx, for example, Marisa takes him to task in the street, drawing on her working-class Latina credentials and ('authentic') experience of the city to underline and undermine his white, rarefied and privileged grasp of it.[8] Ultimately, though, in delivering a happy ending in which the two overcome their differences to embark on a relationship and Marisa's professional skills enable her to pursue a new, more lucrative and rewarding management career in the hotel industry, the film evades a more complex engagement with the contentious nature of the social inequities between the couple. The question is, perhaps, if it didn't, would it still be a rom-com?

~ *The fairytale of New York* ~

Alongside the kinds of rather intangible and mythological meanings of New York outlined here, there are also, as always, other pragmatic, economic and institutional reasons that may account in part too for why filmmakers might choose to film on location in New York City, despite its relative expense, rather than creating their own New York in Vancouver. The city has long been known to hold a solid crew base and to welcome and facilitate film crews with a well organised Mayor's Office of Film, Theatre and Broadcasting, for example, while in 2004 enhanced tax incentives were introduced for film crews completing 75 per cent of their work within New York State and/or the five boroughs (Anon, 2007: 39). Furthermore, as already noted, Hollywood plays a vital role in supporting and feeding the economy of New York: in 2005 alone, 'New York State's film business generated 10,000 jobs and $1.5b in expenditures' (ibid.). It might be said, then, that there is even a sense in which it is in the US national interests as a whole for the film industry to invest there. But more than this, and for the rom-com's purposes especially, there is inescapably something enduringly unique in the New York skyline's instant recognisability and the meanings and connotations crystallised within it. Few cities or spaces or monuments can claim to produce anything like the kind of emotional response that New York does. For Tamar Jeffers McDonald, 'the rote use of the city as iconography in the neo-traditional romantic comedy seems another sign that this type of film has exhausted its inspirations' (2007: 90), but I would argue that it speaks instead to the enduring fascination that the city holds throughout popular culture. While she is right to suggest that the genre, like any other, must continually seek to reinvent and update itself, there is little to suggest that audiences have yet tired of New York in this way, and it remains a living and dynamic city for filmmakers to draw on.

It seems both indulgent and somehow appropriate to end on an anecdote here, since so much of what we understand 'romance' to be is shared and experienced through our stories and the narratives we create. While researching this essay I visited many of the sites referred to above. On a bright Saturday morning in March 2007, I set off for Ellis Island, but the subway was out of action and, along with an endless stream of other tourists, I had to take a replacement bus to the ferry. As we turned a corner approaching our final stop I had my back to the driver, when all of a sudden a collective cry and audible gasp went up from everyone around me. Wondering what had happened I turned round and saw what my fellow travellers had just seen, understood immediately what they had responded to as one and why, and felt the same thrill – the Statue of Liberty had just come into sight. It is this quality, this ability for the city to move us, that Hollywood has helped construct, exploit and perpetuate. The connections between New York's romantic imaginary, the actual history of immigration and the rom-com's simultaneous discomfort at explicitly confronting race issues constitute an arena where there is evidently still much to be explored. What seems clear, however, is the way the genre continues to underline that even (or more than ever) in a post-9/11 climate, the romantic sensibility of New York, and the manner in which this is inextricably embedded in the city's innate 'cinematic-ness', remains just as potent and persuasive a phenomenon as ever.[9]

2 Music, Ritual and Genre in Edward Burns' Indie Romantic Comedies

~ Robynn J. Stilwell ~

It plays something like vintage Woody Allen in a minor key. (Roeper, 2006)

Burns, a shameless Allen disciple . . . plays the notes while missing the music. (Tobias, 2002)

IN REVIEWING *Looking for Kitty* (2006) above, critic Richard Roeper checks off certain similarities between the films of writer-director-actor Edward Burns and the dominant romantic comedy auteur of the previous generation, Woody Allen: ensemble tales of men trying to understand women, distinctive dialogue, New York City as a character. These comparisons have followed Burns closely since his debut film *The Brothers McMullen* (1995). Yet whether by intention or simply by having absorbed the gestalt, Roeper sums up the film with a metaphor that highlights another major stylistic feature shared by the two filmmakers: a pervasive use of music that goes beyond the usual illustrative underscore common to most films, or the collection of pop tunes particularly prevalent in the rom-com genre. Similarly, Scott Tobias (2002) may find Burns derivative – but he still finds him fundamentally musical.

The consistency with which music is mentioned or alluded to in discussions of Allen and Burns suggests not only a kinship to each other but a certain noise in the system. The work of both writer-director-actors is founded on the rom-com genre, while enunciating it in different and shared 'independent' inflections. The rom-com is strongly associated with female stars, spectatorship, and social drives traditionally linked to femininity and the domestic (and big studio productions), as are the popular songs normally associated with romance. However, Allen as the dominant rom-com auteur of the late twentieth century and Burns as an acolyte/heir bring an anxious masculine perspective to a genre that has been defined by 'the woman on top' (Rowe, 1995b: 41). Their use of music creates disruptions of affective and structural norms in the genre, drawing unusual attention from critics and audiences.

An exploration of the rom-com as a musical genre lays a foundation for an examination of how Allen asserts authority within and over his 'nervous' narratives from a conservative ground. Burns' musical palette emphasises his allegiance to an 'independent' aesthetic, both cinematically and musically. His narrative anxieties are transmitted through the confessional connotations of the folk-rock 'indie' musical style that dominates his films. While his male characters control music as Allen's do, the music plays a more dynamic role, more subjective than objective, a stance inherent to the indie rock aesthetic.

Indie music, like indie film, began as a financial definition but became a genre determined more by style and attitude. On the most obvious and literal level, an 'indie' genre is one defined by the financial structures of production. Indie music has come to be associated with a loose grouping of stylistic elements that include (but are not limited to) singer-songwriters, a guitar-driven texture in a basic two-guitars/bass/drums rock combo, fairly square four-beat rhythms, a predominantly 'unplugged' aesthetic that may be augmented by electric amplification and signifying 'noise', and songs that speak of alienation and disaffection, or emotional vulnerability – both states that can be useful in underscoring romantic relationships.

These traits overlap almost entirely with the style of music deemed 'authentic' by most rockist journalism and the audiences it shapes. An independent financial structure is seen as the most amenable to the production of such music, resisting the 'sweetening' of slick production values of major labels and their desire for radio-friendly commercial hits, whereas in reality one can foster such aesthetics in a high-end recording studio in order to target the independent audience just as surely as any other mainstream demographic. As happened with the term 'alternative' in the early 1990s, 'indie' music has migrated from an industrial term to a musical one.

Independent record companies have always been absorbed into larger companies as they become more successful, but this cycle accelerated through the 1990s, alongside the rise of the American independent film. Most boutique labels today are not genuine independents, but smaller divisions of large companies that are designed to capitalise on the rock audience's oppositional stance, just as many major film companies now have their indie arm. The economics of independent film financing and a cluster of issues that circulate within the ethos of independent filmmaking – for instance, the emphasis on identity formation and rites of passage – have led to a generic dependence on jukebox scores and an alliance with indie music. Where Edward Burns' rom-coms differ most strongly from Woody Allen's is in Burns' embrace of a musical aesthetic that reinforces his narrative anxieties rather than ironically juxtaposing them with the music of romantic ritual.[1]

~ The rom-com as a musical genre; genre as ritual ~

The rom-com as a genre has a longstanding history – conventions of the 'meet cute', misunderstandings, and miscues date back to the Greeks, as underlined by Stephen Sondheim's *A Funny Thing Happened on the Way to the Forum* (Broadway musical 1962, film 1966) – and is narratively conservative. Part of the joy for the audience is knowing that no matter the contrivances of the plot, the couple will end up together at the end. Occasional plots that cast at least some doubt on which characters will end up together, like those of *Sabrina* (1954) or *While You Were Sleeping* (1995), are rare. The pleasure is in the details of the journey, just as it is in the details of a conventionally structured 32-bar pop song or its verse–chorus descendants.[2]

Music and romance have an intimate connection – music can be seductive and soothing. The romantic ballad shares many of the musical gestures of the lullaby, though normally with an expanded range and turns of phrase that suggest the momentum and longing of romance and sexuality.[3] This connection is hardly surprising: baby talk is both parent to child and lover to lover, and while the phonemes are the same, the inflections and timbre are different.

Music can function on the most intimate level between two people, or it can join many people into a community through ritual performance – church hymns, school songs, national anthems at sporting events. At another level of engagement, it can elevate speech in religious and theatrical contexts and have a quasi-hypnotic effect, a kind of 'group seduction'; this is, in fact, one of the often-cited rationales for the presence of music in film, rendering the spectators 'untroublesome (less critical, less wary) viewing subject[s]' (Gorbman, 1987: 57–8), while also bonding them to the film and to each other, as an audience.[4]

Music in rom-coms may often be superficial in its specific connection to the narrative – but a rom-com without music is unthinkable. Music is an integral part of Western society's construction of romance. Most popular songs are about romance in some guise (whether subtle seduction or the 'romance' of sexual fantasy), and all of our romantic rituals from courtship to weddings are strongly shaped by music. The pervasiveness of music in the genre is, therefore, understandable. These popular songs have taught successive generations the language of romance. Their very familiarity is part of their ritual quality – rituals, by definition, are repeated. They are conservative by nature. Ideally, the content and the form are one: the repetition of a litany invokes as well as evokes the desired feeling.

Romances, from Shakespeare to Austen to McCarey, are likewise based on our understanding of social rituals. The disruptions common to the rom-com – particularly mistaken identity or misunderstandings/ deceptions that set the primary duo at odds with each other – complicate and prolong the mating rites, and in themselves become common tropes that build the generic field of rom-com.

Since the 1970s, the rom-com has become increasingly aware of itself as a genre. Allen was not the only director to draw on the familiar machinations of the genre to comment on the change in social dynamics, nor even to draw heavily on the musical elements,[5] but his use of music became a distinct fingerprint of his authorial style and influence. This was less an imposition and more a distillation of a generic trope. The decade of the 1930s was a 'golden age' of the rom-com. In his study of this period, James Harvey (1987) describes Irene Dunne as a primary female screwball star; her musical and comedic talents were perhaps never better meshed than in the scene in *The Awful Truth* (1937) where Lucy's laughter at Jerry (Cary Grant) at her recital is integrated seamlessly into a staccato downward passage in her singing. Harvey likewise describes Fred Astaire and Ginger Rogers as an exemplary rom-com couple; their dance numbers are the musical equivalent of the banter between Cary Grant and Katharine Hepburn in *Bringing Up Baby* (1938). The genre of the musical comedy is, structurally, a rom-com with the music shifted from the background to the foreground.

Most genres develop a distinctive musical style; *The Magnificent Seven* (1960) sounds like a Western, even though Elmer Bernstein's propulsive score with its Latin rhythms and soaring, disjunct melody represents a coalescence of a style that stretches back into the pre-cinematic history of depictions of the American frontier. The rom-com is notable as a dominant film genre in that it doesn't have an immediately recognisable style.[6] Perhaps because of the close relationship between musicals and rom-coms – particularly in the key decades of the 1920s, 1930s and 1940s – and the conservative nature of 'ritual' music, the closest approximation to an overarching style would be that of the Tin Pan Alley or mainstream pop song.

Because the drive of the rom-com narrative is more predictable than in most other genres, the need for music to perform such structural functions as foreshadowing, character development and thematic connection is lessened. It arguably becomes more about reflection on emotional states, bringing its purpose closer to that of the classical operatic aria. The strongly melodic and lyric-focused nature of the American popular song of the first half of the twentieth century is well suited to this function, in part because it was so strongly bound to that of the musical comedy; the two developed in tandem – circling each other like a couple dancing in a mutual embrace. While the rock era may have changed the rhythms and diction, the musical style of the love song has been remarkably consistent over the past century.

~ Woody Allen: genre as a ground ~

Analysts of the rom-com speak of Woody Allen's approach to the genre as anxious, insecure, nervous (Babington and Evans, 1989; Krutnik, 1998). While these are not necessarily new traits in the rom-com, they have become less superficial character traits and more thematic tropes. Allen was working in a genre that, while it had changed with the times during the century, had always worked on the presumption of the happy ending. By questioning the fundamental tenet of the rom-com – there's someone for everyone, and they shall be recognised as a couple at the end of the journey – Allen upset the basic narrative paradigm, while keeping other generic elements in place. The alterations are thus thrown into relief.

Perhaps most prominently in Allen's films, banter is retained but the content is varied; verbal conflict is no longer primarily foreplay but an articulation of real anxiety. Music remains prominent as a marker of the genre, but it is most often part of the generic 'ground', literally harking back to the earlier golden age of the rom-com. Whether a compilation of recordings or a newly generated score in a period style, the early New Orleans jazz style and 1930s-era Tin Pan Alley song selection is a distinctive and recognisable element of the 'branding' of an Allen film, as identifiable as his logo-like use of white text in the same classic serif font on black for his credit sequences.

Despite the prominence of music in his films, however, the music rarely functions in the same way as a classical non-diegetic film score, or even a modern jukebox score. Perhaps in part because of the anachronistic style, the music resists the sort of meta-narration of the jukebox score common to most contemporary rom-coms, although the predominance of this scoring option may well be a measure of Allen's influence. While it is possible occasionally to determine oblique connection between plot and the lyrics of songs adapted instrumentally on the underscore, the classical leitmotivic functions of music are surprisingly rare in Allen's films. The music acts as a stylistic marker, as lighting and design do, providing subtle mood inflections.

One of Allen's few films to involve music actively in the storytelling is *Hannah and Her Sisters* (1986). The variety of musical functions are particularly revealing of Allen's larger narrative themes of masculine anxiety and the need for control. A rare musical leitmotiv comes in the thematic, non-diegetic use of a piano version of Richard Rodgers and Lorenz Hart's 'Bewitched, Bothered, and Bewildered' to score Elliot's (Michael Caine) fascination with his sister-in-law Lee (Barbara Hershey). This song selection is on-the-nose, but dependent upon the audience's recognition of the song and its lyrics. Most of the musical function takes place primarily at the level of style, with a definite implication that women are musically incompetent, or at least tasteless. Holly (Dianne Wiest) and Mickey's (Woody Allen) disastrous first date shifts between her musical choice (a punk band) and his (Bobby Short, performing standards), and when they become a couple at the end, her musical tastes have converged with his, in jazz. The artist Frederick (Max von Sydow) and the architect David (Sam Waterston) are strongly associated with Baroque music (Bach, Vivaldi), and they intellectually intimidate Lee and Holly respectively. Perhaps the most dramatic musical moment occurs in a scene in Frederick's loft between Lee and Elliot; she puts on a harpsichord recording of Bach, and in the middle of the heated discussion, an accidental bump of the record player skips the record to a developmental episode in the music, underscoring the rising tension between the two with an unstable harmonic passage of fragmented motivic sequencing. This classic thematic transformation is almost never otherwise utilised by Allen.

However, a trace memory of the earlier period of the rom-com runs through the film, in the narrative background. Performed diegetically, clearly couched in nostalgia, Tin Pan Alley songs characterise the sisters' parents and their problematic relationship. They continually perform the same songs and the same arguments, but repeatedly resolve their differences; they are the persistence of generic memory – a happy ending, if something less than a happily ever after. Allen's musical palette paints a background against which his questioning of the possibility of romance can be read. Annie Hall aspires to a musical career; although it is not acknowledged in the film, her cabaret style is not merely nostalgic but anachronistic: realistically, no major record company A&R man would be scouting an act like hers in 1977. The impossible career echoes the impossible romance, hinging on the classic romantic song – both are of the past.

In most of Allen's films, the Tin Pan Alley song is an element that goes to define the genre; it may occasionally also accrue symbolic meaning, but essentially remains an object that symbolises a character without undergoing the transformation typical of most film music. The songs are an element of the ritual of romance.

Under Allen's influence, but without his sense of irony, the nostalgic popular song remains a marker of the rom-com, particularly in the films of writer-director Nora Ephron, which play on this 'old-fashioned' quality and breathe new life into it. *When Harry Met Sally* (1989) looks back at the genre through the lens of *Annie Hall* to recapture the possibility of romance that was lost in Allen's film. Ephron's younger male contemporary Edward Burns also looks to Allen; however, while Ephron reinforces the romance via the nostalgic musical style, Burns reinforces the anxiety by adopting a more contemporary, and anxious, musical style.

~ Edward Burns: like Woody Allen, only not ~

Sidewalks of New York is like a Woody Allen movie without the intellectual pretension, which is mostly a good thing. (Scott, 2001)

Sidewalks is what it sounds like: a Woody Allen movie. It's a better one than Woody Allen himself has made in a while. (Fuchs, 2001)

I remember when I first saw Martin Scorsese's *Mean Streets* and y'know his use of 'Jumpin' Jack Flash' in that scene when De Niro is introduced, walking down the bar . . . I think that is the moment when I said, 'Oooh, I wanna make movies . . .' The idea was that if I can recreate something that cool, I wanna be in that business. (Burns, 2006)

The persistent comparison to Allen is not wrong inasmuch as it is incomplete. Burns' films, on the whole, are more consistently serio-comedy than comedy, and like Allen, most of his films interrogate generic conventions of the rom-com. *She's the One* (1996), for instance, is about what happens after couples are married, and *Looking for Kitty* (2006) is about letting go of relationships that are over, without providing a happy reconciliation or a new pairing. Burns states assertively that he is not a rom-com fan, but then does not consider Allen's films to fall in that genre either.

Allen and Burns, despite the disparity of their usual operating budgets, are noted for creating images of New York City that are both intimate and spectacular, familiar and fantastic, but the palettes they use are vastly different. Allen's city is either black and white, the sharp-fast silvery-white of art deco, or a sepia-toned wash of nostalgia, warm and affectionate and slightly claustrophobic. Burns' New York is not less romanticised, but it is a more contemporary romanticism, with a nod towards the diversity and history of the city. These two visions of New York City are not mutually exclusive, but they are quite different, rooted in the experience of the filmmakers.

Like Allen, Burns has a quasi-repertory company of actors who appear in his films, in his case often as friendly favours, given the constraints of his budgets. In Burns' earliest films, which are semi-autobiographical examinations of familial relationships, most of the cast belongs to the same working-class, outer-borough Irish-Catholic background. As his stories have grown more complex, so have the ethnicities of the characters. True, African-American and Asian characters are still not very visible, but Italian, Hispanic, Eastern European and Jewish characters are common, and – perhaps more significantly – the range of socio-economic class represented is much broader. This spectrum of representation adds shades of colour to Burns' New York that are missing from Allen's monochromatic city.

Both directors are often accused of mining the same material over and over again. This criticism is one that popular music scholars may well recognise as harmonious with, if not identical to, Theodor Adorno's (1941) dismissal of the 'pseudo-individualization' of popular music. However, those who enjoy popular music may be able to articulate that one of its pleasures is not the 'macro' individuality of innovative structure but the micro-originality of rhythm, local harmonic colour and melodic turn. The varied details of the films' plots offer similar 'micro-originality'.

Burns is certainly more classically oriented in his scoring choices than Allen. His debut film, *The Brothers McMullen*, looked at New York working-class Irish Catholics in a forthright manner. The range of characters and behaviours is supported by an instrumental underscore by Seamus Egan, heavily influenced by Irish folk music. It speaks more directly to the common background of the characters, despite their differences, than the tone or the narrative of the film. The similarly micro-budgeted *Looking for Kitty* likewise has a quirky instrumental score by Robert Gary and P.T. Walkley, although it is more varied in tone: the music has some of the jaunty early-jazz quality of some of Dick Hyman's arranged scores for Allen, but the reliance on mandolin as the lead instrument and certain melodic and harmonic turns also lend the score an air of Italian folk music. This resonates with the Irishness of the *McMullen* score, and even the folksy Italianate underscores of films like *Moonstruck* (1987) and *Big Night* (1996). The music for *Looking for Kitty* underlines the ethnicity of the key supporting character, Abe Fiannico (David Krumholtz), who functions essentially as the leading lady. The film begins with Burns as private detective, Jack, enlisted to help Abe in his search for his estranged wife, Kitty, and develops into a love story between the two men. Although the relationship is clearly platonic and they go their separate ways at the end of the film, Abe's friendship and his nurturing philosophy of life helps Jack come to terms with the death of his own wife. It seems only appropriate that the music should in some sense 'belong' to him.

~ *The leitmotivic song score* ~

> I'm a big music buff, love nothing more than working with musicians,
> and, y'know, how film and music when married can completely change
> the tone and vibe and energy of a scene. (Burns, 2006)

Although he has worked with a number of different musicians, ranging
from rock star Tom Petty to P.T. Walkley, who runs his local guitar shop,
Burns has a similar way of working from film to film. He often cites *The
Graduate* (1967) as his primary model for scoring a film, and one of
the immediate benefits of a $3 million budget for his second feature,
She's the One (as opposed to $25,000 for *The Brothers McMullen*), was
that he could engage Petty to write songs that reflected aspects of the
plot. As with the Simon and Garfunkel tunes in *The Graduate* score,
instrumental versions of the songs follow the plot like leitmotivs or
themes in a classical Hollywood film score, but emerge at certain points
as full-blown non-diegetic songs with words to underline key plot
turns.

This *Graduate* model has become Burns' standard. With *Looking for
Kitty* (shot in 2003, but not released until 2006), Burns began a successful
association with Walkley and his collaborator, Robert Gary. In addition
to the Italianate underscore, each of the musicians provides a theme
for one of the main characters: Gary's theme is for Jack; Walkley's is for
Abe. Abe's theme becomes the song 'Kitty You're the One' as Abe packs
his bags to leave New York – an ironic statement since he is beginning
to let go of Kitty. Walkley and Gary also provide the underscore and the
closing original song 'A Man Who Knows' for *The Groomsmen* (2006), the
song that encapsulates the lead character's journey from a chilly-footed
prospective groom to a man facing his responsibilities and embracing
his connection to his fiancée and their unborn child.

Even when dealing with pre-existing songs, Burns prefers this
leitmotiv technique. For *Sidewalks of New York* (2001), almost all of the
cues are instrumental versions of songs by the band Cake, provided
by the band themselves. Some songs with vocals are heard on the
soundtrack, although it is singer-songwriter Pete Yorn's song 'A Girl
Like You' that assumes the most musical prominence through its
performance by one of the main characters. Benny (David Krumholtz)
is a struggling rock musician who has a day job as a doorman; as the
film opens, he drops in on his ex-wife Maria (Rosario Dawson) yet again,

hoping to impress her with a new song he has written. As his attentions shift to the young waitress Ashley (Brittany Murphy), he pursues her with the hope of playing a song for her. Whether this is another song, or the one he wrote for Maria is unclear, but Benny's ritual of courtship is unwavering. Yet when Benny actually performs the song, it is not to either woman. He sits in his bathroom, sadly strumming his guitar and singing the song, which continues over a shot of Ashley walking down the street. The song ties them together – they are the only couple who have anything approaching a happy ending – and it can be read as a foreshadowing that they will end up together. However, it also reflects an earlier moment in a documentary-style interview segment in which Benny says that his life after divorce is pretty much the same as it was before his marriage – he spends a lot of time playing the guitar and masturbating. The suggested equation can be taken as funny or sad, but it reflects the intimate connection between music and sexuality.

Benny is also the focus of the most significant bit of underscore, in a nearly silent scene. Having broken up with Ashley, Benny is on the street at his doorman job, struggling not to cry. The snippet of Django Reinhardt's solo guitar is anempathetically jazzy. It is reminiscent of a 1920s ukelele solo, one of the most Allenesque moments in any Burns film sheerly due to the musical style. However, the obliviousness of the jaunty music to Benny's predicament creates an emotionally charged contrast that Allen would probably avoid.

Music was in large part the impetus for Burns's ensemble comedy, *The Groomsmen*. Though the plot was generated by Burns's experience as the first of his group of childhood friends to get married and start a family, his hope was to create a movie as widely identified with Generation X as *The Big Chill* (1983) had been with Baby Boomers, including the rediscovery of their music.

While *The Big Chill* is a rare, pure jukebox score, much of the music in *The Groomsmen* is performed onscreen by the characters, reminiscent of a musical. A subplot revolves around the friends' band, Butter Tongue, reassembled to play for the weekend's wedding festivities, performing songs that represent their high-school days.[7] Butter Tongue's repertoire evokes the specific time and space of the characters' adolescence, including Eddie Money's 'Shakin''[8] and the Greg Kihn Band's 'The Breakup Song' – as one band member points out, not the best choice for a wedding dinner. This is not the MTV-friendly synth pop that dominates most visions of the 1980s such as *The Wedding*

Singer (1998) and *Music and Lyrics* (2007), but the white, middle-class American adolescent ritual of the garage band.

The guitar is an important emblem in *The Groomsmen*. It begins as the typical symbol of rock, with all its implications of rampant masculinity, individuality and freedom, but comes to play a part in the maturation of the main characters. The 'phallic' electric guitar enacts a transition, as the most mature of the friends, Desmond (Matthew Lillard), instructs his two young sons on playing riffs from Loverboy songs; the scene depends on a certain dissonance between the posturing arena rock riffs and the tenderness between father and sons.

The more domestic, intimate acoustic guitar guides the two brothers at the centre of the film to reaffirm their commitments to the women in their lives. As his marriage founders on his possible infertility, Jimbo (Donal Logue) tries to recall a song he wrote for his wife in high school. The tune is earnest and naive, cast in a folky Dorian mode with a prominent lowered-seventh cadence; the words lead up to an incredibly lame rhyme about getting into her pants that fortunately is evaded as Jimbo realises how much he loves his wife. After a scene in which Desmond tells Paulie (Burns) how much his children mean to him, we see Paulie playing a soft tune on acoustic guitar before sliding into bed next to his pregnant fiancée, Sue (Brittany Murphy). In that wordless musical moment, Paulie has warmed up his cold feet.

The emotionally intimate moments centred on the solo acoustic guitar in *The Groomsmen* signal an aspect of Burns's aesthetic that can easily be missed if looking through the lens of the traditional rom-com. His almost obsessive commentary on the techniques of shooting on a limited budget underlines his status as an independent filmmaker and the indie aesthetic that emerged in the 1990s.

The alliance between indie film and indie music is both financial and thematic. An orchestral score is an expense few independent films can afford, and the most common instrumental alternative – a synthesiser score – still demands a composer and may create an aesthetic clash with the film, particularly if the film seeks emotional immediacy and/or a raw sensibility. Synthesisers still evoke an emotional distance for most listeners, while the human voice and acoustic guitar – staples of the indie music style – tend to evoke vulnerability, intimacy and emotional honesty.

As Burns's rom-coms turn toward the serio-comic, this musical style becomes more resonant. While Tom Petty is not exactly an indie artist,

She's the One was a studio film, and Burns was encouraged to consider his (relatively) big budget.[9] Petty's roots rock style is, however, a precursor to the indie style, and his rebellious, independent stance and singer-songwriter status give him credibility with the indie movement. Petty resides squarely in the pantheon of rock masculinity reinforced in *Sidewalks of New York* by Benny's choices of LPs that Ashley 'really needs to know'. In a local record store, he picks out the Rolling Stones' *Exile on Main Street*, Bruce Springsteen's *Greetings from Asbury Park* and *Led Zeppelin I* ('the best debut album ever'), choices echoed in the repertoire of Butter Tongue. Benny's own song, 'A Girl Like You' was written by Pete Yorn, a textbook example of a singer-songwriter whose ethos is indie but his record label is one of the true maxi-majors – Columbia (a division of Sony/BMG/Coca-Cola) – and the band Cake was one of the leading lights of the indie movement at the time of *Sidewalks of New York*. Burns's alliance with Walkley and Gary is both a step further into the realm of the independent, and a return to a classical Hollywood model of a leitmotivic score – a model that was never particularly prevalent in comedies, but dominated dramas.

Woody Allen's rom-coms used the classical film genre as a ground from which to question the possibility of romance. His questioning of the basic premise of rom-com was brought into relief by the adherence to – and nostalgia for – the classic period of the genre. The ritual music of romance was still there as an ideal, and the gap between the form and the content was a source of anxiety and of comedy. As our culture has grown less certain of the possibilities of romance, and the concerns of relationships extend beyond the expected resolution, the union of the heterosexual couple – through infidelity, divorce, children, infertility, extended families and, increasingly, homosexual[10] rites of passage, such as coming out and pairing up – Edward Burns keeps the anxiety in the foreground, but the music relinquishes its ironic stance to underscore the emotions more directly.

3   *Après le Coup de Foudre*

Narrative, Love and Spectatorship in *Groundhog Day*

~ *Paul Sutton* ~

ANDRÉ BAZIN FAMOUSLY asserted that, 'the cinema more than any other art is particularly bound up with love' (1953: 72). If this is indeed so then this remark would appear to be even more apposite when applied to the romantic comedy; and yet in fact it is precisely love that remains occluded in the rom-com. While critical writing on the romantic comedy has been attentive to questions of genre, gender, comedy and film form, very little attention has been paid to love itself. It is my intention in this chapter to offer some redress to this and to explore the function and operation of love in the rom-com by looking specifically at love at first sight, a structuring trope of Hollywood romance more broadly.

Love in mainstream Hollywood cinema (for reasons of temporal economy as well as dramatic resonance) is frequently at first sight. Indeed, Mary Ann Doane places it at its structural heart arguing that, 'classical cinema believes in "love at first sight," perhaps because it so conveniently fits within its highly developed system of point-of-view and glance/object editing' (1987: 114). Love is also, of course, reliable in its repetition, allowing (in its endless permutations) for the familiarity and difference so central to Hollywood genre. Love's universality, its formulaic quality, is central to the appeal of the genre for spectators and producers alike, but it is also central to its critical denigration. Love at first sight is, though, subject to a range of narrative obstacles that serve to question and ultimately reinforce the power of this immediate, visual and spectacular form of falling in love. Characterised by a very specific temporal and causal structure, love at first sight or *coup de foudre* in French, like the avowal 'I love you', is a performative construct, only becoming love at first sight in the (present) moment of its articulation; it is structured, as I will argue in more detail later in this essay, by the temporality of 'afterwardsness' (Laplanche's neologism for Freud's *Nachträglichkeit*).[1]

The rom-com, *Groundhog Day* (1993), 'one of the masterpieces of 1990s Hollywood cinema' (Gilbey, 2004: backcover), is structured, much like love at first sight, by a notably complex (for mainstream Hollywood, at least) temporality based on repetition and retroaction, lending itself to psychoanalytic interpretation. My specific interest, however, relates to the film's engagement with a set of spectatorial and psychoanalytic concerns that coincide with my articulation of a theory of cinematic spectatorship, what I refer to as 'afterwardsness' in film. Love in the film is represented as at first sight and a certain kind of remaking or rewriting of narrative proves to be the key to breaching the romantic and temporal impasse that faces its protagonist; the film retrospectively charts the progress of, and the obstacles to, romantic love. Through its narrative of repetition *Groundhog Day* lays bare the preparatory 'work' that lies behind the immediacy of the love at first sight it represents; indeed it is not directly visible in the film, emerging only retrospectively (it is also significantly more motivated than it at first appears). *Groundhog Day* reveals the mechanics of the rom-com and manages to both have its proverbial cake and eat it, by cynically and *com*ically critiquing the rom, while nonetheless having the central protagonists fall in love. At the same time, the film's unusual narrative structure allows it to operate in an arguably more sophisticated register than that more usually associated with the rom-com genre. Thus in this essay I will demonstrate how both the film *Groundhog Day* and spectatorship more generally may be seen to be structured by afterwardsness.

~ Groundhog Day ~

The plot of *Groundhog Day* may be summarised as follows. Phil Connors (Bill Murray), cynical weatherman for a regional television station, sets out to cover (for the fourth time) the town of Punxsutawney's annual 2 February Groundhog Day festival. The groundhog, sharing the name Phil, predicts whether winter will end or continue for another six weeks. Despite Connors' prediction that snow will bypass the area, he and his crew (producer Rita (Andie MacDowell) and cameraman Larry (Chris Elliott)) are stranded in Punxsutawney after a blizzard cuts off the town. Forced to stay overnight, Connors wakes up the following morning to the same tune and banter on the radio as the previous day, soon discovering that the 'boys' are not 'playing yesterday's tape' but rather that today is yesterday. He is living through Groundhog Day again, a day that '[A]s he complains later, . . . is not a particularly good one. At various points, he will redefine the ideal day that he would want to be repeated, and he will try to transform his own cyclical February seconds into that day' (Thompson, 1999: 137). The breaking of the spell requires that Connors, as in all good fairytales (albeit one with a non-traditional shift in gender), be 'rescued' by a princess (Rita). Rita 'buys' Connors at a charity auction that closes the Groundhog Day festivities, after he has finally managed to engineer or (re)construct the perfect (enough) day and, of course, his thoroughly cynical self.

Groundhog Day has been criticised, somewhat dismissively, for its 'self-consciously retrospective cinematic redemption narrative', the referencing of Frank Capra's *It's a Wonderful Life* (1946) in its closing sequence providing partial evidence of this (Davies, 1995: 225). On one level such a description offers an accurate summary of the film, but to see it only in these terms is to fail to read the film with any sense of irony, or in sufficient detail. The overt references to Capra and to *Brigadoon* (1954), as well as to the fairytale (both narratively and visually), are excessive and clearly intended to be so. The film's Capraesque ending is ambiguous in precisely the same way that the lush visuals of Douglas Sirk's melodramas are self-consciously, and therefore self-critically, exaggerated. Indeed, *It's a Wonderful Life* also contains an undercurrent that undermines its seemingly happy ending. While the redemption in *Groundhog Day* occurs in the apparently conservative context of the traditional small town/big city, nature/culture opposition, the film's implausibly romantic, visually excessive ending serves to undermine and to critique easy and ideologically clichéd readings. This foregrounding of the film's fairytale dimension may also serve to bridge the possible 'contradiction faced by the spectator who is no longer able to believe in romance . . ., yet at the same time wishes to do so' (Lapsley and Westlake, 1993: 180). Equally, however, the image of the perfect house set in a perfect garden coated in virgin snow and overlaid with a Nat King Cole soundtrack suggests that Connors' 'It's beautiful. Let's live here' is itself too perfect a resolution after the horror of the endlessly repeated Groundhog Day.[2] It is important to consider, in addition to the film's complex visual texture, the performance of Bill Murray as cynical, disdainful TV weatherman Phil Connors. Murray's 'transcendent languor' makes him the perfect comedian for the role (Romney, 1997: 48; see also Janet McCabe's essay, Chapter 12 of this collection), and although the audience may believe that Phil Connors has redeemed his character by the end of *Groundhog Day*, there is arguably a poor fit between Phil Connors and Bill Murray. A degree of implausibility in this resolution results from the previous (and subsequent) roles played by Murray and from the sheer exuberance and pleasure represented by the cynical as opposed to the redeemed characters he plays. Connors' cynicism is inescapable, despite his apparent conversion to idealism. Thus, while 'Connors is improved', it is:

> For all the wrong reasons and in all the wrong ways. He can become the perfect man purely because he has nothing else to do, having exhausted all the day's other possibilities. Given time, he becomes a god, omniscient and omnipresent, and when that's driven him mad, maybe then he'll settle for being a nice guy. (Romney, 1997: 48-9)

It has been argued that *Groundhog Day* is a classical Hollywood film, despite the fact that 'at first glance it might seem not to be' (Thompson, 1999: 131). The repetition is seen as 'original and a bit daring', but the only radical 'departure from tradition – admittedly a striking one – is the failure to motivate or explain the plot's sudden move into an impossible situation' (ibid.: 131). There is no apparent explanation for Connors' waking up endlessly on Groundhog Day, leading some critics to surmise that the intervention is supernatural (ibid.: 132). A more plausible explanation lies beyond the diegesis. The filmmakers are, very knowingly, playing with the film's spectators, laying bare the mechanism of spectatorship itself, just as in the diegesis the constructedness of love at first sight is also being made visible. In other words, the film is far less classical in this respect than might be imagined. Thompson admits this when she notes that 'The repeated Groundhog Days . . . call the audience's attention to the common practice of making multiple takes during the shooting of a film . . . The film calls attention to its own editing and cinematography to a degree unusual for a classical film' (1999: 141). It might also be argued that *Groundhog Day* knowingly articulates, or performs, the repetition that is central to the appeal of – and cultural representation of – romantic love. Denis De Rougemont, for example, emphasises 'our eagerness for both novels and films with their identical type of plot' (1983: 16) as fundamental to the appeal of the romance narrative. Ultimately, whether the narrative is classical or not, the film certainly self-consciously foregrounds the viewers' spectatorial activity. It lures the spectator, capturing him or her in a mirroring of *Groundhog Day* that compels them to perform their own 'redemption' alongside Connors/Murray. It is only afterwards, as is the case with Connors, that they may become fully aware of the extent to which the film's construction is motivated.

~ Afterwardsness in film ~

I want to argue here that spectators remake films as part of the very process of spectatorship and that beyond the actual cinematic experience they carry a remade and remembered 'film' with them. This view of spectatorship therefore takes afterwardsness as its motivating force.[3] The experience of watching a film coincides also with the temporal directionalities described by Laplanche in relation to afterwardsness (1992). Not only is the spectator left with memories from, and of, the film after it has ended, but any number of (frequently traumatic) enigmatic signifiers or messages may have been unconsciously recorded, requiring subsequent de- and re-translation. Following a Laplanchian model, one might surmise that the spectator develops a cinematic unconscious on the basis of the 'repression' of these messages. This 'repression' occurs as a result of the sheer volume and traumatic intensity of the visual and aural stimuli, which cannot be immediately ordered and understood. These enigmatic messages, structured by the temporality of afterwardsness, provoke the spectator into a process of reconstruction, retranslation. At the same time, the sensory dimension of the cinematic experience may also have an immediate effect on conscious perception or trigger the traumatic recollection of a previously unconscious trauma.

These (traumatic) memories, enigmatic signifiers, the de-translated remnants of one's cinema history are re-translated and remade, engendering a remaking of oneself around these fragments in a process of 'auto-translation', which might also be thought of as a kind of re-narration. Significantly there is an active, almost performative, dimension to this process of transformation. Thus it has been argued that:

Forward movement in life is achieved through a backward movement in memory, but one that is more than a simple regression. In place of the blocked nostalgia or nausea of the perpetual return, the past is transformed in such processes as 'working through' and 'deferred action'. This is . . . *performance* that is iterative and interrogative – a repetition that is *initiatory.* (Burgin, 1996: 273)

The idea of afterwardsness in film is to express the very dynamism of the spectatorial experience, to speak of the reconstructive and creative aspect of spectatorship. This process of spectatorship recreates the films it 'remembers' and articulates a certain kind of love at first sight (always already at second sight) of the cinema, the expression of a kind of *après coup* of the *coup de foudre.*[4] It is through an exploration of the *après coup* of the *coup de foudre* that I will argue that love at first sight has certain transformatory and performative effects on, and for, the cinematic spectator. Before considering *Groundhog Day* in detail, however, I want to explore, briefly, the notion of a cinephilic love at first sight, as a starting point for thinking about loving the cinema or a way of connecting an intellectually sanctioned passion with a more popular romantic one.

~ Loving the cinema/love-in-the-cinema: cinephilia and spectatorship ~

A number of recent studies have tried to demythologise romantic love, although reflection on these has been generally absent from existing work on the rom-com genre. In the field of psychoanalysis Klaus Theweleit (1994) has sought to expose the structures and motivations that underpin romantic love attachments, and Ethel Spector Person (1989) has endeavoured to demonstrate the positive transformatory power of mutual romantic love. Psychoanalysis, in particular, recognised the importance of love early on. Writing to Jung in December 1906, Freud remarked, 'essentially, one might say, the cure is effected by love' (McGuire 1979: 50). For some contemporary psychotherapists, love for the movies can itself function as a means by which the psychoanalytic cure may be effected.[5] The sociologist Anthony Giddens has sought to explore the significance of romantic love for a modern, emancipatory, 'pure relationship' (1993: 2), and in *Fragments d'un discours amoureux*

(1977) Roland Barthes has 'simulated' the loving subject (Heath, 1983: 101). The film *Groundhog Day* may be seen as a privileged site for an exploration of romantic love in the terms set out by these studies and, as I will argue, may offer cinematic spectators different ways of approaching film.

It is striking that all of these studies stress the connection between romantic love and narrative. For Giddens, 'romantic love introduced the idea of a narrative into an individual's life' (1993: 39). Historically, he argues, 'the rise of romantic love more or less coincided with the emergence of the novel: the connection was one of newly discovered narrative form' (ibid.: 40). Spector Person makes a similar point, noting how romantic love 'is the narrative thread not just in novels, but in lives' (1989: 23). Romantic love appears, then, to offer a structuring narrative to individuals or to couples: 'the capturing of the heart of the other is in fact a process of the creation of a mutual narrative biography' (Giddens, 1993: 46). The protagonist in *Groundhog Day* is required to re-narrate (or in Laplanchean terms to de- and re-translate) the same day over and over again.

The primary goal of the film is also that of mainstream cinema more generally, namely the instigation, charting and resolution of a heterosexual romance. In *Groundhog Day* romantic love has a diegetic and extra-diegetic function. Romantic love, at first sight, operates as the structuring narrative both for the story and for the protagonist's 'self-realisation' (Giddens, 1993: 40). Falling in love has been described as 'an imaginative act' (Spector Person, 1989: 31) and as such, romantic love is often seen to possess a liberating function (this is certainly the dominant view in Hollywood). It is a quest 'in which self-identity awaits its validation from the discovery of the other' (Giddens, 1993: 45), but it also 'projects a course of future development', necessitating 'a major reworking of the conditions of personal life' (ibid.). In other words, it projects or performs a narrative ideal that is transformatory in its effects. *Groundhog Day* appears to offer its viewers two conflicting approaches to romantic love. On the one hand it cynically unpacks the 'love story' and the ideal of love at first sight, on the other hand it nonetheless provides the viewer with an affectively satisfying, although excessive, resolution to the romance.

How might a concept of romantic love relate, then, to the rather more specific love of the cinema? It has been suggested by Barthes that 'the first thing we love is *a scene*' (1990: 192). One might argue that in the case of the cinema, the first thing that we love is in fact a *mise-en-scène*. Love certainly requires a *mise-en-scène* in the sense that it requires a narrative and a visual context. As will become evident in the next section, love does not appear simply 'out of the blue'. In fact it becomes clear in *Groundhog Day* that context is more or less all. Phil Connors' most successful day, before the final Groundhog Day, culminates in Rita and Connors falling asleep together, only for Connors to wake again on Groundhog Day, alone. His subsequent attempts to repeat the sequence of events that led to Rita joining him in his room fail, precisely because he cannot quite mimic the very particular *mise-en-scène* of the earlier, almost successful day. The *coup de foudre* appears to occur in the staging of a scene. Thus Barthes argues that:

> Love at first sight requires the very sign of its suddenness (what makes me irresponsible, subject to fatality, swept away, ravished): and of all the arrangement of objects, it is the scene which seems to be seen for the first time . . .. I am initiated: the scene consecrates the object I am going to love. (1990: 192)

In many ways, the cinema provides the perfect setting for this kind of (quasi-religious) love at first sight. While the cinema may offer its spectators fantasies that they can incorporate into their personal narratives, it also 'promises to answer the desire it constitutes through the scenarios it enacts' (Lapsley and Westlake, 1993: 191). It is the cinematic text, in other words, that provides the spectator with a *mise-en-scène* that 'ravishes' him or her, which provokes his or her loving desire, provokes an active, performative engagement with the film; as Laplanche and Pontalis remind us, fantasy 'is not the object of desire but its setting' (1988: 26). The romantic comedy provides a privileged space in which a direct, affective relation with the spectator is actively sought. Thus in *Groundhog Day* the spectator's desire is constituted by the scene of Connors' desire and the obstacles to it, but it is also motivated by the transformatory imperative of both the film's, and the spectator's own, narrative.

~ Love at first sight? The après coup *of the* coup de foudre ~

There is a certain fortuitous coincidence between the French term
for deferred action, *après coup* and the terminology used to describe
the phenomenon of love at first sight, *coup de foudre*. *Après coup* in
French conveys the sense of trauma so central to any articulation of
afterwardsness, while the term *coup* is used in many French phrases,
particularly those that relate to the weather, and often denotes ideas
of shock, suddenness and violence. *Foudre* in French refers to lightning
(or the thunderbolt), thus, while the subject of a *coup de foudre* falls in
love at first sight, he or she also falls in love violently or 'traumatically'.
The 'traumatic' event of falling suddenly in love occurs retrospectively,
the discursive product of a romance narrative popularised in romantic
literature and the cinema, and reintegrated into the personal narratives
of individuals seeking to express the experience of falling in love. The
arrow of love, so to speak, is experienced not as an original trauma but
rather as its secondary manifestation; 'the emotional meaning of the
present determines the emotional significance attached to memories of
the past' (Spector Person, 1989: 43). It may perhaps be more appropriate,
therefore, to talk of love at second sight; 'one remembers the gesture
or the detail as the beginning of the process of falling in love only after
love has been realised . . .' (ibid.). As suggested earlier, the detail may
also become a privileged 'cinephiliac moment'. This moment is itself
a retrospective construction, a love at first sight that is subject to the
same structuring logic of afterwardsness.

Romantic love may be seen to be both caused *by* and revealed *in*
the *coup de foudre*, in the illumination of the lightning bolt and in
the *coup*, the trauma, that brands the observation retrospectively as
important, disruptive, traumatic. This is perhaps the primal scene/
seen of a certain kind of love. Theweleit's remarks on this type of love
remind us to pay particular and proper attention to the weather, an
important theme in *Groundhog Day*, because love at first sight, as he
argues, belies a certain strategy. 'The thunderbolt of love, which', he
notes, 'strikes unexpectedly, finds curiously uniform routes [here]; it's
quite astonishing, enough to make one doubt that it comes from the
blue' (1994: 23). Strictly speaking it does not, of course, come from the
blue; storm clouds afford some advance warning. Ironically *Groundhog
Day* opens with cloud footage and we are introduced to Phil Connors as
he presents a weather bulletin against a blue screen. More importantly

he first sees – and falls for, as we discover later – Rita as she playfully experiments with this same blue screen. There is, as Theweleit suggests, a fundamental anteriority in relation to the love object, frequently in terms of social, cultural and economic factors.

Despite the potentially strategic dimension to love at first sight, it remains a powerful image and represents a popular ideal, the instantaneous, all-consuming love that is entirely coincidental and purely passionate. Giddens (1993) has distinguished between passionate and romantic love, arguing that the former breaks or eschews the rules, whilst the latter seeks in a sense to remake them. It might be argued that love at first sight functions as romantic love's mythical origin, its primal scene/seen, retroactively reinscribed so as to render the romantic dynamic passionate. It is perhaps the origin that romantic love desires for itself, so to speak, the 'out of the blue' that belies its strategic composition. And yet it is always at the same time the story of an origin (and the origin of a story), a 'trauma' only through afterwardsness. To know it as love at first sight one would have to be taking one's second (at least) glance. Barthes appositely describes the temporal and causal gap between love at first sight and its narrative recollection:

> There is a deception [*leurre*] in amorous time (this deception is called: the love story). I believe (along with everyone else) that the amorous phenomenon is an 'episode' endowed with a beginning (love at first sight) and an end (suicide, abandonment, disaffection, withdrawal, monastery, travel, etc). Yet the initial scene during which I was ravished is merely reconstituted: it is *after the fact* [c'est un *après coup*]. I reconstruct a traumatic image which I experience in the present but which I conjugate (which I speak in the past) . . .. Love at first sight is always spoken in the past tense: it might be called an *anterior immediacy*. The image is perfectly adapted to this temporal deception: distinct, abrupt, framed, it is already (again, always) a memory. (1990: 193–4)

Barthes appears to share Theweleit's suspicion that love at first sight may well be more strategic than imagined, arguing that: '[W]hen I "review" the scene of the abduction [*rapt*], I retrospectively create a stroke of luck: this scene has all the magnificence of an accident: I cannot get over having had this good fortune: to meet what matches my desire' (1990: 194, translation modified).

~ *Love, spectatorship and afterwardsness in* Groundhog Day ~

Does *Groundhog Day*, then, reveal through its repetitions of Connors' seduction of Rita, the *après coup* of the *coup de foudre*, the strategic dimension of love at first sight? Connors' love at first sight is clearly retrospective, signalled both by our spectatorial witnessing of its construction and by his assertion that he has loved Rita from the first moment he saw her ('out of the blue' screen); 'The first time I saw you, something happened to me.' For Rita it is a case of a rapid move from initial dislike, to a kind of *coup de foudre* but not quite love at first sight. From Rita's temporal point of view (and to some extent from the spectator's) her falling in love with Connors happens very, almost too, quickly. Initially Rita has to contend with Connors' cynical views on the kinds of 'morons' who might be entertained by the Groundhog Day ceremony and his innuendo-laden comments about his desirability and talent. As Connors is transformed, Rita is – in narrative terms – unaware of his change in character because she is experiencing each Groundhog Day for the first time. Rita appears somehow aware of the new Connors, even though she spends very little time with him on the final Groundhog Day. As Thompson notes:

> The moment in the climax when Rita finally reaches up to accept Phil after having 'bought' him depends on our sense that they have had a romantic courtship – even though during that final day she presumably remembers nothing of these earlier scenes. But Phil does, and we do, and by the end that is enough to give us a sense that they are ready to marry. (1999: 143)

There are in the film two versions of time that overlap. Following linear time – in other words, the perspectives of the other characters (apart from Connors, and later Rita who eventually accepts his bizarre story of temporal distortion) – the love between Connors and Rita is virtually instantaneous. Yet from Connors' perspective – that of repetition, warped time – this love is achieved as a (narrative) process. By learning more and more about Rita he comes to love her, but he only comes to realise this through the work expended on the seduction. We are presented here with the hidden causal factors that underpin the act of falling in love, factors that come into being only after one falls in love.

Connors' love results, then, from the temporal logic of afterwardsness – it happens *après coup*. The trauma of the initial 'thunderbolt' is only activated at a later stage, once Connors has begun the process of transformation and is susceptible to its effects. It is only at this point that love is activated and is understood as the retrospective cause of his love at first sight. Ironically it is Rita's love (at first sight, more or less) that rescues Connors from his condition of repetition. She rescues him by a process that is, strangely, very similar to the means by which he manages to seduce her, to get her to fall in love with him, but this process remains invisible to her. She learns as much about Connors as he learns about her, but in one day. While Connors' literal escape from the repetitive temporal structure of his endless Groundhog Day results ultimately from the agency of a woman, the film makes it clear that his escape is also a result of his active self-transformation. As will be demonstrated, Connors' escape from Groundhog Day is effected by his final performance of it.

The repetition that Connors experiences could also perhaps be conceived of as the projection of an aspect of his psyche, as the compulsion to repeat. The compulsion to repeat is essentially an attempt to remember:

> psychoanalysis was confronted from the very beginning by repetition *phenomena*. . . . Any consideration of *symptoms* reveals that a certain number of them – obsessional rituals for instance – are repetitive in character; furthermore, the defining property of a symptom is the very fact that it reproduces, in a more or less disguised way, certain elements of a past conflict . . . .. In a general way, the repressed seeks to 'return' in the present, whether in the form of dreams, symptoms or acting-out. (Freud, cited in Laplanche and Pontalis, 1988: 79)

Remembering, however, is also possibly the means to a more effective forgetting – once remembered the item is externalised (Phillips, 1994: 24). If this is the case, what is it that Phil Connors is trying to forget? What is it that is causing Groundhog Day to repeat endlessly? Is Connors attempting to forget a version of himself perhaps, a self that needs to be forgotten before another can be conceived of? The ultimate form of forgetting is death, and Connors, unable to commit suicide effectively (he always wakes up again at six the next/same morning), is forced to devise another strategy in order to escape this repetitive trap. Through the knowledge he gains from these repeated suicide attempts and the seductions of Rita, Connors begins a (narrative) project to better himself. In other words, his acting out, his repetition is reinscribed back onto the events repeated in order to retranscribe or retranslate them – to narrate a 'better' story in which he is 'good', cured even, and where 'the mystery has been solved and the spell broken' (Laplanche and Pontalis, 1988: 79). Connors is reconstructing an identity on the basis of a return to the reflective domain of the Lacanian mirror stage, where his actions are directly mirrored in the behaviour of others. He has an image of perfection (ego-ideal) reflected back to himself, an image over which he has total control by virtue of the fact that he is able to rehearse and thus perfect his moves, so to speak. Internalising this image through the love focused on him by Rita, Connors takes on this subjectivity, performs it as an identity, becoming an ideal man for Rita and an ideal community-minded citizen for the residents of Punxsutawney. This process reveals the constructedness of identity, its narrative dimension. The film's audience, clearly intended to identify with the Murray character, arguably shares the afterwardsness experienced by Connors. As viewers of a heterosexual rom-com, the audience witnesses a traditional love story but one that reveals to them, comically, the mechanics of its construction. Nonetheless the revelation of the temporality behind love at first sight also provides the love story with its traditional obstacles, 'the desire does not reveal the obstacle, the obstacle reveals the desire' (Phillips, 1993: 86).

It is the motif of repetition that both reveals the strategic aspect to romantic love and at the same time operates as the 'obstacle' that Connors has to surmount; it is, somewhat ironically, only through the knowledge gained by repetition that Connors' can escape this repetition, this Groundhog Day. The narrative overcoming of these obstacles after so many comic failed attempts provides romantic, visual pleasure for the audience. The film's final montage sequence during which Connors performs the perfect (and perfected) Groundhog Day reveals to the audience the extent of his transformation. Connors' detailed knowledge of the day's events enable him to intervene on a number of occasions – saving the boy who falls from a tree and performing the Heimlich manoeuvre on Buster Green (Brian Doyle-Murray), for example – turning the cynical Connors into a kind of superhero. Thus in the final sequence of *Groundhog Day*, the spectator arguably identifies with, and internalises, the pleasurable images of Connors' omnipotence viewed on screen and thus shares in the reconstruction of both Connors' identity and his or her own.

In terms of cinephilia, or cine-love, it may be argued, then, that the spectator is subject to a certain kind of *coup de foudre*, to the logic of the *après coup* or *afterwardsness*. Cinematic spectatorship must be about being kidnapped or overwhelmed by the image – the spectator must fall in love with the cinema (at first sight and repeatedly). *Groundhog Day* performs and requires the spectator to perform – through its narrative and through its temporal structure – a love at first (and inevitably, second) sight. In loving the cinema, this amorous spectator (re)constructs, *après coup*, the cinematic object of his or her *coup de foudre*. The film comes into being for the spectator by afterwardsness, in and through a certain kind of memory.

Ultimately, *Groundhog Day* may be read as a film about love (and psychoanalysis) as cure. The film stages and restages a love at first sight, a repetition of a romantic and a cinematic love. Perhaps *Groundhog Day* stages a repetition of this psychoanalytic procedure/cure, just as this chapter repeats both the film and psychoanalysis, *après coup*, so as to reveal a 'better', or at least different, version of the film.

4   *Prom-Coms*

Reliving the Dreams and Nightmares of High-School Romance

~ Stacey Abbott ~

Only socio-paths experience their teenage life just once. Everyone else relives them again and again, occasionally with professional assistance, and some of us actually find entertainment value in this process. (Katz, 1998: 35)

THE TEEN COMEDY is a curious genre that has emerged and developed in recent years. While American cinema has been preoccupied by youth in various guises since the earliest days of filmmaking, a genre of comedy devoted to exploring the humorous side of adolescent experience usually set in the American high school emerged in the 1980s.[1] Although not all of these films are romantic comedies (a notable sub-genre of the teen comedy being the sex-quest film best exemplified by *Porky's* (1982) and *American Pie* (1999)), the search for love and romance is a key structuring element of most teen comedies. Some films, like *Pretty in Pink* (1986), *Say Anything* (1989) and *10 Things I Hate About You* (1999) are in many ways conventional rom-coms chronicling the pursuit of romantic fulfilment, albeit with closer consideration for youthful insecurities and the pressures of social standing and individual identity upon budding relationships. Others, including *The Breakfast Club* (1985), *Heathers* (1989), *Clueless* (1995) and *Mean Girls* (2004), are more focused upon exploring the complexity and hypocrisy of the high-school social hierarchy but still present romance as playing an important role in negotiating that environment, either as a way of rebelling against cliquish stereotyping (*The Breakfast Club* and *Heathers*) or as a means of maturing (*Clueless* and *Mean Girls*). What *all* of these teen comedies have in common, however, is a preoccupation with social acceptance and surely there is no better way to represent the achievement of this acceptance than through love and romance, usually attained at the high-school prom, a social event that is presented in film and television as 'nothing less than epochal in the life of a teen-ager' (Elias, 1999: 63). At the prom, according to most teen comedies, love and social acceptance come together in one grand romantic gesture, representing, as Thomas M. Leitch argues, not 'the promise of permanent commitment and social renewal' but 'the timeless apotheosis of teen love' (1992: 45).

The production of teen comedies raises an interesting schism between the creative voice behind the film and its presumed audience. As Timothy Shary points out, since adolescents are usually unable to write or direct mainstream films themselves, 'screen images of youth have always been traditionally filtered through adult perspectives' (2002: 2). In this way we are faced with a genre that is ostensibly for teenagers and about the teenage experience but produced from the perspective of adults reminiscing or revisiting their own teenage years. For instance, Amy Heckerling, director of *Fast Times at Ridgemont High* (1982) and *Clueless*, describes herself as 'stuck in adolescence' (cited in Eisenbach, 1999: 42), while Joss Whedon, the writer-producer of the successful teen television series *Buffy the Vampire Slayer* (1997–2003), has always claimed that his conception of high school as hell in *Buffy* grew out of his own experiences as a teenager (Gross, 2003: 36). It is therefore not surprising, given the perspective of the creators of these teen-oriented series and films, that this genre has often found its audience split between teenagers and adults.

It would be easy to explain this interest by assuming that for adults this genre represents a return to an idealised past and a feeling of innocence, when having a date for the prom was the most important issue of the day. Comic-book and television writer Brian K. Vaughan supports this perspective by stating that 'while you're going through high school, it seems like hell, but once you're old you begin looking back at high school like it used to be paradise' (cited in Wizard Staff, 2007). This explanation does not, however, acknowledge that while teen films usually end with the affirmation of true love, the path to this happy ending is laid with trauma, isolation, loneliness and even horror – the line between teen comedies and teen horror is a fine one. For instance, in response to Vaughan's interview, a group of *Buffy* fans on the whedonesque.com discussion board, each stating themselves to be well beyond their high-school years, exchanged their memories and views on this subject that undermine Vaughan's nostalgic perspective. 'Tamara C' claimed that, 'Twenty plus years after high school I still look back with hate and fury. There was no good in high school,' while Redfern stated, 'I remember a high school teacher telling me "This is the best time of your life" and thinking "Should I kill myself now or wait, just in case he's full of it". Thankfully, he was' (Whedonesque, 2007). What is interesting about this exchange is not only the vehemence of their response but the fact that it is coming from fans of the largely high school-set television series. While the participants in this discussion hated high school, they clearly enjoy revisiting it through the series. The same can arguably be said for adult fans of teen rom-coms, but why? What does the genre offer to the adult fan?

In this chapter I will address this question by exploring how the teen rom-com offers a cathartic re-exploration and rewriting of past experiences for adult audiences. To achieve this, rather than focusing exclusively upon conventional teen rom-coms, I will discuss a selection of recent films, most notably *Grosse Pointe Blank* (1997), *Romy and Michele's High School Reunion* (1997), *Never Been Kissed* (1999) and *13 Going on 30* (2004), that acknowledge and address the grown-up pleasures of the genre. In all four instances, they do this by featuring adults returning to high school and being confronted by adolescent romance. In so doing, these characters re-enter the generic parameters of the teen rom-com, creating a hybrid of the teen and adult genre, in order to confront both the dreams and nightmares of teenage life and, more significantly, teenage romance, but from the perspective of adulthood.

~ Remaking high school ~ .

> Maybe we were better off when we thought less and kissed more. Have we graduated past our ability to find true love? When it comes to matters of the heart, did we have it right in high school? (Carrie Bradshaw (Sarah Jessica Parker), *Sex and the City*)

In the episode 'Boy Interrupted' of *Sex and the City* (6:10), prompted by the renewal of her relationship with her high-school boyfriend, narrator and chief protagonist Carrie Bradshaw questions whether the cynicism of adulthood has undermined the possibility of love and romance that seemed so tangible in high school. Throughout this episode each of the characters reminisces, relives or rewrites their high-school experiences, highlighting many of the pleasures of the teen rom-com. For instance, Carrie nostalgically recalls the wonders of teen love as she makes out with her high-school beau. Stanford (Willie Garson) relives the traumas of teenage relationships as he finds himself without a date for the 'Prom' (a charity fundraiser for the Gay/Lesbian/Bi/Transgender Centre). Finally, both Carrie and Stanford rewrite their past experiences by being crowned Queens of the Prom.

On a more basic level, however, the episode calls attention to the appeal of remembering high school, which, while paradoxical given that these memories are often laced with 'hate and fury' as declared above, is a key attraction to watching teen rom-coms. Through their familiar high-school imagery, these films trigger memories, both good and bad, of our own teenage years. This is a fact that is highlighted by recent DVD releases of *Sixteen Candles* (1984), *Pretty in Pink* and *Fast Times at Ridgemont High*, now packaged under the series label 'The High School Reunion Collection', and thus clearly marketed as a return to both high school and the high-school film.[2] *Romy and Michele's High School Reunion* and *Never Been Kissed* in particular integrate the act of remembering within their narratives as events in the present cause the main characters to flashback to their high-school years. For instance, after hearing about their upcoming ten-year reunion, Romy (Mira Sorvino) and Michele (Lisa Kudrow) flip through their yearbook, sharing memories and comic anecdotes. As they stop on particular pages to comment upon individual students or high-school cliques, the camera swoops down and into each photo, bringing the past back to life as the still image leaps into motion. What is significant about these memories, however, is that they are not presented with nostalgia but are laced with cynicism and horror.[3] While each flashback begins positively as Romy and Michele enthusiastically reminisce, the horrible events depicted, such as the A-group cheerleaders ridiculing their dress sense, or they themselves mocking the C-group honour-roll geeks, call to mind the cruelty of high school.

This aspect is even more apparent in *Never Been Kissed* when journalist Josie Gellar (Drew Barrymore) informs her brother that she has been assigned to go undercover as a student in a local high school. His response is one of shock as he asks her 'Josie, do you *remember* high school?', sparking a flashback to the entire student body chanting

4.1: Drew Barrymore remembers the horrors of high school in *Never Been Kissed.*

'Josie Grossie! Josie Grossie!'. Furthermore, both of these films follow the flashbacks with the protagonists' return to high school, meaning that they are no longer looking back to the past but are *living* it and as a result have once again become the outsiders they were as adolescents. Romy and Michele's attempts to feign success at their reunion results in further mocking as their lie about being the inventors of the post-it is revealed. Josie's attempts to be young and hip on her first day at school, dressed in white jeans and feather scarf, immediately signals her as a loser and results in her becoming an object of disdain for her fellow students who describe her as 'off the chart'. In both cases, the distance between past and present that, according to Susan Stewart, facilitates a nostalgic perspective is collapsed (1993: 145). When Josie looks at herself in the mirror after her first flashback, it is her teenage image that is reflected back at her (see Fig. 4.1).

The most painful memories of high school depicted in these films are, however, those linked both with romance and the prom. The prom, or other forms of high-school dance, often plays a crucial part in the teen rom-com for, according to Lesley Speed, it 'forms an important social sphere for the beginnings of romance' (1995: 27) but also the potential for trauma and humiliation, best exemplified by the high-school horror film *Carrie* (1976). While Romy and Michele's initial memories focus upon how they looked and what they wore, important signifiers for any prom, the memory quickly turns to teen love as Romy successfully asks football player Billy Christenson to dance, making this in her words 'the best night of my life'. This ideal prom experience is, however, shattered when Billy leaves her as he rides off on his motorcycle with his Prom Queen girlfriend. For Josie the prom memories are even more traumatic. Flashbacks reveal that school heartthrob Billy Prince asked Josie to the prom as a joke, which she only finds out when he turns up in a limousine and hurls eggs at her. Josie's humiliation as she collapses crying on the porch, covered in egg yoke is utterly abject. The pain of adolescent unrequited love, which in the context of the teen rom-com has embedded within it aspirations for peer acceptance and social affirmation, is here made the material of nightmares as both Romy and Josie are cruelly rejected by their peers. As a result, these memories of thwarted romance are more humiliating then any witnessed in traditional romantic comedies, for they are overlaid with the pain of teenage isolation.

The presence of these flashbacks serves not only to remind the audience of the horrors of teen love but creates a space in which these defining moments can be re-experienced through the conventions of the teen rom-com, reimagined as a form of adult wish fulfilment. Where in the flashback to the prom, Romy and Michele quietly slow dance together as a means of comforting Romy following her romantic humiliation, at the reunion they triumphantly take centre stage as they join former science nerd-turned-success story Sandy Frink (Alan Cummings) on the dance floor for a balletic ménage à trois.[4] For Josie in *Never Been Kissed* the catharsis of her second high-school experience is even sweeter. Having transitioned from disenfranchised to popular through the intervention of her 'cool' brother Rob (David Arquette), Josie, 'a geek to the core', is able to experience the dream prom night that she was previously deprived of, when asked to the prom by high-school heartthrob Guy Perkins. In keeping with the prom's theme 'Meant for Each Other: Famous Couples Throughout History', Josie and Guy arrive beautifully dressed as Rosalind and Orlando from Shakespeare's *As You Like It*. This not only provides Josie, now dressed as a princess, her Cinderella moment but also indicates for the first time that while her scholarly interest marks her difference from the other girls (dressed as Malibu, Disco and Evening-Gown Barbie) it is an acceptable difference. The approval of her peers is confirmed when she and Guy are crowned Prom King and Queen, dance romantically before the approving crowd, and when Guy – 'that one guy with his mysterious confidence who seemed so perfect in every way' – tells Josie she 'rocks his world'. The perfect rom-com memories are achieved to replace the haunting memories of her first prom.

That this cathartic and revisionist pleasure is one of the factors that attracts adult audiences to the teen rom-com is reinforced within the diegesis of the film by Josie's growing audience at the newspaper after she starts wearing a hidden camera that transmits images back to her editor's office. The prom marks the dramatic highlight for this audience as the technician transmitting Josie's signal brings his own date to watch the proceedings in his van, which he has bedecked with its own disco ball and stocked with champagne while the staff at the newspaper gather together, reminiscing about their own proms, running a pool on who will be crowned Prom Queen and waiting to see how Josie will do. This group of adults, who sit in the dark, eat popcorn and cheer when Josie is crowned, stand in for the adult cinema audiences of the genre, watching a contemporary re-enactment, or remake if you will, of their own past experiences in which past wrongs are righted. This is in keeping with Susan Stewart's definition of nostalgia, which, she claims 'is always ideological: the past it seeks has never existed except as narrative' (1993: 23) and with Claire Birchall's argument that the teen genre 'encourages nostalgia . . . for the teen identity that we never quite achieved' (2004: 184).

While part of the pleasure of these films involves this type of romantic wish fulfilment, their climax, however, often centres on the pain of adolescence through an overt condemnation of high-school cruelty. In *Never Been Kissed*, Josie denounces the teenagers for their malicious behaviour after stopping them from dousing one of the less popular kids with dog food – a moment consciously reminiscent of the shower of pig's blood in *Carrie*. Removing her crown, Josie informs the others:

> Let me tell you something. I don't care about being your stupid Prom Queen. I'm 25 years old. I'm an under cover reporter for the *Chicago Sun Times* and I have been beating my brains out trying to impress you people . . . All of you people, there is a big world out there, bigger than prom, bigger than high school and it won't matter if you were the Prom Queen or the quarterback of the football team or the biggest nerd in school.

This film therefore provides the audience with the satisfaction of achieving a seemingly unattainable teenage goal while at the same time, and with the experience of an adult, denying its importance when Josie is both crowned Prom Queen and later rejects the title. Similarly, at the reunion, Romy enacts the ultimate reunion fantasy by confronting her high-school tormentor and telling her 'I don't care if you like us. We don't like you. You're a bad person with an ugly heart. And we don't give a *flying fuck* what you think.' Both *Never Been Kissed* and *Romy and Michele* deny nostalgia for real high-school experience, instead fostering it in the reimagining of that experience through the conventions of the teen rom-com in which the loneliness of adolescence is replaced by social acceptance but, with the hindsight of adulthood, not at the expense of integrity and individuality.

~ Nostalgia for the 1980s ~

While *Romy and Michele* and *Never Been Kissed* evoke a nostalgia for a fantasy high-school experience, *13 Going on 30* and *Grosse Pointe Blank* consciously construct a nostalgia for a very specific lived experience, most notably the 1980s – the heyday for the teen comedy. These are films aimed specifically at the generation of adults who were teenagers watching *Pretty in Pink* and *Say Anything* upon their original release. For instance, *13 Going on 30* is replete with references to 1980s pop culture, most notably represented through the music of Pat Benatar and Michael Jackson. *Grosse Pointe Blank* evokes classic 1980s teen films *The Sure Thing* (1985) and *Say Anything* through the casting of John Cusack as Martin Blank, a hired assassin returning to his hometown for his high-school reunion, celebrating the class of 1986. The film, and its reunion narrative, serves to position the audience alongside Blank both in general terms, looking back at what they have done and who they have become since they left high school, and quite specifically by harking back to the iconic image of John Cusack from these 1980s teen rom-coms.

Similarly, *13 Going on 30* invites the audience to reflect upon their own teenage past alongside the film's stars who, as part of the film's marketing campaign, were made to share their personal adolescent memories both in the press material for the film's release and in the 'I Was a Teenage Geek' special feature on the DVD, which includes photos of each of the film's main stars, Jennifer Garner, Mark Ruffalo and Judy Greer, as teenagers. *Never Been Kissed* similarly includes teenage photos of the entire cast and crew in the film's final credits. By integrating the past of the actors and crew into the film, these films reinforce the notion that part of the appeal of the teen film is in looking back and recognising a shared experience – we've all been teenagers, we've all been to high school – and also a shared reimagining of that experience. *13 Going on 30* in particular presents an overtly sentimental look at high school and romance largely because it is from the point of view of a character who has missed that experience and therefore still harbours all the romantic ideals of one who is anticipating their perfect prom and their first love.

The film tells the story of Jenna, a 13-year-old girl who, through unexplained magical intervention, is propelled from 1989 into her own life at the age of 30, with only her yearbook, including photos of her as Prom Queen, to inform her about her high-school life. In this way the film uses Jenna (Jennifer Garner) as a link to the past of its largely adult audience. Much like *Never Been Kissed* this is mirrored in the effect Jenna has on the adults around her. They respond with a wistful nostalgia for the past that she evokes through her youthful enthusiasm and guileless charm. She has yet to take on the cynical qualities that, from the point of view of the teen movie, are the defining features of growing up. For instance, in the films of John Hughes, as Leitch argues, 'the whole system [adults] represent is so hypocritical, alienating, and meaningless that growing up would mean the end of the world' (1992: 45). This view is memorably expressed in *The Breakfast Club* when Allison Reynolds (Ally Sheedy) tells the others, 'when you grow old your heart dies'. *13 Going on 30* both reinforces and reverses this attitude by reminding the adults what it is to be a teenager by awakening rose-tinted memories of their own teenage years. The best illustration of this is in the scene where Jenna livens up a company party by asking the DJ to play Michael Jackson's 'Thriller' and urging the surrounding crowd to join her in performing Jackson's famous dance moves. Initially too self-conscious and mature to respond, the crowd are gradually won over by Jenna's dancing and by the iconic quality of this bit of 1980s pop culture as everyone, including Jenna's gruff editor-in-chief and her coldly duplicitous 'best friend', get up and dance. The joy of embracing the past is all the more idealised by the beautifully choreographed quality of the sequence, for the group not only dance to 'Thriller', they dance it well. This sequence challenges anyone who was a teenager in the 1980s to resist the urge to get up and dance (see Fig. 4.2).

Jenna, however, not only evokes nostalgia for youthful ideals but youthful romance. Throughout the film, she has been renewing a relationship with Matt (Mark Ruffalo), her teenage best friend and first

4.2: Dancing to 'Thriller' in *13 Going on 30*.

love whom – in the past she doesn't remember – she rejected due to peer pressure, causing the two to grow apart as adults, a fact he remembers all too well. The nostalgia that Jenna evokes therefore is also for the promise of first love before the full impact of high school and adult social pressures. While Jenna causes the others around her to remember their youth, she rekindles Matt's romantic idealism and desire to find a soul-mate in Jenna, a fact that is specifically signposted by their youthful antics as they dance to 'Thriller', share favourite childhood candies, and play on the swings. Screwball comedy's extolling of 'play as a means of establishing the companionship so essential to contemporary love' (Lent, 1995: 322) is here made quite literal through the hybridisation of the rom-com with the teen comedy as the characters re-enact favourite games from their childhood as part of their courtship, resulting in a re-ignition of the intense emotions associated with teenage love. Matt later tells Jenna, 'I have felt things these past few weeks that I didn't know I could feel anymore.'

In the build-up to his own wedding to his fiancée Wendy, signposted as a 'wrong partner' by her insistence that he move to Chicago despite his obvious reticence, Matt, however, rejects his ideal relationship with Jenna in favour of the adult pragmatism associated with the 'nervous romances' of the 1970s or the contemporary independent rom-com when he tells Jenna,

> but I have realised in these past few days you can't just turn back time . . . I moved on. You moved on. We've gone down different paths for so

long. We made different choices. I chose Wendy . . . You don't always
get the dream house but you get awfully close.

Here he rejects the nostalgia for the past and looks to the future with
Wendy, even if it is less than ideal. Through this decision Matt both
undermines mainstream rom-com tradition by not walking out on the
wedding to pursue a relationship with 'right partner' Jenna – a popular
convention of the genre from *It Happened One Night* (1934) to *Four
Weddings and a Funeral* (1994) – and conveys the invasion of cynicism
that the teen rom-com rejects, proving *The Breakfast Club* assertion
that 'when you grow old your heart dies'.

That isn't the end of the story. For Jenna, her experiences as an
adult cause her to realise that she loves Matt, which incites her to
return to the past to right the wrongs of her teenage years and restore
Matt's romantic idealism in the process. Here Jenna reasserts the
film's position as a teen rom-com for, as Leitch argues, the genre is
distinguished from its adult equivalent by the fact that the obstacles
to romance are largely external and need simply be removed in order
to provide 'the satisfaction of successful wish fulfilment' (1992: 45).
In so doing, however, Jenna, like Josie in *Never Been Kissed*, also gets
to reject high-school social hierarchy and admonish her peers with the
hindsight of adulthood by sacrificing social acceptance and choosing
the unpopular Matt instead. The film therefore ends with the 'happy
ending' we generally expect of both the teen and adult rom-com as
Matt and Jenna find social acceptance in each other and end up happily
married. As Hilary Radner points out in Chapter 15 of this volume,
however, the fantasy nature of this ending, as Jenna and Matt literally
move into her pink 'dream house', calls the idealism of this resolution
into question. As such the film gets to embrace nostalgia for the perfect
high-school romance while subtly questioning its attainability.

In contrast to *13 Going on 30*, *Grosse Pointe Blank*, through its
reunion narrative and darkly comic tone, takes a more cynical look
at the attraction of returning to high school and the high-school film.
While the film traces through its lead character Martin Blank a similar
desire to go back and right past wrongs, which is, as I have argued, a key
pleasure of the teen comedy, the film deliberately problematises this
fantasy by contrasting the seeming normality of Blank's hometown, and
high-school past, with his current life as a contract killer. Going back
to confront his past, he finds himself to be an anachronism in Grosse

Pointe – decidedly out of place with his questionable morals, suspicious behaviour and lone gunman appearance. However, the extremity of his remoteness from his surroundings – asking his therapist 'What am I going to say "I killed the President of Paraguay with a fork. What do you do?"' – humorously highlights the tensions experienced by all the characters returning to the reunion, each confronted by the disparity between who they are and who they were. Rather than romanticise the process of returning to high school, this film raises the question: can, or should, *anyone* go back?

This tension between past and present is made all the more transparent through Martin's attempt to renew his relationship with high-school sweetheart Debi Newberry (Minnie Driver), the girl he stood up on prom night as he ran off to join the army, leaving her waiting in her $700 dress and wondering what she had done to drive him away. Here is a prom night as traumatic as Josie's in *Never Been Kissed*. The Grosse Pointe reunion is their opportunity to regain that lost prom experience, but is met by both parties with trepidation. Should she trust him again? Can he feign normality and resist the urge to bring a gun? Can the past be recaptured or rewritten, which is the promise of this hybrid genre? As Martin and Debi strategically negotiate the reunion, deciding who to talk to, who to avoid, how best to justify their lives, they rediscover their romantic dynamic by slipping into teenage behaviour as they slow dance in the gymnasium and later have clandestine sex in the nurse's office. Their teenage euphoria is, however, disrupted when Martin's real life comes crashing in and he is attacked by a fellow assassin, whom he kills in self-defence only to have Debi find him next to the body covered in blood. As Lesley Speed argues, the film negates any nostalgia for the past through the 'violent collisions between [Blank's] past and present' (2000: 27). Discovering the truth about Martin, Debi finally tells him 'You don't get to have me,' echoing Matt's rejection of Jenna in *13 Going on 30*, because the past can't be recaptured. Even more than Jenna and Matt, Martin and Debi have 'gone down different paths'.

Like *13 Going on 30*, *Grosse Pointe Blank* does have a 'happy' ending in this case as Martin decides that he wants to give up his life of crime in order to be with Debi, reconciling his psychosis in the process, and confirming her earlier angry assertion 'I'm part of your romantic new beginning' (all of this while rescuing her father from would-be assassins). While the idealisation of the ending of *13 Going on 30* can be read ambivalently as I have suggested above, the romance of Martin's proposal in *Grosse Pointe Blank* is overtly presented as questionable by the film's dark humour as Martin declares, 'Debi, I'm in love with you and I know we can make this relationship work,' as he wipes his face clean of the splattered blood of the man he has just shot. The intercutting of Martin's declaration of love with a violent, if comic, shootout clearly undermines the idealisation of this high-school relationship and begs the question 'upon what is this relationship based?'. Unlike Carrie in 'Boy, Interrupted' who ends the episode alone but looking to the future, Debi does end up with her high-school boyfriend, as they drive out of town – and away from their past. Debi's final narration, however, leaves the film with a sense of uncertainty rather then romance as she declares 'Some people say forgive and forget. I say forget about forgiving and just accept . . . And get the hell out of town.' Here the restoration of the high-school couple does not suggest the promise of youthful romance associated with teen rom-coms but rather an acceptance of compromise over idealism and as such the film questions what kind of future they will have together.

By putting the conventions of the teen rom-com on display and narratively situating adults within the generic parameters of the teen film, these hybrids demonstrate how the genre touches upon familiar adolescent experiences while at the same time reimagining them in ways that betray the adult perspective of their creators and audiences. They are simultaneously familiar and unfamiliar, lived experience and fantasy wish fulfilment. While high school is often discussed as either the best of times or the worst of times, the teen rom-com brings these two types of imagery together in a glorious mix, offering an ambivalent exploration of the pleasures and horrors of re-experiencing adolescence and high-school romance.

5 The Healing Power of Romantic Love in Popular Indian Romantic Comedies: Raja Hindustani

Home Elsewhere and Elsewhere Home

~ Sean Redmond ~

IN THIS ESSAY I intend to explore the way contemporary Indian romantic comedies attempt to come to terms with what are imagined to be the divisive footprints of globalisation, (post)modernity and social and gender inequality as they manifest themselves in Indian society today. It will be my contention that Indian rom-coms look to the power of romantic love to heal or make invisible social divisions, overcome amoral desires and to unite social groups otherwise differentiated by income, wealth, caste and diaspora distance. Romantic love is represented as a utopian force that confirms the superiority of Eastern/Indian ways of being and belonging, shaping and informing the (inter)national imaginary of India.

Indian rom-coms are largely free of irony and self consciousness (unlike many American post-classical rom-coms, for example). The romantic love that burns at the core of these films is represented as pure, eternal, authentic and, in the religious sense, mythological. Indian heroes, villains and heroines appear as excessive conduits for the representation of love and romance. Through fabulous song-and-dance numbers, hyperbolic poetic monologues, and fantasy/dream scenarios, the romantic love that emerges is rendered spectacular, visually and orally extraordinary, with iconic stars heralding its transformative powers. Contemporary Indian romantic comedies suggest that devotional love is a magical force that will find a way, and it is a traditional, pre-postmodern version of love that will save India (and Indian migrants around the world) from emotional chaos and wretched Otherness.[1]

Contemporary Indian rom-coms utilise comedians, stock comedic characters and comedy situations to counter-balance the emotional intensity and 'truthfulness' of the romantic encounters. Such is the power of romantic love that it often needs a complementary force to temper its kinetic, smouldering energy. The use of comedy, then, is one such cross-generic device used to ground the 'higher-order' metaphysics of romantic love (Nayar, 2004). Comedy also works to 'distract' the audience from the ideological glue that sits behind or beneath the representation of romantic love, through what can be considered to be a different type or 'flow' of corporeal catharsis. Comedy and romance can be argued to work in both complementary and contradictory ways.

In summary, I would like to establish that the aesthetic and ideological nucleus of popular Indian rom-coms is, in the end, about recentring and reconfirming traditional (repressive) forms of engagement and bondage; it is also about the fantasy of the homecoming ('home-elsewhere'), and of successfully staying put ('elsewhere-home') for the Indian diaspora. In this essay I take the rom-com to be a concrete product or generic form in popular Indian cinema. However, that is not to elide the fact that a great many popular Indian films are multi-generic 'Masala' hybrids, or a heady mixture of action, melodrama, comedy, romance, and musical elements. The films that I am concerned with, nonetheless, always return the 'story' to the over-determining force of love and laughter.

The central textual case study for the essay will be *Raja Hindustani* (1996), the first Bollywood rom-com to achieve widespread crossover appeal in the West, particularly the UK, where it reached number one at the box office (the first commercial Indian film to do so). *Raja Hindustani* can be argued to be a Bollywood film explicitly aimed at the Indian dispora; a text so saturated in nostalgic yearnings that it particularly spoke to those who live(d), or were born outside, India. *Raja Hindustani* is a film, then, that offers up a powerful sense of the home-elsewhere and elsewhere-home motif that I argue is central to the ideological underpinning of contemporary Indian romantic comedies.

~ *The healing power of romantic love* ~

What can romantic love do? *Everything.* It has the power to cross social divide, class, caste and religion. It has the power to shape subjectivity, arouse the senses, fuel the emotions and direct action. The power of romantic love is such that no obstacle – spiritual, cultural, ideological, historical, geographical – can stand in its way once it has been ignited. In cinematic terms, romantic love is a utopian force that brings together two people, usually a heterosexual couple, who are destined to be together. Cued by both representational and 'non-representational' signs such as colours, textures, clothes, sounds, expressions and 'feelings' (Dyer, 1999: 371–81), the lovers act as an expressive healing conduit for the social ills of the age. As Frank Krutnik suggests in relation to the Hollywood rom-com:

> Conceptualisations of love may constantly be in flux – along with the broader configurations of romance, sexuality, gender identity and marriage – but the genre routinely celebrates it as an immutable, almost mystical force that guides two individuals who are 'made for each other' into one another's arms. Love is shown triumphing over all manner of obstructions, over all kinds of differences in social status, cultural background and personality. (2002: 138)

The force of cinematic romantic love is such that its transformative powers extend beyond the loving union of two protagonists, reaching out to family, friends and the wider society in both the film world and the 'real' world it connects with and interprets. Romantic love is meant to be the very sense-based, cardiovascular material that makes the whole world a better (more loving, joyous, harmonious) place.

Contemporary popular Indian romantic comedies utilise the encounter between two fated but 'different' heterosexual people to make or prove the case that India (through its particularly religious and devotional version of romantic love) is a better place to be (in love, at home, under the 'spell' of its imagined community). Often based on a narrative pattern in which the hero, 'separated from the heroine by barriers of caste, status or wealth, does a good turn – so that the family, in the last scene, willingly give their girl in marriage to him as a reward' (Gokulsing and Dissanayake, 1998: 24), the Indian rom-com employs a mixture of realist and fantasy scenarios, often framed by spectacular song-and-dance routines, and aural-dramatic encounters, to communicate its complex message about the type of place India is for those (good and evil, romantics and Machiavellians) who live within/without its borders. This devotional message is delivered through distinctly excessive forms of visualisation ('song picturisation') and oration, both of which are particular to the way in which the arts and culture have developed in India (Gokulsing and Dissanyak, 1998; Mishra, 2002; Nayar, 2004).

The representation of romance and of the romantic coupling is a truly dazzling and hyper-intense affair, with a romantic hero and love-struck idealised female embodying the heart and soul of the modern nation state. The hero is the personification of perfected masculinity. He is physically strong, athletic, brave and courageous, but unlike his American romantic-heroic counterparts, for example, he is not silent, silenced, inarticulate or uncertain. The romantic hero of popular Indian cinema is a poet who delivers impassioned speeches and monologues, and sings songs on love, honour, duty and obligation. For example, in *Raja Hindustani*, Raja (Aamir Khan) sings these lyrics to Aarti (Karisma Kapoor), the 'modernised' woman he is destined to transform, pacify, and marry:

Your speech is like that of a nightingale,
Your innocent face is like a sculpture.
Don't go into the garden lest I worry
That some thorn will pierce your feet.
I hope I won't go crazy, won't lose my head in the things you say!
Flying cloud, flowing water, that's how this drunken love sees it.

The Indian romantic hero is a healing life force, one whose affirmative 'cultural' power effaces or negates the deep structures of difference he comes across. Raja is but a lowly taxi driver, Aarti the daughter of a wealthy businessman; in the end, this matters naught in the mythicscape of *Raja Hindustani* – Raja and Aarti love one another and his/their love is coded as transcendent, above and beyond class and caste differences. Nonetheless, while the romance imparts a new equality between them, it is conservative in nature, since he is so often represented as a version of Rama (an incarnation of the god Vishnu) from the *Ramayana*, an Indian biblical epic that sets out the power relations between men and women through clearly defined and absolute notions of good and evil. Popular Indian films often adopt the *Ramayana* and populate the *mise-en-scène* with iconic figures from this sacred text. According to Gokulsing and Dissanayake, Indian audiences are raised on the iconicity of the *Ramayana* and immediately recognise its central narrative trajectory whenever it is adapted for film (1998: 13).

In the *Ramayana*, the heroic Rama defeats the evil (ten-headed, with 20 arms) demon Ravana who had abducted his beautiful wife Sita. Sita is the incarnation of the goddess Laxmi – virtuous, noble and passive. She is juxtaposed against the love-stricken demon, Soorpanaka (sister to Ravana), who covets Rama's love. Soorpanaka has her nose, ears and breasts cut off before Rama defeats her and her army of demons with his golden bow. Near the end of the epic, having rescued Sita from the evil clutches of Ravana, Rama refuses to take her back because she had stayed in a 'stranger's' house. On hearing this, Sita throws her (now worthless, 'vile') body into a fire, only to be rescued, or reborn, by the fire god Agni, thus proving her purity to Rama, who now accepts her back as a dutiful and loving wife. The Indian rom-com is often found repeating this diabolic *ménage à trois* with the same sort of power-saturated binary opposition confirming the righteous place of the heterosexual and patriarchal couple within the Indian imaginary. At the end of *Raja Hindustani*, for example, Aarti proves her fidelity to Raja and they are reunited as only true and good romantic lovers should be.

The character of Sita is more directly embedded in the ideological drive of the Indian rom-com, through both allusion (for example, through the female lead being juxtaposed against religious figures or paintings) and the literal naming of good women (daughters are often given this title). Sita is the ideal woman and the ideal wife who shows selfless devotion (*Sati*) to her husband and the bonds of marriage but is also immersed in an all-consuming and absolutely pure, eternal love for her suitor/ husband. Given that the *Ramayana* dictates 'that a wife's god is her husband: he is her friend, her teacher. Her life is of less consequence than her husband's happiness' (Gokulsing and Dissanayake, 1998: 75), Sita engages in romantic love only to fulfil her essential, spiritual place within the patriarchal order. Gokulsing and Dissanayake suggest that this type of romantic love is also tied to other epic texts:

> In classical Indian texts, the love of Radha or Krishna is all-consuming, absolutely pure, and eternal and this is the kind of romantic love depicted in mainstream Indian films. Women who seek to live by the traditional norms find happiness, while those who dare to transgress them are punished and victimised. (1998: 76)

In *Raja Hindustani*, Aarti offers to sacrifice everything – her family, independence, wealth and modernity – for Raja once she is sure his/ their love is real. When Raja refuses to live in the house provided by Aarti's rich father, who wants to fulfil his function as patriarch and sole provider, she responds by saying that, 'I can sacrifice 100 houses for your sake, but if you ever talk of leaving me again I will kill myself.' Raja responds, 'You love me that much?' Romantic love, then, is defined in absolute terms, with a rigid gendered framework for its consummation and success. As suggested in the *Ramayana*, wives will sacrifice themselves if love (their husbands) demands it.

The love that is shared and enunciated between two fated lovers often takes place in an extended song-and-dance number where realist and fantasy codes collide, clash and merge. The feeling(s) of romance established through these sequences suggests that love becomes a porous sentiment that touches every aspect of the *mise-en-scène*. Love and romance or 'the inner reality of feelings, emotions and instincts', to appropriate Richard Dyer's examination of the Hollywood musical, 'are given metaphoric and symbolic expression through the means of music and dance' (1999: 380). The sensuous poetics of the romantic song-and-dance routine is played out in the elaborate, ostentatious and glittering sets; the fantastic costumes, fabrics, objects and foodstuffs; the heavy make-up; the awe inspiring 'global' outdoor locations (often populated with a cast of thousands); and the over-investment in the representation of emotion through exaggerated performances and the use of close-ups on the eyes in (almost) every dramatic moment. The sensuous poetics of the song-and-dance number gives expression to feelings that could not otherwise be articulated in words only. As Jha suggests:

Song spaces provide an excess that opens up moments that cannot be uttered at the diegetic level. In other words, the highly stylized performance of the songs furthers the plot and gives voice to untold stories in the mise-en-scene. This can be articulated by indirection through the spectacle of the sudden and unexpected outburst of song and dance during the film. (2003: 48)

At an intimate and decidedly phenomenological level, one can argue that in popular Indian rom-coms love burns a hole through the transparency of the narrative, so that its 'flavours' directly assault its spectators, causing them to taste with these feelings. At an ideological level, such an embodied simultaneity ensures that not only the message of proper romantic coupling is communicated, but that its cardiovascular and sense-based qualities are experienced. At a cultural level, one can make sense of this romantic flavouring through the theory of rasa, the central way that classical Indian drama and art has been organised for over two millennia (Patnaik, 2004: 1).

Rasa theory suggests that in making a piece of art, one should be attempting to capture or 'embody' a particular emotional state. Rasa is the art of emotion or more literally the blissful, delectable 'tasting of flavour'. Each emotion – of which there are eight main ones, including Eros, the comic and heroism – has a distinct tone or flavour. The art object should itself be emotional; the intention of art is to carry this emotion to the viewer (to achieve a state of rasa-hood). This is what makes art meaningful, the emotional connectivity between text and reader/viewer. The consequences of achieving rasa-hood, however, are again ideological in application. In popular Indian rom-coms the spectator is meant to not only taste the love (the Eros) cooked up between the loving couple, but to taste the 'real' India, the India of the devotional and the mythological tale that is very rapidly being eroded by modernity and the secular, Western threads of globalisation. In tasting real India one is being asked to remember the taste(s) of yesteryear and to digest and internalise something that is sanctified but under threat. It is implied that in tasting the authentic Indian flavours of romantic love all other modernist and globally inflected tastes will be felt to be dull in comparison.

In *Raja Hindustani*, for example, Raja and Aarti declare their love for one another in a song-and-dance number that oscillates between reality (together in the same space, in realist time) and dream/fantasy (there in the same space but in an imagined and enchanted time, where location/setting/temporality shift repeatedly). The two lovers are found dancing atop a mountain, proclaiming their desires alongside fountains and in the interiors of fire-lit temples bathed in moonlight. Aarti's costume changes with each location, as does her hair, jewellery and make-up. Colours, textures and elements (fire, water, earth, sun and moon) help create a *mise-en-scène* of tastes, textures and feelings that not only speaks to but senses the love being consummated in the scene. Aarti has hitherto been constructed as a modern woman: one who wears Western clothes – including a provocative short, red dress – smatters her conversation with English and identifies herself as economically independent. However, in this narrative-defining song-and-dance number the love that begins to burn brightly between them 'transforms' her forever. As she feels with these feelings and lets the healing, rasa-like power of them enter her, communicated as they are through Raja, her would-be lover, she senses (and the spectator senses) that modernity will come off second-best from now on.

At the beginning of the sequence Raja generally directs the looking relations in terms of who is looking at whom. Once the song-and-dance number has been cued by a 'spontaneous' invitation to sing about their 'friendship', the film elliptically cuts to a shot of Raja and Aarti, in a 'new' real/present time, walking in front of ornamental waterfalls. The shot is bathed in natural light, Aarti is wearing a blue sari; she is smiling. As she walks out of the frame, leaving Raja in a standing position, hypnotised by her movement, the sequence abruptly cuts to a fantasy/daydream image – same location but a different temporal and spatial dynamic. Raja watches an eroticised Aarti dance in slow-motion, midriff exposed, between, behind and in front of the gushing waterfalls. The shot is now awash with an expressionistic blue hue and, given the fact that the image has been slowed down, Raja (and the viewer) can spend time desiring her, falling in love with her, sensing her presence. She is his vision of idealised Indian perfection. Raja is 'making her up' in this sequence so that the romantic love that emerges is (in part) built on his wishful fabrications. Nonetheless, this is complicated by Aarti, who aligns herself with the dreamscape scenario. By the end of the sequence, as the difference between the real and fantasy realms blur and conjoin, she comes to see herself fully, taste herself, through Raja's longing, desiring, hope-filled eyes and sexualised musings. By the end of the sequence Aarti is the dreamscape: in a hyper-real setting, as rain, thunder and lightning engulf the bewitched pair, they kiss, fully immersed in the fantasy that they are lost-and-found Indian romantic lovers.[2] One can also define their relationship, then, as a form of romantic nostalgia, or a longing for an imagined past of heterosexual and patriarchal certainty, a past that can be reborn in the intoxicating senses and sentiments of romantic love as it is made real in the present. As Krutnik suggests, in relation to Western rom-coms: 'The dialogue with the past takes on almost obsessive proportions as the films seek to bridge the gap between then and now, identifying love as something from a long-lost era that needs to be rediscovered in the modern world' (2002: 140).

The song-and-dance routines are, of course, oral in nature: it is the words, the lyrics that matter (particularly to audiences who invest a great deal of time in memorising and replaying/singing their favourite lines, in domestic and public contexts), and which carry the concrete signifiers and emblems of romantic love from hero to Sita and back again. As Nayar suggests, 'Hindi films are "anti psychological"; there is no "interior" story. Nothing exists within a character that is not said' (2004: 17). This *will* to say and to share feelings, dilemmas, aspirations and worries between agents and across formal and informal sites in popular Indian rom-coms connects the genre to an Indian oral tradition that is particularly 'collective' in nature. As Nayar argues:

> . . . because the fabric of oneself in oral cultures is transmitted by word of mouth, from one person to another, from the previous generation to the next, what this also implies is that self-preservation is an inherently *collective* affair, a group endeavour. As a result, communal structures of personality are fostered, with things being 'we'-inflected rather than 'I'-inflected. (2004: 20)

It can also be seen as a way of confirming community and commonality, and of ensuring that an imagined, romanticised India emerges out of the fictional landscape. The spectator/reader/listener – be they 'home' or 'away' – is orally interpolated into the utopian arms of the nation state. The sharing of (what is often heightened and hyperbolic) language confirms one's place in the collective psyche of the nation. *Raja Hindustani*'s final reunification song between Raja and Aarti:

> You have come into my life like the spring;
> remain in my heart forever, having become love, love itself!
> You are settled into my eyes, (the answer to) a thousand dreams;
> remain in my heart forever, having become love, love itself!
> Each flower bud was veiled, it had yet to be poured into colors;
> and the winds were neither lively nor fragrant.
> Now what an intoxicating season has come upon us!
> Forever remain in my heart, having become love, love itself!
>
> You have come into my life like the spring.
> The city of my spirit was empty: the branches lay dry and withered,
> the colors of Holi faded, Diwali was lightless.
> You became the rain, and pattered down...
> Remain forever in my heart, having become love, love itself!
> You have come into my life like the spring;
> you have settled into my eyes, (the answer to) a thousand dreams.
> Remain forever in my heart, having become love, love itself!

is a triumph of tradition over modernity, the dutiful woman of honour over the new Westernised woman of suspect morals, and of love and matrimony over hate and discord. It is fitting, given the importance of the 'coupling' song-and-dance sequence earlier in the film, that Raja, confused by the 'truth' that he has just been told – that Aarti is innocent and loves him unconditionally – calls out for her in and through song. Of course, he sings not only to her, for her, but to the journeyed viewer, so that she can be fully reborn to us; pure, simple and dutiful.

~ Journeying romance ~

According to Vijay Mishra, 'Bollywood' in its contemporary incarnation as a late cultural industry and exotic Eastern signifier, has emerged out of the needs of the Indian diaspora found in Western Europe and North America. Mishra contends that:

> The present situation, at least in the settler states and in the metropolitan centres of Europe . . . has to be linked to the new global Indian diaspora of late capital which . . . has effectively produced Bollywood, the cultural phenomenon as we now understand it, in response to a dislocated diaspora youth culture's need for an accessible, unproblematic and sanitized India. (2006: 10)

The version of the mother homeland often found in popular Indian rom-coms is one that clearly and directly speaks to those whose Indianness provides a source of identification and belonging, and the prejudicial label of Other or outsider, in the Western nation states they arrive at or are born in. Rom-coms provide the space for both the Indian disapora to fantasise about returning home, while staying put (home-elsewhere) and for successfully engaging with their migrant difference by making their migrant home 'Indian' (elsewhere-home), 'commodified and globalized into a "feel good" version of "our culture"' (Rajadhyaksha, 2003: 37). The utopian representation of romantic love is meant to fulfil a yearning for Mother India that resides in the disenfranchised diaspora and to create a 'home' space in an away space that they can be proud of and interpolated into. This 'diasporic nationalism' is romantic in all its senses: India is romanticised as a breathless nation state; love is romanticised to be pure and perfect; caste, class and religious differences are romanticised so that they become insignificant – purified – in the game playing of romantic coupling; and the people of the diaspora are romanticised as 'lost' children looking back at their mother, who welcomes them 'home' with open arms.

Romantic comedies are in part about journeying: the interiorised journey one takes to find romantic love, the realist journey that one takes to chase love down and the fantastical journey one takes to be delivered in and through love. In *Raja Hindustani*, the lovers are separated because of familial sabotage (Aarti's mother-in-law dupes Raja into believing that Aarti has been unfaithful, and Aarti into believing that Raja no longer loves her). The film asks the viewer to 'journey' with both Raja and Aarti through the Machiavellian complexities of the plot, until its final conciliatory dénouement. This journeying romance must resonate with people whose identities are tied up with the myth of the migrant's journey, a journey that is interior, exterior, real and symbolic and full of the 'romance' of journey storytelling.

Rom-coms, of course, also help produce a conservative form of Indianness abroad, instructing its 'children' about the right and proper modes of conduct for Indian men and women. For example, *Raja Hindustani* instructs Indian women on the perils of letting modernity turn them away from their essential role in life as dutiful mothers, wives and daughters. When Aarti first puts on a Western red dress, a dress she chooses and buys with her own money, she is verbally abused by a rowdy group of young men. Raja, visibly upset at her wanton display, viciously attacks them, upholding her honour, and in effect forcing her to face the consequences of her own embodied transgression. Aarti, recognising that romantic love is what she really wants, turns away from Western culture, turns to Raja, her Rama-in-waiting, and turns into Sita, taking up her rightful role in Indian culture.

There is, nonetheless, often a tension in the way modern India is nostalgically romanticised through the purity of the traditional heterosexual coupling. This tension is built on a desire for popular Indian film to let elements of modernity and globalisation into its discursive imaginary, not least because its diaspora children are in part the product of the global flow of capital and technology. Populated by successful businessmen, the motifs and settings of international travel and the objects, furniture and decor of Western consumerism, the 'benefits' of late capitalism can be seen to enable these films to feel glamorous and Western-exotic. Of course, the tension is often resolved through the way they sanitise and appropriate the Western so that they come to mean, feel, particularly Indian and 'local'. The fusion of styles within a grand narrative that celebrates the traditional Indian imaginary can be argued to transform the modern so that it appears 'traditional' or 'authentic', in the magical way that films in general can *bricolage* history.

~ Comedic catharsis ~

As is the case with rom-coms in general, popular Indian romantic comedies are tangibly based on a generic tension: the clash or collision between the serious business of romantic love and the funny business of the comedic performances and comic interludes that (sporadically) punctuate the narrative. Both schemas supposedly require different aesthetic values and spectatorial responses. The high drama of love is performed, scored and edited differently, and requires a sentimental, exhilarating and tearful response from viewers. The anarchy or absurdity of comedy, of course, asks viewers to laugh out loud and at/with those who suffer prat falls, struggle with the mundane and the ordinary, and who are at the mercy of the irony, wit and sarcasm of language games. The sounds of violins, cellos, mandolins and sitars rise up from a romantic scene, while the variant 'internal' (biological) sounds of the comedy routine dominate the comedic scene. The idealised bodies of the romantic leads are sharply contrasted with the deviant/over/under-sized/ugly bodies of the comedic characters, whose bodily liminality overall is in sharp contrast to the perfected lines and mass of the film's heroes and heroines.[3] In *Raja Hindustani*, the two comic leads, Balvant Singh (Johnny Lever) and Kamal Singh/Kammo (Navneet Nishan), are diametrically opposed in physical appearance to Raja and Aarti. Balvant is overweight, clumsy, and loud, while Kammo is coded as stereotypically unattractive, imperfect, if obedient and utterly loyal.

Nonetheless, both romance and comedy require an embodied response from viewers (Williams, 1991) and, in terms of shared convention, both romantic leads and stock comedians are outsiders or, in terms of the former, will become outsiders if they dare to covet a Sita from a different caste position. Similarly, at the level of emotional involvement and of feeling, both forms immerse the viewer in their respective exploration of the senses, although the mythology of romantic love claims it is tied to higher modes of being, while the sensations of comedy are considered to be of the lower-order (Jenkins, 2003: 91–104). The clash or collision between these two forms is often managed or assuaged through narrative/narrational devices (scene signposts and segues) and through character differentiation, including the stock 'comedians' whose job/ role it is to be funny and to provide the comedic moments between the spectacular song-and-dance routines and the intense romantic and dramatic encounters. Both romantically cued song-and-dance routines and comedic mishaps are anti-narrative, or at the least they offer a self-contained version of narration since they have their own internal logic, codes of enunciation, and emotional rhythm. Taken together, romance and comedy are sensory and narratively complementary.

At an ideological level, romance and comedy seem also to complement and support one another in a number of ways. First, as briefly noted above, it is often the case that the romantic-heroic lead and his comedian friend(s) will be both coded as 'outsiders'. The hero will be of lowly caste or of a 'minority' religion, while his comedic side-kick will be an outsider precisely because he is funny (to look at and/or hear) and because his body challenges the norms, rituals and overall social order of everyday life. Krutnik suggests that the film comedian is:

> Generally cast as an outsider or misfit in some way (and) presents a spectacle of otherness by serving as a conduit for energies that are marginal, non-normative or antisocial. The resultant conflicts between the comedian and the (social) world may also be played out through intrapsychic divisions, with the comedian located as an eccentric individual who . . . disrupts conventional modes of behaviour, thought and identity. (2003: 3)

Nonetheless, in popular Indian rom-coms, both the romantic hero and his comedic side-kick are recuperated by the social order by the end of the film, and in so doing symbolically prove that India is a fair, inclusive and harmonious society where outsiders, once they have been proven to be worthy (of romantic love) or where they assist in the success of the heterosexual coupling (one of the functions of the comedy side-kick), are drawn into the ideological core. The lower-caste hero marries the beautiful Sita, with the blessings of both families, and the comedic characters become part of this 'new' extended family, their eccentricities now accepted. At the end of *Raja Hindustani*, Balvant Singh and Kamal Singh/Kammo, the comedic duo who have acted as supportive conduits to Raja and Aarti's desires and woes, join the blessed couple on a lush green mountain top, in the final song-and-dance sequence of the film, collectively proclaiming:

> Hey, where did you come from?
> You seem like a stranger to me.
> Amidst my own family, I am an outsider.
> I see the whole truth now.
> I collided with a statue of stone -
> A good thing that I regained my senses!
> I'll tell everyone what's really going on here; I won't be ashamed
>   to do it!

Finally, though, the dominant ideological function of the comedy characters/moments may actually be to mask or efface the explicit work that 'ideology' is performing in these films in relation to the rigid proclamations on patriarchy, tradition and heterosexual norms. It can be argued that the cathartic function of comedy, and the reduction of 'difference to laughter' (Krutnik, 2003: 3) enables an imaginary 'free zone' to emerge that – albeit momentarily – takes spectators away from the sermon-like monologues, duets and interpersonal encounters that structure nearly all of the romance sequences. Of course, to complicate matters, comedy is often an explicit ideological form with the terror or spectacle of difference at its cardiac centre. For a diaspora audience, this spectacle of outsiderdom, of being reduced to comedic otherness, chimes perfectly well with their experiences of living in a home-elsewhere space that constantly pokes fun at them. At the end of the popular Indian rom-com, when the comedic side-kick(s) are drawn into the centre of the extended family of modern India, the diaspora viewer feels/senses a profound moment of subjective alignment: they feel at home again.

Popular Indian romantic comedies take their audiences home again: home to a pre-modern India that nonetheless recognises and appropriates modernity and speaks to those who find themselves adrift in the late global order. The films are explicitly heterosexist and patriarchal, and while they openly explore the issues of difference, difference is sanitised in and through the golden bows of a healing, unifying romantic love.

6   *A 'Special Relationship'?*

The Coupling of Britain and America in Working Title's Romantic Comedies

~ Annabelle Honess Roe ~

TOWARDS THE END of the 1988 film *A Fish Called Wanda* there is a scene where Archie is being hung by his feet out of a window by Otto. Archie (John Cleese) is an uptight, erudite British barrister; Otto (Kevin Kline) is a stupid, crass and violent American. In this scene Otto is forcing Archie to apologise for his retort about the debacle of the Vietnam War – a retort prompted by Otto's comment that if it wasn't for the Americans the British would all be speaking German. This scene is the culmination of a film's worth of verbal sparring between Archie and Otto, sparring that usually centres on their national identity. The film gains most of its comic mileage by playing on the commonly held, stereotypical characteristics of the British and the Americans.

The essence of these comedic exchanges between Archie and Otto highlight the question of the 'special relationship' between Britain and America. This term was coined by Winston Churchill in his 'Sinews of Peace' speech in 1946, in which he articulated the close political and military ties between the two nations. In using this phrase Churchill was acknowledging the importance of a close bond between Britain and the USA in defeating common enemies. With Fascism only just thwarted, Churchill was drawing attention to the looming threat of Communism to the global stability recently established through, primarily, a coordinated British–American effort. Subsequently, the extent and nature of this 'special relationship' has been greatly debated, but something that is generally acknowledged is that, whether it be primarily a cultural, financial or political relationship, this is not a relationship of equals.

Awareness of this inequality in terms of Britain's political and military position on the world stage has been highlighted in the twenty-first century. Following the election of George W. Bush as president of the

United States in 2000, Britain's relationship with America, it has been suggested, has become one of increasing subservience. British Prime Minister Tony Blair became widely regarded as Bush's 'lapdog' in matters of foreign policy, most importantly in the decision to support Bush's aggressive move for military action in Iraq in 2003. This post-millennial state of affairs could be argued as feeding into an already battered sense of British self-worth, one that has been diminishing since the fall of the empire and the concurrent adjustment of Britain's status on the global stage of international relations. As such, the already confusing matter of British national identity has been further complicated in the twenty-first century.

In addition to being played out in the arena of global politics, the special relationship between Britain and the USA can be examined at the level of cultural economy. The two film-producing nations have long enjoyed a cultural reciprocity. It was a British filmmaker, William Horsley, who made the first film in California in 1911 (Parker, 2002: 5) and from the mid-1920s Hollywood depended on the UK as its most lucrative foreign market (Thompson, 1985: 127). In turn, Britain relies on America as its most remunerative overseas territory (UK Film Council, 2005–6). The British government recognised this reciprocity in the Film Acts of the 1920s and 1930s, which were specifically structured to permit, and even encourage, American investment in the flailing British film industry (Glancy, 1998).

Despite this cultural cooperation between the two countries, the British film industry has long been in the shadow of Hollywood. Historically, various attempts have been made to redress this balance, through the installation of quota requirements in the 1930s and the Eady Levy in the 1950s that, respectively, demanded that a certain proportion of all films shown in UK cinemas be British and that a percentage of exhibition receipts be reinvested in British film production. However, when these attempts faltered or were withdrawn, the British industry faltered with them. Since the 1980s film activity in the UK has cycled in a boom-and-bust pattern with little success at creating a self-sustaining industry. This is despite the inception of the UK Film Council in 2000, which distributes state funding to individuals and companies via a central organisation. However, as Film Council chairman Alan Parker observed in 2002, this organisation was always intended to support the industry, not *be* the industry, and it continues to be debated whether any such industry exists to be supported (2002: 3).

As well as being bolstered by the Film Council, the British film industry is dependent on Hollywood, primarily because of Hollywood's global dominance in terms of distribution and exhibition. In the UK there is a tension between wanting to make specifically British films, ones that 'talk about our own unique experiences' (Cox, 2003) and 'the need to stimulate the growth of an industry that embraces the international market' (Parker, 2002: 8). Success in British cinemas alone is not enough to support the indigenous industry, especially when most of the box-office receipts go to distributors based outside the UK. Yet with regard to producing internationally competitive films there is a further struggle. In terms of a film's style and content there is little point competing with the studios, yet British films must still appeal to an audience attuned to the conventions and attractions of Hollywood cinema.

The extent of Hollywood's financial input into, and control over, the British industry has been a cause of anxiety. 'British films continue to be inextricably bound up with American capital, leaving some commentators with an uneasy feeling that should this be withdrawn, "our industry would effectively become a cottage industry overnight"' (Dyja, 2001, cited in Street, 2002: 214). Along with this sense of unease there is an acknowledgement that the success of a British film often depends on approval from the American cinema-going public (and hence, American distributors). As Neil Watson has observed, 'The UK distribution and exhibition sector tends to take its lead from the US and British screens are dominated by films which have already proved to be hits across the Atlantic' (2000: 85).

However, one company that seems to have successfully negotiated the British film industry's creative and economic relationship with Hollywood is Working Title Films. The London-based company, helmed by Tim Bevan and Eric Fellner, is undeniably the most successful British film production company of recent years. Described as 'the jewel in the crown of British film production' (Parker, 2002: 6), the company 'bestrides the industry like a giant' (Dyja, 2001: 18). Furthermore, unlike other (often sporadically) successful UK film companies, Working Title receives no state funding or support. Whereas other companies lurch through the boom-and-bust pattern common to British production, Working Title manages to output a steady number of films, many of them incredibly successful both in the UK and overseas.

Four Weddings and a Funeral (1994) was the company's break-out success overseas. The film was first released in the USA and, when it proved successful in the States, it was released in Britain, advertised as 'America's No. 1 Smash Hit Comedy!' *Four Weddings* went on to take nearly $250 million worldwide (*Variety*, 2006). This film provided a model for what has become recognised as the characteristic Working Title rom-com: it centres on the coupling of a bumbling, ineffectual British man with a beautiful, successful American woman within the upper-middle-class milieu of an idealised, idyllic Britain and it features quick verbal humour often derived from transgressing particularly British social conventions. This pattern was later repeated in *Notting Hill* (1999) and *Wimbledon* (2004). All three of these rom-coms can be seen as playing out the 'special relationship' between the USA and the UK in the central romantic relationship of the leading characters. As I explore below, the 'special relationship' is also directly commented on in Working Title's 2003 ensemble romantic comedy *Love Actually* where the British prime minister and romantic protagonist played by Hugh Grant challenges the heavy-handed attitude of the US president and of US politics more broadly. Furthermore, the films allegorise the political relationship between America and Britain as well as the way the British industry is positioned in relation to Hollywood – something that is particularly apt considering Working Title's financial structure.

Several British producers and production companies have brokered distribution and financing deals with American studios over the last decade. In 2003 British production company DNA Films entered into a five-year deal with Fox Searchlight wherein the American studio took a 50 per cent stake in DNA (Dawtrey, 2003). Producer Michael Kuhn struck a distribution deal with that same studio in 2002 for films made by his new company and David Heyman, British producer of the *Harry Potter* franchise, signed a first-look deal with Warner Brothers in 1997. The most significant Hollywood–London alliance, however, is the one that was struck between Working Title and Universal in 1999.

Working Title was established by Tim Bevan and Sarah Radclyffe in 1984, growing out of their music video business. PolyGram Filmed Entertainment, a UK-based financier and distributor that provided an alternative to Hollywood support, invested in the company in the early 1990s. At this point Radclyffe left and Eric Fellner joined as co-chairman. When PolyGram was sold to Seagram in 1998 the Dutch drinks company was only interested in the music assets. PolyGram's film interests were sold to the Hollywood studio Universal (Working Title Films, 2003). In 1999 a much-publicised deal worth a reported

$600 million was made between Working Title and Universal whereby the British company retained the power to greenlight up to five films a year with budgets under $25 million (BBC News, 2004; Dawtrey, 1999). Such a financial arrangement was unprecedented in the British industry. In just over 15 years Working Title had gone from a small independent Soho production company, making such small-scale films as the socially astute *My Beautiful Laundrette* (1985), with its exploration of an interracial relationship between two men against the backdrop of Thatcherite Britain, to become the most commercially oriented film set-up in London, producing international box-office successes financed from across the Atlantic and featuring major American stars. By the late 1990s this jewel of a British production company had become a self-proclaimed 'Hollywood producer' (Working Title Films, 2003: 18).

Andrew Higson has suggested that one way of defining a national cinema is in terms of representation. In looking at national cinema this way one can question how certain films 'dramatize the fantasies of national identity' and what role 'they play in constructing the sense or the image of a nation' (1995: 5-6). According to Higson, there are two ways of looking at the question of representation in national cinema. On the one hand, there is the argument that 'cinema simply reflects or expresses a pre-existing national identity, consciousness, or culture'. An alternative consideration of representation is that 'national identity is constructed in and through representation'. He goes on to argue for a conceptualisation of national cinema that takes both of these arguments into consideration: 'films will draw on identities and representation already in circulation – and often they will naturalize those identities. But films will also produce new representations of the nation' (Higson, 1995).

The Working Title rom-coms under discussion here all construct some kind of unified national identity through the naturalisation of stereotypical British characteristics. What is specific to these films is that they achieve this by positioning the American as a foreign Other. In all these rom-coms the Britishness of the British characters is drawn in marked contrast to the Americanness of the American characters. Generally the difference being observed is along the lines of the already circulating national identities of, for example, British reserve versus the American free spirit or British class and propriety against American freedom and spontaneity. Furthermore, the suggestion in these films is that the possession of Britishness is more desirable than the possession of Americanness.

This construction of Britishness is quickly established by *Four Weddings and a Funeral.* When the endearingly awkward and romantically hopeless Charles (Hugh Grant) first sees Carrie (Andie MacDowell) he comments to his friend Fiona (Kristin Scott Thomas) that she's pretty. 'American', comes Fiona's disparaging one-word reply, as if nothing else need be said, and later, 'slut'. In her ostentatious hat, Carrie stands out at the fusty English country wedding. This demonstration of her physical self-assuredness contrasts markedly to the awkwardness embodied by Charles, with his scruffy appearance and frequent tendency to make inappropriate comments. This difference is exemplified in Charles' and Carrie's respective last-minute entrances to the wedding at which they first meet. While Charles amusingly mutters expletives as he rushes into the church, struggling to do up his tie and stealing a flower for his buttonhole, Carrie swans coolly in, turning heads in her aforementioned attention-seeking hat. With her apparent arrogance and self-confidence she displays attributes of Americanness that are implied, in these early scenes, as being undesirable.

Notting Hill may initially seem to be catering to the US audience with the casting of American star Julia Roberts as Anna Scott, the Hollywood prima donna who steals the heart of William (Hugh Grant), a down-to-earth bookshop owner. However, as Robert Murphy has pointed out, 'the film makes cheekily few concessions to Hollywood' (2000: 9). The film frequently suggests that the quirky, underachieving ways of the Brits are preferable to the aspirations and success of Americans, embodied by Scott: 'It is not just the way in which the film industry is represented as crass, cynical and superficial . . . it is the assurance with which a messy, unambitious, British lifestyle is shown as preferable to the gloss and glamour of Hollywood' (Murphy, 2000: 9). In a scene where the characters compete for a brownie by bemoaning the 'crapness' of their lives, the comforting restrictions of the British class system and the failure of personal enterprise among the British are represented as preferable to the pioneer attitude and self-promotion of the Americans. While William's British friends try to claim the prize with stories of romantic and professional woes, Anna (quite literally) takes the biscuit when she tells them, 'I've been on a diet every day since I was 19,' that her love life is regularly splashed on the front pages of the tabloids and that despite her nutritional self-deprivation she's had multiple plastic surgeries to obtain, and maintain, her good looks. Furthermore, Anna reminds them that her fame will be short lived; when her looks fade she will become merely 'some sad middle-aged woman who looks a bit like someone who was famous for a while'. As such, American ambition is wrapped up with the superficiality and impermanence of Hollywood (and beauty) and its dream-factory fantasy is effectively undermined.

Love Actually contains the most obvious assertion of British superiority in a moment that, according to the *Guardian* columnist Polly Toynbee (2003), raised a cheer from cinema audiences in the UK. Hugh Grant plays a bachelor prime minister who at the beginning of his term meets the president of the United States (Billy Bob Thornton) to discuss unspecified international issues. Initially the prime minister disappoints his cabinet by refusing to break the previous government's pattern of subservience, reminding them that 'America is the most powerful country in the world.' However, the prime minister later unexpectedly stands up to the president in a press conference speech.

The press conference scene directly references the special relationship between the two countries when the prime minister claims that it has 'become a bad relationship', one that is based on America's needs only. He accuses the president of 'casually ignoring all those things that really matter to Britain' and suggests that the USA has become a bully, rather than a friend. Accompanied by a swelling orchestral score, the prime minister vows to be stronger and in putting his foot down to the demands of the larger country shows that smaller in stature does not mean smaller in pride. Significantly, this show of British pride by the prime minister is a direct response to the president's sexually predatory behaviour. The prime minister has taken a shine to the tea lady at Number Ten and when he walks in on the president making advances on her his hackles are raised. It is this instance of sexual harassment that spurs the prime minister to make his political stand.

Another of *Love Actually*'s romantically challenged characters seems to do just as much to assert British dominance over the Americans. Colin Frissell (Kris Marshall) is totally incapable of 'getting a shag' on his home soil. The young man naively travels to America (the Mid-West), telling his friend how American women always fall for 'the accent'. We laugh at Colin, at this naivety, and assume that he will soon come running back to Britain with his still-virgin tail between his legs. However, Colin achieves unparalleled success in the Mid-West, picking up a trio of beautiful women on his first night who invite him to share their bed.

The three Americans, who simper at Colin's accent, are portrayed as stupid and superficial, falling for Colin because of how he talks and where he comes from.

With these films' references to the battle for superiority between the USA and Britain they can be seen as playing out a fantasy that reverses the political position of the two countries. In this fantasy Britain is the dominant partner in the 'special relationship'. By exerting such British characteristics as good manners, self-deprecation, propriety and a general incompetence that belies their integrity, the characters in these films are repeatedly seen getting one up on the Americans. The British are united by virtue of being not-American. In this way a kind of negative national identity is constructed. By showing what the British are not – American – and by painting American characteristics (stupidity, crassness, self-promotion, ambition) in broad strokes these films allow the British audience to imagine and idealise Britishness by giving them a privileged position of superiority over these American characteristics.

Andrew Higson (1995) discusses how films that represent a nation to itself construct imaginary bonds between the peoples of that nation. These bonds are constructed by, among other things, dramatising current fears and anxieties. In *Love Actually* one of these fears and anxieties is being walked over by the Americans. In *Notting Hill* the fear is of becoming too successful or self-serving (read: American). Thus these films, by playing on beliefs popularly held by the British about Americans, invite the 'diverse and often antagonistic' audience to 'recognise themselves as a singular body with a common culture, and to oppose themselves to other cultures and communities' (Higson, 1995: 7).

However, further reflection shows that this unification of the British against the otherness of America is complicated by the narrative in Working Title's romantic comedies. While British audiences are being invited to feel superior towards Americans and to unite in their not-Americanness, Americans represent the romantic goal for which the British characters are aiming, even if they may not realise it at first, and the leading characters ultimately achieve happiness and fulfilment through unity with an American. This is most clearly seen in *Notting Hill* and *Four Weddings and a Funeral*; in both cases Hugh Grant's character actively spurns the offer of love with a fellow Briton in favour of an American. In *Four Weddings* Charles dumps the very British, upper-crust

Duck-Face at the altar after Carrie suddenly reappears in his life. In *Notting Hill* even the perfect British girl, embodied by Emily Mortimer, cannot cure William of his heartbreak over Anna Scott. Similarly, *Love Actually* demonstrates the British longing for all things American when the luckless lover Colin turns down the prospect of seeking love in Britain in favour of the hot, sexually forthcoming American chicks he finds in the Mid-West.

In *Wimbledon*, Working Title's most recent rom-com to follow in this vein, Paul Bettany plays Peter Colt, an ageing, mediocre tennis player who is spurred on to victory at his final Wimbledon tournament by his romantic entanglement with Lizzie, a younger, much more successful American champion (Kirsten Dunst). This film not only articulates the 'special relationship' between Britain and American, but again constructs the British as relative underachievers, and it plays on long-held British resentment at failing to succeed internationally at one of their national sports.

Once again, the American provides the romantic goal for the British character and in this case the final scene in New York City shows Peter eschewing his native land and opting for geographical unity by decamping to America. However, throughout the film, Peter is represented as the more likeable character, with the more likeable family. In quintessential and stereotypical outspoken American fashion, Lizzie, channelling John McEnroe, throws temper tantrums, alienating other players and officials. When we first see Lizzie on court she is abusive to the umpire, firing herself up by accusing him of making a bad call. Conversely, Peter is good natured and self-deprecating, displaying sportsmanship and manners both on and off the court. In his first match he makes friends with the ballboy and, rather than lashing out, he keeps his frustrations about his game to himself.

Lizzie is dominated by her father, who insists that she put her game before her personal life. He is pushy and demanding and when he suspects that Lizzie is falling for Peter he threatens Peter to stay away, accusing him of distracting her from 'what we've been working towards all these years, what she's always wanted'. In contrast, when we first meet Peter's family, who live in an idyllic, rambling country house, his feckless younger brother makes sarcastic references to his Wimbledon 'grand finale' and his losing streak. Peter's parents are more concerned with their own petty feuds and the fact that Peter hasn't secured them tickets for the tournament. Whereas Peter's family and his relationship with them is eccentric in a gently amusing way, Lizzie's relationship with her father is dysfunctional and threatening.

Once again, British characteristics are shown as being more desirable than American characteristics. Yet, what ultimately allows Peter to achieve his highest sporting goal is his union with Lizzie and his adoption of a more aggressive, competitive (that is, more 'American' and more similar to Lizzie's) attitude on the court. In his final match against the obnoxious American youngster Jake Hammond he responds to his opponent's jibes about his back injury with an accusation that Hammond has a 'weak mind'. Yet Peter's newfound determination is still tempered by his British manners, as demonstrated when Hammond's aggression towards a ballboy (the same one Peter befriends in his first match) riles his sense of propriety. However, it is not until Peter is reconciled with Lizzie halfway through the match, until he admits to himself and her how much he loves her, that he can win the tournament. In *Wimbledon* the union of Britain with America is seen as not only desirable for romantic happiness, but necessary for British success. Furthermore, while Peter's game is raised by his love affair with Lizzie, her performance suffers. In this story, the British succeed on the international stage (of tennis) at the expense of America.

This representation of America and Americans as the aspiration of the British complicates the unified national identity created by the simultaneous negation of Americanness in Working Title's rom-coms. Britishness is constructed as something desirable, as something that is superior and preferable to being American. Contrary to this, the British are also represented as desiring Americans or America. This ambivalence can be seen as articulating the broader cultural ambivalence of the British towards the USA, one that manifests itself in Britain's attitude towards its political relationship with America.

Indeed, the relationship between Working Title and Hollywood is one that causes unease within the echelons of the British film industry. Tim Bevan's attitude that 'if you are going to work in the film business you have to have an ongoing and solid relationship with Los Angeles' (Working Title Films, 2003: 13) and the company's success both at home and abroad is a cause for consternation among some British filmmakers and critics. In the UK 'they are considered commercial sell-outs to Hollywood', and reviewers – who often 'accuse WT of playing it too safe' – are quick to condemn their less successful films (Dawtrey, 2005). The anti-Hollywood attitude within the industry was displayed in 2003 when there was a backlash against Alan Parker's suggestions that the British industry had to become more international in scope, in short, more like the American. 'Well, we mustn't,' replied Alex Cox, because 'we know exactly what America thinks of any culture other than its own' (Cox, 2003).

Furthermore, this distaste for American commercialism and Hollywood is actually articulated in *Notting Hill*. Anna Scott is dissatisfied with her career status as a star of mindless Hollywood genre films. She longs to do more serious acting, by which she means British period drama, although she lacks confidence in her ability to pull off such weighty fare. In the rooftop scene in which William helps Anna learn lines for her upcoming action flick she laughs at the facile dialogue and notes that, 'You never get anyone in *Wings of a Dove* having the nerve to say "inform the Pentagon we need black star cover".' William coaches her through her lines and in the end Anna achieves professional and personal fulfilment when she is reconciled with William after pulling off a role in a British historical costume film. While Working Title's chairmen may extol the virtues of an alliance with Hollywood, this film suggests an underlying distaste for the commercial, genre-based films produced by their financial backers and the superiority of the heritage tradition of British filmmaking as a marker of cinematic 'quality'.

While the British unease at their political relationship with America and their film industry's economic relationship with Hollywood is evidenced in these films it must be questioned to what extent Working Title's rom-coms are offering any unified sense of national identity. As has been demonstrated in the preceding discussion, the coherent sense of Britishness that is constructed through a negation of Americanness is already complicated by the romantic narratives in which the British want nothing more than to live happily ever after with their American love interests. The notion of a unified British national identity is further complicated when one considers the criticism levelled against these films for failing to represent the cultural diversity that is contemporary Britain.

Around the time *Love Actually* was released in the UK, the *Guardian* newspaper ran several pieces with a comic tone that described ironically what they call 'Curtis Britain' (after Richard Curtis, the writer of *Notting Hill, Four Weddings* and writer-director of *Love Actually*). In these films 'English people rarely go into work, and if they do they generally carry out their jobs with an endearing incompetence. They just happen to believe there are more important things in life, like swearing and snow' (Dowling, 2003). The articles draw attention to the oft pointed-out fact that the Britain, or more specifically the London, in these middle-class rom-coms is nothing like the London milling outside the safe confines of the movie theatre. In the London of *Love Actually* there are 'smiling faces all around, people being knocked over by love rather than renegade cyclists . . . Nobody gets mugged and doorways aren't the boudoirs of the homeless' (Appleyard, 2003). The films gloss over the aggression and social inequity that abound in the capital as well as its ethnic diversity. Criticism of this latter omission was particularly directed at *Notting Hill*, for eliding the ethnic make-up of the capital, particularly given that the area of London in which it is set, and from which it takes its name, has historically been a centre for London's West Indian community. Instead they paint a chocolate-box Britain populated by white, middle-class Oxbridge graduates where the Christmases are always white and love is all around.

This critical backlash against the Working Title representation of Britain contained within their romantic comedies could in part explain why *Wimbledon* was considerably less successful at the box office than the other films discussed above. Whereas *Love Actually* scored the highest opening weekend of any British romantic comedy with a weekend total of approximately $10 million (BBC, 2003) *Wimbledon* managed to amass only a slightly higher figure ($12 million) over the entire course of its UK run (*Variety*, 2006). Critics, as well as audiences, had also arguably tired of the now predictable Working Title formula of transatlantic love. Philip French complained in the *Observer* that the film was a 'feeble successor' to the company's Hugh Grant films and that the 'American screenwriters cull most of their scenes and situations' from *Notting Hill* (2004b).

The Working Title rom-coms discussed here can be seen as constructing a British national identity at the cost of neglecting the cultural and ethnic diversity of contemporary Britain. By unifying the British audience against the fear of being American and the anxiety of losing their Britishness these films are constructing a national identity that arguably does not exist. However, evidence of discomfort with this unified national identity can be seen in the films themselves through the frequent construction of America as the ultimate goal for the British characters. It seems, then, that the British ambivalence towards Americans is also displayed in the films' ambivalence towards the possibility of a unified British national identity. Made during a period when Britain was perceived as increasingly subservient to the USA, both in terms of politics and culture, the films' confusing invitation to a 'diverse and often antagonistic' British audience 'to recognize themselves as a singular body with a common culture' (Higson, 1995: 7) can be read as symptomatic of the time of uncertain national identity in which Working Title's rom-coms were made.

7 Transatlantic Exchanges and Influences

Décalage horaire (*Jet Lag*), Gender and the Romantic Comedy *à la française*

~ *Brigitte Rollet*[1] ~

♡ WHILE LEVI-STRAUSS NOTED the link between genres and nations by saying that 'narrative [is] a culture's way of making sense of itself' (cited in Hayward, 1993: 9), Jane Feuer has highlighted the fact that 'shifts in the film genre correlate to changes in culture outside' (Feuer, 1987: 143). Both views need to be considered when thinking of the romantic comedy within a French context. Despite Angelique Chrisafis' assertion regarding contemporary French cinema in the British newspaper the *Guardian* that, 'It's *oui* to rom-coms and *non* to art house as *cinéphiles* die out' (2007), the rom-com in France is an extremely rare and recent phenomenon. Yet love is a key element in French films whatever the period concerned, from the classical age of *réalisme poétique* with its recurrent tragic heroes falling in love with the 'wrong' woman and often dying at the end (as in the roles played by Gabin in the 1930s), to the sexually emancipated youngsters of the New Wave and beyond. Nevertheless, the specific genre at the centre of this volume – romantic comedy – is not (yet?) an established part of the narrative traditions of French cinema.

In more recent years, however, more and more French films could be said to fit the category of the rom-com. These include *Prête-moi ta main* (2006), *Hors de prix* (2006), *Toi et moi* (2006) and, the subject of this essay, Danièle Thompson's *Décalage horaire* (*Jet Lag*), released in France in 2002 and starring Juliette Binoche and Jean Réno. Unsurprisingly, the phenomenon can be linked with the French and worldwide success of Jeunet's *Le Fabuleux destin d'Amélie Poulain* (or *Amélie*) in 2001, although the film was never explicitly called a rom-com in France – a clear sign that the genre remains unusual there, as does the use of the expression to define it. Whether this recent development is part of the

Americanisation of French culture and cinema dreaded by some will not be considered here. Instead, after discussing how the rom-com is untypical of the French cinematic context and suggesting some possible explanations for this, this essay will briefly consider the genre from the perspective of gender, before contextualising and concentrating on Thompson's comedy. *Jet Lag* is particularly suited to a discussion of 'transatlantic exchanges', an expression by which I mean movements, interactions, correspondences and hostilities as well as attractions between cultural traditions (in the widest possible sense of the terms). At another level, the 'transatlantic exchange' dimension in Thompson's film is also obvious, from its use of stars that have 'crossed over' into popular US cinema, to the very location of the film – the airport – which immediately suggests the themes of international exchange and the global market. In what follows, then, I will examine how *Jet Lag* reworks and adapts the traditional ingredients of the Hollywood classic rom-com for a French audience, while also offering a closer reading of the film in order to highlight Thompson's innovations regarding gender roles and social and national identities.

~ *No rom-com please, we're French!* ~

So *Amélie* is not considered a rom-com in France at least[2] and one won't find the genre included among the many categories commonly used in Paris' popular film guides such as *Pariscope*. Similarly, major academic publications devoted to French cinema in both French and English do not refer to romance (even less to rom-com as a genre) in chapters or books dealing specifically with cinematic genres in a French context (see Hayward, 1993; Pinel, 2000). In two recent encyclopedias on French and European cinema (Vincendeau, 1995 and 1996), for example, the only entry on 'romance' is for the actress Viviane Romance (1909–91)!

A distinction has to be made here between the graphic and 'relaxed' Gallic representation of (female) nudity and sexuality on the one hand, and sentimental or 'corny' love stories on the other. As noted by Geneviève Sellier, it is the contemporary French auteur cinema, indirect heir of the New Wave, that has taken over the field of intimacy and love relationships rather than French popular cinema (2004a).[3] But exploring love or sex is not the same as telling love stories or producing rom-coms. While being a recurrent theme in French films, love is not presented and constructed here in the way it is most typically seen in the mainstream Hollywood rom-com. Rather, characters are often already established in a couple, married or not. Furthermore, in the stories told, love – which can often be a painful and complicated process – is rarely the main focus of the film. Other films deal with passionate love, often as intense as it is short-lived. However love is treated, it does not often bring a fairytale 'happy ending', if by this we mean the familiar ending that the rom-com so often drives towards: a resolution marked by the creation of a monogamous, heterosexual union. As I explain in more detail below, cinema in France is not seen by the cinephilic critics and cinephilic audiences as entertainment but as an art form. The only 'good' films are auteur films. Rom-coms, like other Hollywood popular genre films, are seen as the worst of all 'bad' films by cinephiles. Although a significant majority of the French public enjoy these films, many directors (and audiences) internalise the taboo against Hollywood-like films.

Apart from disdain for its alleged mechanical format and narrative, could resistance to the implicitly reactionary ideology of the traditional rom-com, demonstrated by the recurrence of this resolution, be a reason for its absence in French cinema? One possible explanation for the absence of the genre and its generic categorisation in French cinema could therefore be cultural; French culture does not place the same importance on or view marriage as the USA traditionally does. It is worth noting that the famous French popular genre on stage and the big screen known as the vaudeville does not aim to bring people together and end with a marriage. Rather, it usually starts long after the wedding and deals mostly with finding a way of keeping the marriage together, as well as maintaining the appearance of bourgeois domestic happiness, while practising adultery, be it on a small or large scale. Moreover, as noted by Ginette Vincendeau (1989), French directors since the 1930s have long favoured what she calls the 'incestuous couple': an older man with a – very – young woman, a scheme that Noël Burch and Geneviève Sellier have identified in subsequent decades too (1996).[4] In other words, these films and characters are far from typical in terms of the characterisation and narrative of the more traditional rom-com.[5]

Another cultural reason for the absence of the genre in France is arguably the fact that the rom-com, like most Hollywood genres, has a fairly consistent 'recipe'; French cinema does not make genre films (or at least so the *cinéphilique* doxa would like us to believe). Despite the popularity of US remakes of French films, French cinema has indeed very little in common with US cinema and there is no equivalent in France to the Hollywood system and its development of genres. Furthermore, the opposition between *cinéma d'auteur* and popular cinema initiated by New Wave directors in the 1950s is still very strong in France and has led to a clear dichotomy between cinema as art (auteur cinema) and cinema as mere entertainment (commercial cinema).[6] Genre films (that is, films that rely on codified structure and recurrent ingredients) belong to the latter and are therefore consistently neglected when they are not explicitly despised by French critics (see Sellier, 2004b). What François Truffaut and the other 'Young Turks' of the New Wave found interesting about some Hollywood film directors such as John Ford or Alfred Hitchcock, was not the various genres they mastered, but their capacity to be or remain auteurs within/despite the commercial/Hollywood system and framework. The French cinephilic critics who today defend cinema as an art, follow the path of the *politique des auteurs*, and only pay attention to genre films when the formulaic format nonetheless allows a subjective/personal artistic expression from the directors, as well as formal and aesthetic innovations. This does not mean, however, that French films do not heavily rely on genres: since the early days of cinema, comedies and crime dramas in particular have always been extremely popular with French audiences, and their popularity has not diminished.

~ Women film directors, feminism and rom-com ~

Like many other popular genres (and comedy in particular, as analysed by Kathleen Rowe, 1995b) the rom-com has long been seen as an ideologically conservative genre that is not always 'woman-friendly'. It also generally provides the audience with a type of 'happy ending' that many feminist theorists object to, especially when marriage was/is, or seems/ed to be, the ultimate goal of the rom-com. As Jackie Stacey has observed, 'romance narratives typically revolve around a potential heterosexual love relationship which must overcome a series of obstacles before being fulfilled ... whatever the problems, they are ultimately overcome and a relationship established which may result in marriage or promised permanent monogamy' (1990: 345). She notes further that, 'will they or won't they (or how will they) live happily ever after is the question that sustains narrative tension' (ibid.). Nevertheless, though feminist theory in film and literature may have initially criticised the traditional constructions of gender implicitly sustained in romance and based on the model of the fairytale and the myth of everlasting love, some later research has concentrated on the various pleasures romance gives female readership and audiences (see Radway, 1984; Stacey, 1990).

In French and French-speaking cinema, women film directors emerged in great numbers in the 1970s and followed the general trend of women's cinema elsewhere: their main concern was to criticise the fallacious myth of – heterosexual – eternal love and the pink legend of marriage. Although most chose to create and explore a female gaze and subjectivity cruelly lacking in French films at the time (without necessarily making 'feminist' cinema, another rarity in French cinema), some expressed this idea more clearly than others: Yannick Bellon's *La Femme de Jean* (1976) is arguably one of the most interesting cases of the decade in this regard.[7] There were therefore very few love stories in films made by women in France following the May 1968 period. A long decade later, Coline Serreau's *Romuald et Juliette* (1989) reworks the scheme of the fairytale, adding social and racial concerns to the initial model. Her film tells the improbable but nevertheless plausible love story between an upper-middle-class married manager and the black, plump cleaning-lady of his company, a single mother of five children by five different fathers. Far from condoning and reproducing the conservative ideology of the traditional rom-com, Serreau infuses it with her own feminist and utopian agenda.[8] In a completely different style, Catherine Corsini's *La Nouvelle Ève* made ten years later (1999) offers interesting variations around the figure of a 30-something single woman with an extremely active sexual life (one often shared with complete strangers) who rejects conventional life and rules. An archetypal unruly woman she escapes the 'Bridget Jones syndrome' as she does not want to find Mr Right and only accepts the idea of (unconventional) coupledom based on her own anti-conformist way of life; it is clearly not marriage she desires. Despite showing her infatuation with a married man, the film does not conclude with the union of the two lovers and opts instead for an open ending with Camille heavily pregnant and unsure about the identity of the father of her child, bumping into her former lover in a shop without clear hints being given of what will happen next.

Comedies dealing with love made by women directors in France in the 1980s and 1990s borrowed from Hollywood genre films, such as the rom-com in the case of Serreau (key ingredients of which include the fairytale dimension, the opposition of contrasted characters and the creation of a heterosexual monogamous couple at the end) and the screwball/ slapstick comedy for Corsini (with her eccentric female protagonist getting involved in unusual romantic or social situations). However, their films are ideologically far removed from these genres. In contrast to the predominant traits of mainstream Hollywood, these directors always choose to give their female characters the lead, in respect of both the narration and the gaze. This female subjectivity allows them to express 'alternative' views about love, sex and the couple, or how and why women should get romantically or sexually involved: the conditions are usually set by them and do not always follow the implicit or explicit ideological rules of the traditional Hollywood rom-com. This is especially true of *Gazon Maudit* (or *French Twist*) the first ever French 'lesbian comedy' made by Josiane Balasko in 1995, which ends in a utopian manner, with the lesbian lover, her girlfriend and her girlfriend's husband all living under the same roof in the couple's house.[9]

It can be deduced from the discussion above that before Danièle Thompson made *Jet Lag*, other French-speaking female auteur-directors had already ventured into the field of a kind of tentative rom-com. Some had even previously relied on 'transatlantic exchanges', if only in the places and casting, such as Chantal Akerman's *Un divan à New York* (1996), starring Juliette Binoche – before her international career took off – alongside William Hurt. Hurt later appeared in Tonie Marshall's *Loin du paradis* (2001) together with Catherine Deneuve. If Marshall's film could be seen as more of a 'comedy of remarriage' (Cavell, 1996), as the two protagonists are former lovers who meet again in New York, Akerman's is more clearly in the tradition of later Hollywood rom-coms. I have noted elsewhere the hybridity some French directors bring to genre films; thus Balasko, Marshall and Serreau, for example, blend popular genres to make 'comedy thrillers' or 'comic road movies' (Rollet, 1999). Similarly, the films they make that could be described as rom-coms are not just that. The interest some French female directors (unlike their male counterparts) show in the genre could be linked to the potential transgression it allows: all the films mentioned above offer an alternative to the dominant model of the traditional 'boy meets girl' format. The focus on female characters in the rom-com can be understood as exploring the expression of unconventional female subjectivity, especially in a country like France, where gender roles are still very conservative.

~ *(French) Food for thought?* Jet Lag *and the rom-com* ~

Famous in France for the comedy screenplays she wrote with and for her father Gérard Oury (including the biggest best-selling film *La Grande Vadrouille* in 1966), Danièle Thompson made her directing debut in 1999 with *La Bûche*, a bitter-sweet comedy of manners which was a big commercial and critical success. Her second feature-length film, *Jet Lag*, offers a different style of comedy, directly influenced by the traditional Hollywood model of the rom-com, but also with a distinctive 'French touch'. The website filmsdefrance.com summarises the film as follows:

> Félix, the head of a frozen food empire, is on his way to Munich to attend a funeral and maybe start afresh with his ex-wife. Meanwhile, Rose, a self-obsessed beautician, is about to catch a flight to Mexico, so that she can start a new life, far away from her bullying boyfriend Sergio. Their separate itineraries cross at Paris airport.... They are complete opposites with nothing at all in common, so they couldn't possibly fall in love – could they ...? (http://www.filmsdefrance.com/ FDF_Decalage_horaire_rev.html)

The film casts two major stars of French and international cinema who both play against type: Jean Réno is Félix, the neurasthenic French cook living in the USA who suffers recurrent panic attacks, and Juliette Binoche is Rose, the heavily made-up beautician trying to flee France and a violent boyfriend in order to work at a holiday resort in Acapulco. At first sight the film seems to uphold all the necessary and expected ingredients of the genre (and I use the word 'ingredients' purposely, since food and recipes are an important aspect of the narrative as I will demonstrate): the 'meet-cute', the clash of personalities, the recurrent accessory – here a mobile phone – and the mistakes it generates (he gets her phone calls and she gets his) (see Jeffers McDonald, 2007). Thompson does not miss a single element. She even appears to allude to the Hollywood classic rom-com *It Happened One Night* (1934), by placing a man and a woman virtually unknown to each other in the same bedroom for a night.

More interesting in my view is the fact that *Jet Lag* is so far the only French rom-com that offers the audience all that can be expected from such a film, while at the same time reflecting on it in an almost parodist manner. From the opening to the closing credits, the film seems to mock what it is doing: it opens and ends with two voiceovers that directly and explicitly comment on Hollywood rom-com in a fascinating tongue-in-cheek fashion. At the beginning, over a still image of what looks like a sky at night (before a zoom out at the end of the monologue reveals that it is the sleeping-mask Félix is wearing), a female voice (Juliette Binoche) is heard. She recounts a memory from when she was a schoolgirl:

> la gifle que je me suis prise; ils m'ont chopé à la sortie de *Vacances Romaines* devant un cinéma rive gauche qui passait des vieux films; non seulement j'avais séché mais en plus j'avais pas le droit de voir des films américains. Mon père disait que c'était débile et ma mère disait que ça donnait une idée fausse de la vie; bon d'accord, les pauvres deviennent riches, les riches ont la vie dure; les sans-papiers trouvent des papiers, les guerres s'arrêtent, les morts reviennent même quelques fois et les putes épousent des millionnaires, d'accord . . . ah si tout ça pouvait être vrai.

> [The English subtitles read: Did I ever get slapped! They caught me coming out of *Roman Holiday* at a Left Bank cinema. Not only did I skip school, but American movies were off-limits. Dad found them silly and Mum said they weren't true to life. OK, the poor get rich, the rich have problems, immigrants get legalised, wars end, even the dead come back to life and whores marry millionaires. If only it could all be true!]

At the end of the film, Félix starts his long message to Rose on the mobile phone answering machine, with the same type of references:

> Une nuit, un aéroport, un homme, une femme[10] eh bien non, je ne veux pas être un souvenir Rose, fuck la logique, d'accord la vie c'est pas un Hollywood movie, les happy ends c'est du bullshit, d'accord j'arrive pas à parler une seule langue à la fois mais qu'est-ce qu'on en a à foutre!

[A night, an airport, a man, a woman, well I don't want to be just a memory, *fuck* the logic. OK life is not a *Hollywood movie, happy ends* are just *bullshit.* OK I can't speak one language at a time but the hell with it!¹¹]

Apart from serving as a neat, self-referential framing device and giving a sort of symmetry and equivalence to the female and the male characters regarding romance and their involvement in it, these two quasi-monologues distance the American model. While the characters and Thompson rely on the traditional format and situations inherent to the genre, their explicit foregrounding of these conventions works a little like a direct and 'knowing' address to the audience. Thompson thus manages to make her subject, the genre she uses and the story she is telling acceptable to a larger French audience as well as to the critics. In other words, by being deliberately reflexive or self-conscious about the genre, the filmmaker elevates the film to more than a genre film, or at least to superior genre fodder. Consulting the reviews written in serious and *cinéphile* publications, suggests that on the whole this 'strategy' worked and the film was generally well received.

By choosing an anonymous place like an airport, Thompson also blurs the boundaries of space and time (hence the title) and allows her characters to be in a sort of 'no-man's or no-woman's land' where everything is possible (it is even possible for a French director and two French stars to shamelessly copy an American genre). Airports all over the world look increasingly alike and the adverse weather conditions that ground Félix and Rose's planes could have occurred in any country. Thompson, however, chooses the strike – something that foreigners often presume to be a typically French pastime – as the troublemaker that soon becomes a matchmaker. Airports are conventionally seen and used as thoroughfares, but events can sometimes force passengers to spend longer there than planned and subsequently to meet and talk to strangers (something that happens infrequently in France). Strikes are common enough in France to function as a narrative device¹² and airports are also clearly associated with global movement and transatlantic exchange. In *Jet Lag*, the character of Félix is probably the best illustration of the latter. His consistent use of *franglais* and Anglicisms when speaking is the first sign of this tendency, which is reinforced by his obsession with the idea of quality food, proper ingredients and his fighting against the *malbouffe* in a stereotypical French fashion. At the same time, he is fanatical about smells and sanitised environments, something usually associated in France with the USA.

Food is indeed a significant motif in the film as it allows the director to contrast the two characters in a very subtle manner and to introduce sexual or more intimate elements between them. The first dinner scene they share in Félix's hotel room is an interesting example of Thompson's skills at introducing serious matters into what is sometimes an apparently frivolous film. This sequence is worth examining in more detail here, since it is a climactic scene that serves as a transitional point for the characters and the narrative.

The protagonists are in totally different moods: Félix is jetlagged, grumpy and complaining about the food, while Rose seems just simply joyful, looking forward to an unexpected and much-needed meal. This contrast between them is emphasised when they both place their order. After calling room service and fastidiously checking the freshness of each ingredient from the menu, Félix finally ends up with a simple meal of bread, tomatoes and ham, while Rose asks for a complex dish with a long and sophisticated name (one which was probably just an industrial pâté). This juxtaposition in their culinary tastes stands as a signifier of their different outlooks and sensibilities. Since the atmosphere is slightly tense and heavy, when their meal arrives Rose engages in light conversation by talking about food, while Félix wants to know what prompted her to leave her violent boyfriend. Rose reflects that since they don't know each other and will never meet again, he might just as well ask her what he really wants to, and the conversation shifts, becoming frank and personal. They start talking about intimate things and exchange some unpleasant truths about each other, he in a brusque manner, she with a fake naivety which belies a perceptive understanding of who and what he really is. Félix becomes extremely offensive when Rose tries to give him some of the vinaigrette she has prepared, and the climax comes when, knocking against her, he accidentally throws the dressing in her face. At this exact moment his mobile phone rings and he is able at last to talk to his ex, Nadia, distracting him from apologising or helping Rose, who stands, horrified, dripping in oil.

While an agitated Félix tries to persuade Nadia to let him come to her grandmother's funeral, Rose listens before going to the bathroom. When she emerges, without make-up and with her hair washed and wrapped in a towel, the atmosphere tangibly shifts. The music changes from typical international hotel muzak tunes to a slow and romantic string theme as he looks at her and is clearly taken aback by her transformation and the realisation of her natural beauty. As for her, the incident (or the conversation between Félix and Nadia she has overheard) has changed not only her physical appearance. Her voice is more confident, she becomes more assertive and she seems more on equal terms with him. The colder and surer she is, the weaker he appears and he even sheds a few tears as he begins to open up to her about his pain. It is unclear, though, whether the salad-dressing incident or the conversation on the phone is the cause of the sudden changes they both experience. From this moment on, their relationship shifts and they become increasingly closer and more intimate. At another dinner (which Félix prepares for them in the hotel kitchen) they talk about their childhoods and their secret wounds. While exchanging personal memories, they also reflect on more essential aspects of life regarding freedom, loyalty and cowardice, in a long exchange of dialogue that was seen by some web commentators reacting on the imdb.com forum, to be in typically French 'talkative' fashion (Dennis, 2004). Indeed, if the rom-com has its own tradition of being very talky, French cinema is often criticised abroad for often replacing action with dialogue.

Thompson does not limit the narrative to love and how to find or keep it. Class as well as inter-generational relationships are key elements that contribute to the definition of her characters. Rose comes from a communist background where her dreams as a little girl were criticised as 'bourgeois', while Félix left home and walked out on his chef father's kitchen after clashing with him over a new dish he had created (which could be seen as a culinary version of the seventeenth-century battle of the 'ancients' versus the 'moderns'!) Both made choices in their lives against their parents' wishes and milieux, although their family heritage is still, and despite everything, an important aspect of their current lives and personalities. In other words, Thompson develops the psychological, social and sexual dimensions of her characters far beyond what is usually expected and found in many mainstream Hollywood rom-coms.

Moreover, just as Félix declares when cooking his gourmet dinner for the two of them in the hotel kitchen that, 'il faut sublimer le produit, le reste c'est du bullshit' ['you got to sublimate the product, the rest is *bullshit*'], Thompson 'sublimates' the initial and somehow 'raw' product of the rom-com. Amusingly, it seems that the director does with the romantic comedy the exact reverse of what Félix does with French cooking in his job: adapting a specific diet – French food – for a palate used to other foods and flavours. Félix tries to sell French cooking to US clients just as Thompson adapts the rom-com to French audiences: she uses well-known ingredients (national stars) and adds flavours that can make it more digestible (a woman from a communist family named after the revolutionary Rosa Luxembourg, who has style and a weakness for the Popular Front; a bullying man who happens not only to have a heart, but also to be a great cook with an obsession with authentic country produce).

More interesting, in my view, is the way she introduces a feminist agenda, as Rose is developed into a more multi-dimensional character than the stereotypical frivolous woman she seems to be at the beginning of the film. While giving her female character knowledge and an understanding of human weaknesses, and the kind of depth and complexity that is sometimes missing from the genre in Hollywood, Thompson progressively sets Rose free from all her ideological, social and sexual constraints. She starts the film an unhappy woman and a victim of domestic violence, but eventually emancipates herself from the man who ruled her life. Unlike Cinderella, whose attractiveness hidden under rags is revealed at the end, Rose undergoes the reverse process. By the end of the film, she – willingly this time – removes the make-up we have just seen her applying meticulously, and opts instead for a more 'natural' form of beauty. Her aesthetic transformation parallels her journey in the film: she liberates herself from society's implicit rules regarding femininity, just as she previously escaped a familial, social, political and cultural environment she did not share, and a damaging, alienating love relationship, to at last become herself.

One could argue, however, that by the end she is 'completed' by finding her new love – it seems she is compelled to find another relationship right away – and again, it is with a man who is evidently troubled by personal problems, albeit in a different way from her ex. Also, it is this man who prompts the latter part of her transformation – *he* initiates the moment we first see her without her mask of make-up. This would problematise a feminist reading of the film for enlightened audiences and critics anywhere but in France and in French cinema, where the implicit ideology regarding gender roles and identities remains very conformist, even in films made by women. Unlike 1970s women's cinema, very few films by female directors from the 1980s onwards explicitly question the unwritten rules of femininity and male-female relationships or actually offer alternatives for female characters beyond the creation of a couple and the 'compulsory' heterosexuality denounced by Adrienne Rich (1986).

It emerges from what I have argued here that the same ingredients used in the same recipes do not always produce the same dishes. The French rom-com, to create a new generic category, is far from the Hollywood model from a cultural, ideological and national point of view. More than other popular genres 'imported' from Hollywood and adapted for the taste of French audiences in recent years, the rom-com seems to embody the problematic relationship and differences between the two nations from a socio-cultural as well as from a cinematographic point of view. Although love and relationships constitute a familiar topic in French cinema, the genre encompasses issues that are specifically at the core of French society and cinema. *Jet Lag* in particular exemplifies the opposition between the cinephilic critic's taste and conception of what is a 'good' film, with the growing interest of the general public in France for Hollywood-like films. It simultaneously provides traditional rom-com pleasures for the regular cinema-goer, while evidently being self-referential and critical enough to alleviate the objections of the cinephilic critics. Despite having a resolution familiar from the Hollywood model, it also allows for the expression of alternative masculinities and femininities as well as gender relations, something that is not particularly common in French cinema. Whether the genre will go on to provide other French female directors with the possibility of transgressing the existing rules on gender and sexuality remains to be seen.

8 Romantic Comedies and the Raced Body

~ Karen Bowdre ~

In his 2002 book *Romantic vs Screwball Comedy: Charting the Difference*, Wes Gehring examines the 'seriousness' of romance in romantic comedies. He argues that while rom-coms have comedic moments, these films are nevertheless serious about the idea of love and finding one's soul-mate (ibid.: 67). As an example of a serious romantic moment, one might look to the exchange in *You've Got Mail* (1998) when Nelson Fox (Dabney Coleman) is talking with his son Joe (Tom Hanks) about relationships. Nelson has just ended one relationship and is calculating how quickly he can get into another. He tells his son, 'I just have to meet someone new, that's all. That's the easy part.' Joe sarcastically replies, 'Oh right, yeah, it's a snap to find the one single person in the world who fills your heart with joy.' Nelson laughs as he says, 'Well, don't be ridiculous. Have I ever been with anybody who fit that description? Have you?', underlining how despite the genre's reputation for lightness, the search for a soul-mate can be heart breaking, frustrating, and sometimes elusive. In the next scene, Joe is going to see Kathleen Kelly (Meg Ryan) with a bouquet of daisies, her favourite flower. It is evident that he has finally come to the realisation that Kathleen is the one single person in the world who fills his heart with joy. Interestingly, these serious romantic moments are missing in most Black romantic comedy films, demonstrating how Gehring's account does not recognise how inconsistencies exist across the genre on this matter.

In this chapter I will argue that Black bodies disrupt romantic comedy conventions and that since the mid-1980s it is evident that rom-coms with African-American casts consistently differ in fundamental and significant ways from those with Caucasian casts. Analysis of recent Black cast rom-coms reveals that the highly sexualised and comical meanings placed on African-American bodies in the context of the United States, and their historical representation in Hollywood cinema, inhibit filmmakers from creating roles where Black characters are romantic and take romance seriously. Black cast films do not adhere to many of the conventions that audiences have come to expect of the genre, such as the 'meet-cute' and the overcoming of a series of obstacles that enables the couple to unite at the end (Neale, 1992: 287). Even a cursory look at reviews from sources such as the *New York Times*, *Variety*, studio websites and the Internet Movie Database (www.imdb.com), reveals variance regarding how African-American films are defined and positioned within the category of romantic comedy.

One of the reasons why it is difficult to label these films is that when most films with Black casts are distributed the industry and critics alike typically focus on the race of the characters, and perhaps the location if they are situated in urban environments, as a means of defining them. Films with African Americans that are not gangster or 'hood films' are difficult to categorise because Black films are often viewed as a genre unto themselves (Cripps, 1978). For example, *The Best Man* (1999) is labelled as a rom-com by film critics such as Janet Maslin and Wesley Morris, a comedy/drama on IMDb, and a romance by the film's distributors on the Universal Studios website. Meanwhile in a DVD commentary its director, Malcolm D. Lee, describes the film as being an 'ensemble film' that was inspired by movies like *The Big Chill* (1983), *Four Weddings and a Funeral* (1994), and *Diner* (1982).

Though genre categorisation can be a problem for African-American rom-coms, it is sometimes a problem for white cast films as well. *Jerry Maguire* (1996), which might be considered a dramatic film that contains a romance narrative, is often described by critics and theorists as a rom-com. Interestingly, for white cast films, categories arguably become more obscured when the protagonist is male. When the protagonist is a woman and is played by a female star typically associated with the genre (such as Julia Roberts, Meg Ryan, Sandra Bullock or Drew Barrymore), the category is in less flux. In this chapter, I will take the term 'Black romantic comedy' to mean films with predominantly African-American casts. Though this definition can be contested because the writers and directors of these 'Black' films may not be of African descent, using this criterion is consistent with scholars such as Bogle (2003), Cripps (1978), and Guerrero (1993).[1]

At present there has been relatively little theoretical or academic work performed on contemporary rom-coms. Theorists such as Cavell (1981), Harvey (1987), Byrge (1987), Gehring (1986) and Lent (1995) focus on films produced in the 1930s and 1940s. Additionally, as scholar Mark Reid notes, most genre studies do not engage with the topic of race (2003: 472). Yet African-American bodies are understood in very specific ways in the USA both culturally and in film and television. Longstanding stereotypes of Blacks in visual culture depict them as having diminished intellectual capacity and being natural musicians and comedians. Thus the strong historical emphasis on comedy in Black representation is consistent with images still circulating in popular culture. Some of the most popular African-American actors in early film were Stepin Fetchit and Willie Best, both of whom usually portrayed Black men as mentally challenged, lazy and constantly frightened. Typically Fetchit and Best were objects of derision and side-kicks to white male stars like Will Rogers (Cripps, 1993). Even today, many popular and noted African-American male actors started in comedy – for example, Eddie Murphy, Will Smith, Martin Lawrence and Jamie Foxx. While these comedians are stars in their own right and not side-kicks, many of their roles have been in comedies. This limited view of Black actors and actresses as comic relief has its history in pre-filmic venues such as minstrelsy and vaudeville. Unfortunately, understanding African-American performers in this fashion circumscribes what roles they play and how they are perceived by wider culture. Consequently, it also makes it difficult for filmmakers, both Black and white, to conceive and portray African Americans in romantic situations.

In addition to being comedically overdetermined, Blacks are also perceived as being hypersexual (hooks, 1981: 51–86; Jones, 1993). This belief in African-American exaggerated sexuality has its roots in the racist ideologies that justified slavery. Though slavery officially ended in the United States in 1863, the racial ideologies that perceived Black men as physically and sexually threatening and Black women as sexual temptresses continues to circulate and maintain racial hierarchies. Hollywood, which to some degree reflects the USA culturally, has continued this mythology in its portrayals of Blacks from the inception of cinema to the present day, while other visual media, including television and video games, also continue to circulate sexual and violent images of African Americans. These visual and cultural histories of Black bodies naturalise comedic or sexual representations of African-American characters, with the result that they are not permitted to exercise the full range of humanity that is available to their white counterparts. Since Blacks generally play static stereotypes, their characters are typically denied narrative arcs where they could be seen to be learning from previous mistakes or making sacrifices for individual or collective good.

I will now critically compare the content of Black and white romantic comedies and analyse two films, *Booty Call* (1997) and *Two Can Play That Game* (2001) to this end. *Two Can Play That Game* is a battle of the sexes rom-com that is reminiscent of screwball comedies of the 1930s and 1940s. *Booty Call* is representative of comedian comedy films (see Harbidge, Chapter 13 in this collection) such as *The Wedding Singer* (1998), *There's Something About Mary* (1998) and *Wedding Crashers* (2005), in which the protagonists are played by established comedians, or what some scholars refer to as 'romantic comedies for boys' (Jeffers McDonald, 2007: 108; see also Chapter 11 in this collection). With a dearth of theoretical frameworks examining either contemporary rom-coms or the impact of race on the genre, it is necessary to turn to texts that examine issues of race and representation. Using Richard Dyer (1988) and Ed Guerrero (1993), I will elucidate how race disrupts the rom-com structure. Dyer notes that,

> power in contemporary society habitually passes itself off as embodied in the normal as opposed to the superior. This is common to all forms of power, but it works in a peculiarly seductive way with whiteness, because of the way it seems rooted in commonsense thought, in things other than ethnic difference. (1988: 45)

This normalcy manifests itself in the area of representation in that 'being white is coterminous with the endless plenitude of human diversity' (Dyer, 1988: 47). For example, films with white actors are thought to be universal narratives whereas films with people of African or Asian descent or Latinos/as are read as 'Black', 'Asian' or 'Latino' films. Further complicating the notion that whiteness has an 'infinite variety' is the fact that stereotypes of ethnic others are malleable; they 'are seldom found in a pure form and this is part of the process by which they are naturalised, kept alive' (ibid). Hence, the racial ideology of white supremacy as described by Dyer is used as a particular strategy to maintain racial hierarchies in entertainment and other visual venues.

Examining how racial ideologies operate in popular culture is essential in seeking to address or eradicate stereotypes that limit opportunities for actors and actresses of colour and to eliminate racial falsehoods that circulate in broader society. Guerrero's work is significant to my analysis because he deconstructs how the ideology of white supremacy affects African Americans on macro and micro levels in film. The subtlety of the hegemonic power of whiteness not only affects who plays what role in a film but also how different racial groups view one another and themselves onscreen and in the real world. Hegemonic whiteness also regulates how roles are played when bodies are not the perceived white norm. In rom-coms specifically, racial bias closes off the possibility of most African-American characters being able to take romance seriously.

One example of how characters function according to the race of the actor is the 'rake' male lead in romantic comedies. Recurrently, in white rom-coms, this male lead is an incorrigible and lecherous individual, who is initially the antithesis of the male ideal in this genre. However, the rake eventually comes to the realisation that he has met his soul-mate and changes character. Moreover, this character usually makes sacrifices to demonstrate his love to the heroine. However, in African-American rom-coms the male lead is rarely put in a situation where he has to make a noble sacrifice or change his behaviour in order to win the love of his life, thus proving his integrity and winning classical heroic status.

The narrative structure of the rom-com is broadly: boy meets girl, boy loses girl, boy gets girl. This modality has been a staple of Hollywood film from the time the genre first made its mark in the mid-1930s in the form of screwball films. Though the genre has altered over time with various cycles or sub-genres (screwball, sex comedy, nervous comedy and new romance), Jeffers McDonald argues that since the late 1980s the neo-traditional romantic comedy has been the most dominant cycle produced in Hollywood (2007: 86). In these neo-traditional rom-coms, the romance and struggle (the 'boy meets, loses, (and) regains (the) girl') of the heterosexual couple has returned as the focus. Typically these rom-coms close with the hero and heroine in an embrace and kissing, often with the implication that they will legitimise this relationship with marriage. These romantic norms are so intrinsic to these comedies that it is assumed they operate consistently, regardless of the cast. Surprisingly, though, this 'boy meets, loses and regains girl' structure is often not in operation in films with Black casts. In rom-coms with African Americans since the late 1980s, the leads usually either already know one another as a romantic couple – thus, there is no meet-cute or romantic longing or wooing that is an important element of this genre

- or the comedic aspects of the film are so strong that the romance is marginalised.

Mark Brown's *Two Can Play That Game* is the story of Shante Smith (Vivica Fox), a successful senior advertising executive and self-appointed relationship expert. Shante is constantly giving advice to her girlfriends about how to control their undisciplined and sometimes philandering boyfriends. While having dinner with her girlfriends, Shante discovers her boyfriend, Keith Fenton (Morris Chestnut), has violated one of her relationship rules. Keith and Shante were supposed to have dinner that evening but he had to cancel because he was working late, which according to Shante is the number one excuse for a cheating boyfriend. Keith actually was working late with an attractive female colleague and they went to dinner at a place where Keith and Shante often frequent. Discovering Keith on the dance floor with another woman drives Shante to get Keith back in line by punishing him for his error.

The film's leads, Fox and Chestnut, play straight woman and man to their best friends, who are played by well-established comedians. Wendy Raquel Robinson, who plays Karen, is known to audiences for her comedic turns as a series regular on *The Steve Harvey Show*, a situation comedy that ran on the WB from 1997 to 2002. Tamala Jones, who plays Tracey, is known for her comic skills on television shows like *For Your Love*, a situation comedy that ran on the WB from 1998 to 2002 and films such as *Booty Call* and *The Wood* (1999). Mo'Nique, who plays Diedre, is a stand-up comedian also known for her role as Nikki Parker on the UPN situation comedy *The Parkers* (1999–2004). And Chestnut's Keith Fenton has one buddy, Tony, portrayed by Anthony Anderson, who is known for his comedic work in films such as *Big Momma's House* (2000) and *Romeo Must Die* (2000). Thus it is not surprising that the comedic interactions between the leads and their friends constitute some of the film's most memorable moments. However, the film does not provide much romance between the leads.

When the audience first sees Keith and Shante together, she has come by his office for a visit. In the previous scenes, Shante has explained the man problems of her girlfriends. As she goes to greet Keith, she tells the audience, 'I don't have a problem with my man. He behaves very well.' It soon becomes apparent that the two are aroused by one another as they quickly retreat to his office for sex. These scenes of Shante and Keith's interaction with one another are played farcically and this incident continues the outlandish tone of the film. Unlike most couples in recent romantic comedies, particularly neo-traditional rom-coms, the pair have an active sex life and it appears in this film that sex is used as a substitution for romance and love. For example, after their afternoon tryst, Tony comes into Keith's office to tease him about what just happened. Keith is gentlemanly enough not to state what actually occurred in the office but simply states that 'I will say this, there is nothing that you or anybody can ever say to make me leave that woman, man.' It is difficult at this point in the film to discern whether this post-coital declaration is indicative of Keith's true feelings for Shante or merely a reaction to the moment. His friend Tony further undermines any romantic implications in his declaration. When Tony enters Keith's office he starts sniffing the air as if he can smell the sex. He continues to ask Keith if he and Shante had sex using the vernacular, 'Did you hit it?' and ends his banter by asking his friend if he smacked Shante's bottom. These remarks add to the heightened sense of comedy and help erase the potential for romance in the scene.

A brief romantic moment does occur when Shante recalls how she met Keith. She explains through a flashback sequence that she was out at a nightclub with her girlfriends; 'There were lots of good-looking men in the place. Then he looked at me and for a second everyone else in the place disappeared. He was fine but there was something else about him, you know, that something that makes your head light and your stomach tight.' Thus in their first meeting, Shante and Keith do experience an attraction at first sight and such moments are a cornerstone of the genre. After their good-natured banter, the scene returns to the present. For the remainder of the film, the focus is on Shante's manipulating and punishing Keith, and romantic moments or the subject of love are not addressed again until the film's conclusion.

Though the film does have a battle of the sexes element that is common in screwball comedies, it is difficult to place the film in this category. Keith and Shante are an established couple but they are not married. If they had been, and had they harboured deep resentment for one another, the film might perhaps have borne comparison to classic 'comedies of remarriage' (Cavell, 1981) such as *The Awful Truth* (1937) or *The Philadelphia Story* (1940). While Keith and Shante are together at the close of the film, their not being married distinguishes them from these past screwball films. Moreover, Keith and Shante's reconciliation to mere couple status even falls short of more recent films considered screwball or having screwball elements such as *Runaway Bride* (1999) where the lead couple marry or become a committed unmarried couple as in *Four Weddings and a Funeral*. There is the possibility that Keith and Shante's relationship at the close of the film may be similar to Charles (Hugh Grant) and Carrie's (Andie MacDowell), but neither Keith nor Shante make the kind of grand romantic gesture that we see in *Four Weddings*. Though Keith does profess his love for Shante and forgives her for her antics, this claim is slightly jarring because love has not been discussed in the rest of the film. The audience does not really know what it is that make Keith and Shante a special couple. In contrast, at the close of *Four Weddings* Charles asks Carrie '[do] you think not being married to me might maybe be something you could consider doing for the rest of your life?', to which Carrie responds, 'I do.' Hence, though the two will not marry, he has proposed, she has accepted and they will live 'happily ever after' as most rom-com couples do.

Booty Call shares a structural similarity with *Two Can Play That Game*, in that there is an over-emphasis on the comedy at the expense of romance. The film follows a date with two friends, Bunz (Jamie Foxx) and Rushon (Tommy Davidson), and their companions, Lysterine (Vivica Fox) and Nikki (Tamala Jones). Rushon and Nikki, the best friends of Bunz and Lysterine respectively, have been dating for seven weeks. As we meet the characters, Rushon is looking forward to consummating his relationship with Nikki later that evening. Though Rushon does get his wish at the close of the film, there are several obstacles to fulfilling his desire. For example, Nikki is very conscious of sexually transmitted diseases and insists on using condoms. When Rushon gets one, it slips from his hands and Nikki's dog gets it. Rushon and Bunz, who is about to have sex with Lysterine, then have to go to the store to get condoms and saran wrap (cling film). Neither Bunz nor Rushon know how to apply it properly, instigating a lengthy and farcical sequence in which Rushon starts wrapping his head with the saran wrap. The physical and visual humour of this scene is similar to other over-the-top scenes throughout the film. Based on their earlier conversations, the audience is aware that Bunz and Rushon are not the most intelligent men, though they believe themselves to be hip and cool. This scene is similar to other slapstick performances in comedian romantic comedies, such as Ben Stiller as Ted Stroehmann in *There's Something About Mary*. However, unlike Ted, who throughout the film states his wish to marry and be in love, neither Bunz nor Rushon demonstrate a serious desire for love and marriage and seem merely to be looking for sex, with Rushon willing to maintain but not progress to a deeper commitment in his relationship with Nikki. As is the case with Keith and Shante in *Two Can Play That Game*, Rushon and Nikki seldom have memorable tender moments. Most of their behaviour is comedic or provocative in order to reach their mutual goal of seduction. Though the film ends with Rushon and Nikki finally having sex, it is not clear whether either have intentions or desires for one another beyond sex. The stability of their relationship also seems uncertain, given that their best friends are serial monogamists, constantly looking for new partners.

Just as Black comic stereotypes prevent Black male characters from gaining heroic status, African-American female characters are denied being the heroine. In rom-coms, Black female protagonists are rarely shown thinking about or articulating the qualities of their ideal mate. Furthermore, it is uncommon to see Black women being emotionally moved by the realisation of being in love. Even the manipulating Andie Anderson (Kate Hudson) from *How to Lose a Guy in 10 Days* (2003) has moments in that film where she realises she is falling in love with her 'pawn', Ben Berry (Matthew McConaughey). In this film both Andie and Ben have bet others that they can either lose a man, or make a woman fall in love, in ten days. Nevertheless, despite her hidden agenda, Andie is genuinely touched when Ben brings her to meet his family and she finds out she is the only woman he has introduced to them. Moreover, after their idyllic day together, Andie and Ben have sex for the first time thus signifying sex as the climactic culmination of romance.

In contrast, in Black rom-coms attraction between men and women is almost always immediately acted upon in a physical manner. Shante and Keith sleep together on their first date, as do Bunz and Lysterine. While this inability to portray African-American characters as romantic is consistent with the Black stereotypes outlined here, it also perpetuates perceived differences between African Americans and Caucasian Americans. One of the problematic ramifications of these (and indeed of any) representations is how they might be understood as being not merely portrayals but as constituting 'reality'. Though many US audiences consider themselves sophisticated media viewers and consumers, many still nevertheless learn about ethnic and racial communities beyond their own from the media.

While white rom-coms do, of course, have comedic elements, their romance nevertheless stays central to the plot. For example, in *Never Been Kissed* (1999), the protagonist, Josie Geller (Drew Barrymore) is on her first assignment as an undercover reporter in a Chicago area high school. Unfortunately, going back to high school causes Josie to relive the humiliations of her past. However, her interactions with teacher Sam Coulson (Michael Vartan) cue the audience that despite the obstacles created by these other storylines the couple will end up together. In these films, comic misunderstandings abound but the romantic narrative line always stays prominent. Dyer's concept of whiteness and its invisibility or naturalness (1988) accounts for why the romantic elements are not lost in white rom-coms. Since white bodies do not carry the racial meaning that other 'raced' bodies do, Caucasian bodies do not disrupt the genre format and the narrative focus remains on romance. In contrast, Black characters are denied the kind of 'mature' relationship that our culture reveres and thus the access such relationships bring to achieving heroic or 'human' status.

Though the characters in white films exhibit sexual desire too, for them this longing is synonymous with wanting a committed relationship, one that often leads to marriage but is at the very least signalled as monogamous. Some of these white films cast the lead male as so desiring of a real relationship that he is willing to make great sacrifices, demonstrating that this must truly be love. For example, Tad Hamilton (Josh Duhamel), the famous and popular movie star in *Win a Date with Tad Hamilton!* (2004) leaves Los Angeles in order to pursue a relationship with Rosalee Futch (Kate Bosworth), the woman from West Virginia who won the date with him. Prior to his date with Rosalee, Tad dated and slept with many women and embodied the lifestyle of a handsome single male movie star. Being exposed to a pretty woman with values, quite at odds with the shallow people in Tad's world, causes Tad to re-evaluate his life as a famous celebrity. He wants some of Rosalee's 'goodness to rub off on him' and even buys a farm in her small rural town in West Virginia so he can get to know her better. When the movie role he covets is given to him, Tad is willing to refuse the job to remain with Rosalee. These gestures – leaving Hollywood, coming to West Virginia and buying a home there – along with his wooing Rosalee, have made Tad's manager and agent alarmed at his seemingly irrational behaviour. While Tad may not have completely reformed from his womanising ways, his actions (and the reactions of those close to him) are cues to the audience that this may be true love for him; and, by extension, that he has the capacity to grow, mature and be transformed by love.

Similarly, in *Two Weeks Notice* (2002) for most of the film spoiled millionaire George Wade (Hugh Grant) is self-centred as well as morally questionable in his dealings with women. As the film closes, he finally comes to the epiphany that he is in love with long-time associate and lawyer, Lucy Kelson (Sandra Bullock). In order to pursue this relationship, George goes to Lucy's office, admits his mistakes and professes his love for her. Realising that Lucy is his soul-mate means George must relinquish his position in his family's company and stand up to the unethical business tactics of his mercenary brother. Since George has been a womaniser before, acknowledging his errors and seeking Lucy out in order to state his love for her are all demonstrations of the authenticity of his love; and of how this newfound capacity to love selflessly hastransformed him , like Tad Hamilton, into a 'better' man.

Crucially, then, the 'seriousness' eventually reached by these white male protagonists stands in contrast to the actions of their Black male counterparts. Ironically, Tad and George are not stellar examples of men. Both have been serious serial monogamists or players like Bunz. In spite of this flaw, they are nevertheless allowed to reform and win the affection of the heroine (even if only temporarily in Tad's case). However, this should not be surprising considering the operation of whiteness and the consistency of Black stereotypes detailed above. Whiteness enables rogue white males to always have the potential to change and grow, and thus, to take up the mantle of classical hero. In contrast, the shadow of the tropes of Black foolishness and sexual excess are so powerful that the African-American male protagonist is not given the opportunity to evolve or be reflective; to re-evaluate his life, realise he has found his match and selflessly pursue her regardless of the consequences.

Black female characters are also not given the humanity and depth of the roles played by their white counterparts. In rom-coms this manifests itself as Black women not being given the opportunity to idealise love and romance. Hence, though they may be financially successful like Shante and her friend Karen, they are usually not permitted to be vulnerable in ways that define white femininity. As Keith and Shante reconcile at the close of the film, she does not overtly apologise for her behaviour.

Throughout the film, Shante has shown she can be and is an independent woman. Hence, the audience did not see Shante as vulnerable; she did not even confide in her girlfriends regarding her concerns about Keith. I do not mean to suggest here that representations of Black femininity need to imitate those of white femininity, which has its own set of representational problems. Rather, what I am stating is that hegemonic notions of African-American women normally portray them as over-sexualised and 'strong' to the point of isolation. Just as Black men need to be given the chance to be fully human and demonstrate a range of emotion, Black women need similar opportunities.

What this series of representations demonstrates is that the stereotypical straitjackets of racial hegemony continue to inhibit how African-American characters are portrayed in film and television. My analysis has shown how Black bodies in rom-coms disrupt genre conventions. Ideologies of hyper-sexuality and visual histories of comedy continue to curtail the producers of romantic comedies from creating roles where African-American characters desire, find and pursue idealised love. While it can be argued that the love presented in neo-traditional rom-coms of the past two decades is a fairytale that is not realistic, it is also culturally revered, an aspiration many hope to achieve. If this dream is only offered onscreen to those who are white – and most of the world's population is not white – this dream evidently needs to be expanded.

9 *Armed and Fabulous*

Miss Congeniality's Queer Rom-Com

~ Claire Hines[1] ~

NEAR THE END of *Miss Congeniality* (2000) there is a small but significant moment when a character's queerness is acknowledged and even applauded. At this stage in the film FBI agent Gracie Hart, played by Sandra Bullock, has successfully gone undercover as a contestant in the Miss United States beauty pageant in order to combat a terrorist bomb threat. As the final ten contestants are whittled down to the top five, eliminated competitor Miss New York (Karen Krantz) seizes the opportunity to address the audience, shouting, 'I just want to let all the lesbians out there know, if I can make it into the top ten, so can you!' At the same time as a security guard removes her from the stage, she adds, 'Tina, I love you baby!' From amongst the crowd, Tina jumps up and responds with equal fervour, 'Oh God, I love you, Karen!' Following this romantic declaration, Gracie joins the audience as they enthusiastically clap to signal their support while, powerless to prevent its impact, the pageant organisers can only look on in dismay. However minor, this brief moment of narrative disruption calls attention to *Miss Congeniality*'s general preoccupation with roles and performances of gender and sexuality that, I will argue, can be understood as queer. For the purposes of this essay, the scene could also be said to work metonymically, as it is representative of the way that queerness is a source of pleasure in the rom-com. So, just as the diegetic audience applaud the moment of queer revelation within the film, we as viewers can applaud the queer interlude that this popular genre provides for us.

~ *Queer rom-com* ~

Like the pleasures of film comedy, 'queer' is a critical term that is notoriously hard to define. Building on earlier achievements in gay liberation, it was in the context of AIDS activism in the 1980s that the formerly abusive word 'queer' (most often used in homophobic discourses) was first re-appropriated as a positive term in popular culture and in theory (Spargo, 1999). In culture, queer was reclaimed as an inclusive, unapologetic and oppositional identity that celebrated and encouraged diversity. As a potentially transgressive response to marginalisation, queer shares resonances with the parodic, excessive theatricality of camp. In common with camp, queer theory emerged to reject normative categories of gender and sexuality, instead offering a range of alternative approaches that sought to recognise and to include difference (N. Sullivan, 2003). However, critics continue to debate camp's status as an oppositional strategy as it has been increasingly co-opted into heteronormative discourses (see Meyer, 1994).

Within Film Studies, queer theory provides a way of reading against the grain that enables multiple interpretations of a film at all levels of the text (textual, subtextual, extra-textual and intertextual). As always, though, this process can be thought of as problematic because any exploration of an alternative reading runs the risk of reinforcing the privileged position of the dominant reading. This problem is acknowledged by Alexander Doty, whose work applies queer theory to issues of textual production and reception, in order to locate 'queer elements' or 'moments' of narrative disruption within mainstream films. His argument that 'basically heterocentrist texts can contain queer elements, and basically heterosexual, straight-identifying people can experience queer moments', not only stresses the complex ways in which we engage with cinema, it also highlights the queer erotics of our viewing experiences (Doty, 1995: 72). In the case of *Miss Congeniality*, Miss New York's coming out provides a literal moment of queer narrative disruption that reminds us how often we make assumptions about sexuality based on appearance, and exposes the alternative layers of meaning discussed by Doty. As such, this essay upholds his assertion that queer readings are just as 'there' as those readings preferred by the dominant culture, and exist in the ongoing dialogue between texts, readers and the social world (Doty, 2000: 2).

Writing on 'Queerness, Comedy and *The Women*', Doty has employed 'queer reading strategies' to discuss what he sees as the inherent queerness of film comedy (Doty, 2000: 81). He says, 'Let's face it, as a genre, comedy is fundamentally queer, since it encourages rule-breaking, risk-taking, inversions and perversions in the face of straight patriarchal norms' (ibid.). Indeed, I would argue that this queerness is especially true of the rom-com, which has always explored tensions surrounding gender roles, desire and identity between the sexes. Kristine Brunovska Karnick and Henry Jenkins link comedy to Bakhtin's concept of carnival, a time where 'fixed social roles were abandoned in favour of a more fluid conception of identity' (Brunovska Karnick and Jenkins, 1995b: 271). Brunovska Karnick and Jenkins draw attention here to the rom-com's function to provide its audience with a carnivalesque space in which the social world is temporarily turned upside down, and where transgressive behaviour and queer play is celebrated. Consequently, 'romantic comedy becomes a particularly potent site for . . . queer reception practices, since it deals so directly with the issue of sexual desire and its influence upon our personal interactions' (ibid.: 280).

Yet, despite a period of textual freedom and rebellion, the comedy film's generic ending is often conservative, since as Doty says, 'most comic gender and sexuality rule-breaking is ultimately contained or recuperated by traditional narrative closure' (2000: 81). In the rom-com, this closure is achieved through the joining of the heterosexual couple, who have overcome a series of obstacles and emotional conflicts to move towards their happy union. But in *Miss Congeniality* this drive towards union is given a queer twist. The relationship that develops between FBI agents Gracie Hart and Eric Matthews (Benjamin Bratt) is marginalised to the extent that their coupling appears arbitrary. Therefore, in this essay I use textual and subtextual analyses to argue that the marginal status of heterosexual romance in the first film encourages us to find pleasure instead in a series of alternative romances, focused around the queer character of Gracie. This queer reading is reinforced by the sequel *Miss Congeniality 2: Armed and Fabulous* (2005), which trades on the strong sexual chemistry between Gracie and her new female FBI 'partner', Sam Fuller (Regina King) and the title of which itself ('fabulous' having been co-opted into a kind of camp vernacular) signals the film's queer sensibility.

~ Tomboy agent Gracie Hart ~

Miss Congeniality opens with a prologue set in New Jersey, 1982. In a school playground Gracie is shown as a little girl, conspicuous in that she is the only child sitting alone reading a Nancy Drew novel. Across the playground, she sees a boy being bullied. She comes to his rescue, expertly knocking out the bully, only to be rejected by the boy she saves, who complains that now everyone will think that he needs a girl to protect him. Hurt, Gracie responds by hitting him as well. Not only does this brief prologue foreshadow Gracie's character and relationships as an adult, it also establishes the gender stereotypes that both *Miss Congeniality* and *Miss Congeniality 2* begin to explore, problematise and in effect queer.

Years later, we learn that the adult Gracie remains a social misfit who exhibits few feminine attributes and very little style. In a sequence that parallels Gracie's earlier childhood response to her rebuff in the playground, as an adult she reacts to a bad day at work by boxing furiously with the punch bag that permanently hangs in the middle of her cluttered bachelorette pad, suggesting its centrality to her single life. Frustrated by her relegation to desk duty, having failed to follow orders on an assignment, Gracie still uses violence to deal with her emotions. She has also stayed plain looking, wearing the same sort of dark rimmed glasses, baggy clothing and unruly braids that she sported as a little girl. Grown up, Gracie shows no interest in her physical appearance and owns neither a dress nor a hairbrush. As a result she is informed by Eric that she 'look[s] like hell' and she jokingly complains of suffering from 'a bad hair day . . . Bad hair decade, really'.

At the beginning of *Miss Congeniality* it is thus made clear that Gracie is far from Grace-ful. Instead, she exhibits typically masculine characteristics: she is physically tough, resourceful and independent, behaving more like one of the boys than a woman. To illustrate this, having been selected to enter the beauty pageant, Gracie asks Eric, 'Is it a woman thing?' This question is posed in the FBI gym during the kind of fight one would expect between two men rather than a man and a woman. Gracie has Eric in a headlock at the time; he responds by knocking her to the floor saying, 'Don't kid yourself. Nobody thinks of you that way.' She also displays 'masculine' tastes, favouring junk food, beer and sensible shoes over focus on her body image, make-up or wardrobe. Gracie appears distinctly unfeminine: she stomps and

9.1: Pre-makeover: tomboy agent Gracie Hart in *Miss Congeniality.*

she snorts, she is clumsy and unkempt. Her distaste for femininity is further demonstrated by her scathing attitude to beauty pageants in general. They are, she insists, designed to pander to 'some misogynistic Neanderthal mentality' and she has no desire to join the ranks of what she refers to as a 'bunch of bikini stuffers who only want world peace'. Unsurprisingly, devoted pageant organiser and former Miss USA Kathy Morningside takes an immediate dislike to Gracie, labelling her as one of those 'feminists, intellectuals and ugly women' who mock both the institution and its contestants. This is especially ironic considering Morningside is played by Candice Bergen, in reality one of the 'feminist intellectuals' of second-wave feminism that her character is so scathing about.

In this way, *Miss Congeniality*'s opening scenes introduce Gracie as a feminist tomboy who does not fit the traditional social definition of femininity. Critics have identified the tomboy as a central image in the history of lesbian representation (Creed, 1995; Halberstam, 1998; Tasker, 1998). For example, Judith Halberstam examines the tomboy within her survey of butches on film. Halberstam describes the tomboy as 'pre-butch', who fails 'to assimilate to the demands of femininity' and is part of an order of masculine women who wear 'the wrong clothes' and who are 'very often associated with clear markers of a distinctly phallic power' (Halberstam, 1998: 186-7). In line with this account, Gracie's tomboy attitude and appearance at the start of *Miss Congeniality* visibly tend towards the butch: when walking she strides instead of glides;

she wears men's clothing, and as one of the other characters observes 'in place of friends and relationships, [she has] sarcasm and a gun'. As this description suggests, the use of these familiar signifiers mean that Gracie may be viewed as a queer coded character.

For an audience sensitive to narrative silences as well as disruptions, the vagueness and mystery surrounding Gracie's past romantic life only adds to this queer coding. This is later confirmed by her poolside confession that although she has dated, 'both times it was totally screwed up', revealing that her romantic encounters have been both infrequent and unsuccessful. In this respect, Linda Mizejewski's comment that 'Gracie needs a makeover to "pass" as a girlie girl for the pageant' is revealing, since the notion of passing implies that she must learn to act as something other than what she is (Mizejewski, 2004: 169). Passing has a particular significance in queer culture, as it refers to the ability of a person to succeed in convincing others through their behaviour and dress that they are members of a different social group. This could mean passing as a member of the opposite sex, or if queer, it could also mean passing as straight. So therefore, not only is Gracie in urgent need of the 'gender makeover' recommended by Mizejewski, but in order for her to perform the role of a romantic heroine convincingly in *Miss Congeniality* she, like Miss New York, must also learn to pass for straight by marrying the masculine with the feminine aspects of her identity.

~ *From butch to babe: transforming the tomboy* ~

As already noted, *Miss Congeniality* has as its central device a makeover. In *The Makeover in Movies*, Elizabeth A. Ford and Deborah C. Mitchell write that in film a makeover enables the central female character to 'journey from blah to beautiful. Her physical self must be transformed before she becomes an effective person' (2004: 3). Indeed, the makeover is a device commonly used to unite the couple in the rom-com, where in films like *Pretty Woman* (1990) and *She's All That* (1999) the beginning of closure is usually signalled by 'the reveal'. In *Miss Congeniality*, Gracie's own queer makeover begins inside an airport hangar, a space used to suggest the tremendous size and scope of the task that lies ahead. We are next witness to a lengthy montage sequence during which, starved of food and sleep, she is forced to undergo an extensive range of beauty treatments that reveal the hard work involved in creating the feminine ideal. Having surrendered herself to endure this painful process, Gracie's emergence from the hangar is designed to celebrate the spectacular effects of her outward transformation. Presented in slow motion, the hangar doors are opened and an assembled crowd of FBI beauty technicians' parts to reveal her looking gorgeous – she is newly waxed, plucked and manicured and wearing a figure-hugging blue dress, high heels and perfect make-up. Gracie's image as the stereotypical ideal woman is, however, swiftly and comically undercut by her characteristic hostility to her fellow (male) FBI agents and the fact that she soon falls off her heels. Nevertheless, it is during this protracted moment of visual pleasure and performance that hints of a reluctant femme are first uncovered hidden beneath her aggressively butch exterior. This dual identity reflects Bullock's acting career to date, which includes both rom-coms (*Forces of Nature* (1999) and *Two Weeks Notice* (2002)) and action thrillers (*Speed* (1994) and *The Net* (1995)). In this way, her command of pratfalls and physicality are key aspects of her star persona as both screwball comedienne and tomboy action hero.

Moments like Gracie's transformation and emergence from the airport hangar are used, together with *My Fair Lady* (1964), *Shampoo* (1975) and *Up Close and Personal* (1996), by Ford and Mitchell to trace the story of *Miss Congeniality* back to the Pygmalion myth. In each of these films 'men try to control female transformations completely' (Ford and Mitchell, 2004: 6). However, unlike these other Pygmalion makeovers, it is significant that *Miss Congeniality* does not depend on a romantic

9.2: Post-makeover: gorgeous Gracie's spectacular reveal in *Miss Congeniality.*

relationship between Gracie and the man who transforms her. Instead, Michael Caine plays veteran pageant consultant Victor Melling as a 'gay Henry Higgins', whose interest in his creation is purely professional (Tookey, 2001: 53). Throughout *Miss Congeniality* it is Vic who instructs Gracie how to appear feminine, so that, as Ford and Mitchell note, in this film 'a queen teaches Hart how to become a beauty queen' (2004: 166).

Within this concept of disguise, transformation and masquerade lies the idea of gender as performance that is key to unlocking *Miss Congeniality*'s queer pleasures, and it is this aspect I will now turn to. Gracie's transformation suggests the notion of 'Womanliness as a Masquerade', first introduced by Joan Riviere in her 1929 essay of the same name. The montage sequence cited previously reveals that Gracie's femininity is a disguise, 'assumed and worn as a mask . . . to hide the possession of masculinity' (Riviere, 1986: 38). According to Riviere, the exhibition of masculine traits is highly problematic, as society has traditionally disapproved of masculine display by women as threatening to patriarchy and therefore displays of femininity are rewarded (see ibid.). In *Gender Trouble*, Judith Butler draws on Riviere's work to argue for the performative character of identity – particularly of gender. She questions binary divisions of sex, gender and desire to reveal the artificiality of these culturally constructed categories that we use to define ourselves. This idea of gender as performance implies the constructedness of gender roles and stereotypes. It follows that, 'There is no gender identity behind the expressions of gender; that identity is performatively constituted by the very "expressions" that are said to be its results' (Butler, 2006: 34). In other words, women do not necessarily behave in a 'feminine' way, as there is no essential 'femininity' in the concept of 'woman', and female behaviours are socially constructed rather than natural.

The idea of gender as 'a reiterated social performance' rather than an essence has proved influential in queer theory (Butler, 2006: backcover). *Miss Congeniality* illustrates the constructed nature of gender performance as we are made witness to, and take pleasure in, Gracie's process of transformation from tomboy FBI agent to beauty queen. It is then possible for us to understand and enjoy this process as queer in a number of ways. First, as noted above, it is ironic that a gay man is given the task of teaching Gracie how to conform to society's codes of acceptable feminine behaviour. The skill Vic requires to achieve this goal is evidenced by his proud statement that 'I have taken a woman without a discernable smidgen of oestrogen and transformed her into a lady.' His insider knowledge of the pageant and its conventions plays on stereotypical associations between gay sensibility and style that have since featured in contemporary TV shows such as *Sex and the City* (1998-2004) and *Queer Eye for the Straight Guy* (2003-), and which are repeated in the figure of witty camp advisor Joel (Diedrich Bader) in *Miss Congeniality 2*.

Second, Gracie's transformation permits her entry into pageant life and the 'girl world' she had previously been excluded from (and that she had no wish to join) (Tasker, 2004: 4). Beauty pageants themselves can be read as a paradigmatic space for highlighting the performance of gender and femininity. For this reason they can also be seen as a particularly camp space, and a site for the enactment of hyper-femininity. This is therefore shown to be an environment heavily reliant on learned acts and gestures, which the contestants dutifully submit themselves to rehearse and repeat. It is a regime that *Miss Congeniality* continually mocks, as we share in Gracie's disbelief when the women ritualistically join together and sing the 'Miss United States' pageant song, or mechanically echo a desire for 'world peace'. In this camp setting, Gracie's role-play as Miss New Jersey is a source of comedy founded on Butler's account of gender as performative, and much of the film's humour derives from the disjunction between her on- and off-stage personas. On stage, as Miss New Jersey, she must act like a lady, appearing well spoken, elegant and composed. But off stage, Gracie's true (tomboy) character frequently returns: she hides a gun underneath her evening gown; stashes donuts in her bra; and her idea of 'girl talk' is a beer and pizza night.

Increasingly, comedy also stems from moments when Gracie publicly brings together elements of these two contrasting personas. For example, when asked by the pageant host, 'What is the one most important thing that our society needs?' Gracie's instinctive answer, 'That would be harsher punishment for parole violators,' is greeted only by stunned silence as it departs dangerously from the contestants' standard responses. Aware of her failure to conform, Gracie quickly adds the generic answer 'world peace' to obtain audience approval. Significantly, however, at the same time that she performs these small gestures towards conformity, those around her also learn to value her individuality and difference (Kord and Krimmer, 2005: 48). As a result, any early resistance gradually gives way to acceptance as Gracie's queer character is increasingly admired by the audience, the contestants and of course her male romantic interest, Eric. For instance, whereas the other contestants' conventional 'talents' consist of singing, dancing and baton twirling, Gracie's unconventional self-defence demonstration instantly receives rapturous applause. In return, she acknowledges the impact that the pageant and its contestants have had on her, announcing that this has been 'one of the most rewarding and liberating experiences of my life'.

Thus, third, and most importantly, Gracie's transformation is a way for her to finally find love. At a textual level, this means that during *Miss Congeniality*'s closing scenes the friendly but antagonistic relationship she shares with Eric throughout the undercover operation develops into a tentative romance, as they kiss and arrange a future date. But perhaps more lastingly, it is after this brief exchange that a subtextual, female-centred marriage ceremony occurs. Having won second place in the contest and having saved Cheryl (Heather Burns) from an exploding pageant crown, Gracie is presented with the 'Miss Congeniality' award by her fellow contestants. This marks her out as the 'nicest, sweetest, coolest girl at the pageant', who is loved by them all. Standing on the podium to receive her award, Gracie's appearance has subtly shifted from her awkward tomboy incarnation to someone more at ease with herself: although she is out of her beauty queen disguise and back in her standard FBI suit, the fact that she has become 'very aware and proud of [her] breasts' means that her shirt is now buttoned much lower, her hair is groomed and she is wearing make-up. As the film closes we leave Gracie surrounded by a circle of adoring women. This group also stands in for the film's audience who share in this moment of queer union. At the end of *Miss Congeniality* everyone is in love with Gracie and these alternative love affairs overwhelm the token heterosexual coupling (given relatively little emphasis and limited narrative space), and prefigure the queer pleasures of the follow-up film.

~ *Armed and fabulous* ~

Miss Congeniality 2 begins three weeks after Gracie Hart's undercover work at the Miss United States pageant. The central characters and story of the follow-up film largely adhere to the formula established by the original; once again we follow Gracie as she is first given an FBI makeover, after which she is sent on a mission that forces her to throw out the rulebook, go back undercover and rescue Cheryl for a second time following her kidnapping in Las Vegas. Vegas provides the sequel with a camp setting equal to *Miss Congeniality*'s beauty pageant. It is a location where gender performance is also everywhere, expected and accepted as normal, emphasising the film's queerness. Comedic effect in the second film derives from Gracie's post-pageant fame, her celebrity status and public image as the new 'face of the FBI', which still contrasts with her frustrated personal life. For, while the balance between action and comedy remains the same, an important difference between the two films is that the sequel is free from heterosexual romance. Instead, *Miss Congeniality 2* features a queer romance between Gracie and her butch black female bodyguard and 'partner'-to-be, Agent Sam Fuller. Unlike the first film, significantly the sequel is usually described as a buddy movie (see Glasser, 2005: 62; A. Smith, 2005: 66; Toumarkine, 2005: 41). As there is already an established critical connection between single-sex bonding, homoeroticism and intimacy in the buddy film, this classification underlines rather than undermines its subtextual queerness (see Cohan, 1999; Fuchs, 1993; Griggers, 1993). However, I will argue that *Miss Congeniality 2* should be read principally as a romance, and that this film is therefore a queer rom-com, even more so than the original.

Some ten minutes into *Miss Congeniality 2*, the unconvincing relationship between Gracie and Eric Matthews, used to provide traditional narrative closure to the first film, is brought to an abrupt ending. In an awkward phone call Eric dumps Gracie, suddenly cancelling their forthcoming date and thus accentuating the sense that their union at the end of the first film was an entirely arbitrary one. Hints at an inadequate sex life are made; 'Is it the sex?' Gracie hesitantly enquires, 'Because I could get a manual or something.' With the end of their brief romance Agent Matthews vanishes, but in line with the conventions of the rom-com, he is soon replaced by a new love interest in the form of Sam. An exchange is then made. As Eric transfers out of the FBI department and Gracie's life, Sam simultaneously transfers in. This swap effectively forces a comparison between the two characters in terms of their romantic role in the narrative. Not only is Sam introduced in the scenes that immediately succeed Eric's break-up with Gracie, but the pair's first heated exchange also corresponds to a previous moment of conflict between Gracie and her former boyfriend outlined above. Both scenes are set in the FBI gym and use a combination of verbal and physical sparring to illustrate the couple's initial antagonism towards one another. Again, such scenes are characteristic of the rom-com, as these spats convey the chemistry that fuels Gracie and Sam's passionate love/hate relationship; verbal jousting has long been utilised by Hollywood as a kind of coded foreplay. This type of interaction was a convention of screwball comedy when the Hays Code restricted any suggestion of sexual behaviour onscreen. Thus in the same way that a subtextual reading was required because of restrictions on the representation of straight sex during the era of the code, today similar restrictions are imposed upon the representation of homosexuality in this mainstream genre.

Following their first confrontational meeting, Gracie and Sam continue to argue and fight about everything. Much of their early antagonism stems from Gracie's second makeover, as she becomes the irritatingly superficial 'face of the FBI', a role she adopts following her failure in heterosexual romance. Increasingly, though, as Gracie is transformed again, Gracie and Sam are shown to be very much alike: as well as displaying similar tendencies towards violent and aggressive behaviour, they are also both intelligent and highly motivated career women trapped in a world of ineffectual men. This shift from antagonism to empathy and affection begins to occur when the couple are forced to sleep in the same room one night after refusing to drop the case and return to New York together. As Gracie and Sam lie talking on adjoining couches, their first intimate discussion reveals their parallel lives and past experiences. They confide that they have had similar childhoods and that they have each suffered the loss of a parent with whom they shared an especially close bond. Tellingly, both women also admit to already having spent some time investigating one another, voicing their mutual curiosity and acknowledging the potential for attraction.

From this point onwards, we see Gracie and Sam start to build a close relationship. Their growing harmony is signified as they twice go undercover together (this enactment of role-play, concealment and disguise paralleling the processes of masquerade and performance.) First they disguise themselves as an elderly woman and her carer in order to infiltrate a retirement home; second, they perform in a drag club. In the drag club, accompanied by Joel, Gracie and Sam must win the audience over by masquerading as a Las Vegas showgirl and a Tina

Turner lookalike respectively. Before going on stage, Sam calls attention to the queerness of this undercover operation. She protests, 'I am not going out there as a woman pretending to be a man, pretending to be Tina Turner. I can't afford therapy on my salary.' Returning to Judith Butler's notion of gender performance, this imitation can be read as subversive. Butler uses drag as an example of performativity, because '*in imitating gender, drag implicitly reveals the imitative structure of gender itself*' (Butler, 1990: 187, emphasis in original). In Gracie and Sam's case, the queerness of their double-layered drag (as women imitating men imitating women) is heightened by the dance act that they perform. In the musical genre, episodes of dance are thought to stand in for a couple's romantic and sexual relationship (see Altman, 1987). Arguably, Gracie and Sam's stage appearance in *Miss Congeniality 2* works in the same way, informing us of the pattern and course of their relationship. They start by bumping into one another and are uncoordinated. But this soon changes as they quickly adapt the timing of their steps and movement to coordinate a dance routine. In the context of this film, the increased synchronicity of their drag queen performance symbolises the increasingly close emotional and physical bond that has developed between them. Their ability to anticipate each other's move confirms for us that they are indeed a natural fit.

Like the first film, then, *Miss Congeniality 2* is about transformation. As Gracie's love affair with Sam flourishes, so does her sense of self. Having lost herself amid the trappings of stereotypical femininity and fame during the first part of the film, Gracie is recovered by Sam, whose partnership enables her to 'feel like the real Gracie Hart' again. For Gracie, this means the rejection of her superficial 'FBI Barbie' image and the return of her standard FBI suit to mirror Sam. In a scene that echoes and reverses Gracie's spectacular reveal in *Miss Congeniality* (and foreshadows their synchronised performance in the drag club), the butch couple stride in slow motion across a gas station forecourt: their steps are in unison; they are dressed identically; they put their sunglasses on with the same gesture and simultaneously turn to look at one another. As before, a shift in Gracie's appearance is used to indicate a wider shift in the dynamics of her character and relationships. With Sam at her side and her butch equilibrium back intact, Gracie has transformed to become 'armed and fabulous' once more.

In a truly romantic final gesture, after helping Gracie to find herself, Sam also saves her life. After Gracie rescues Cheryl, in a moment resonant of an Orphic rescue tale in which a loved one is brought back from the jaws of death, Sam heroically retrieves Gracie, who is still trapped underwater in a sunken pirate boat in the Treasure Island hotel complex. Not only does the film's action end with the couple united on the quayside, there is also a postscript that shows us their continuing life in New York. As their 'partnership' is formally announced by Agent McDonald (Ernie Hudson), Gracie responds by teasing Sam with the same sing-song chant that she used to flirt with Eric in *Miss Congeniality*. In the first film she says: 'You think I'm gorgeous / You want to date me / Love me and marry me.' In the second film this has changed to: 'You're my new partner / You have to like me / And back me up if someone is shooting at me.' This is particularly important for a queer reading, as viewers familiar with *Miss Congeniality* can recognise when it is repeated with the identical tune and similar phrasing. This, in turn, forces a comparison between the playful contexts of its delivery, and evokes echoes of the romantic dynamic that underlined its use. After a brief supportive exchange Gracie and Sam temporarily separate to begin their work, but we sense that the pair will remain together for a long time. We sense this because they get on so well together that if they were a man and a woman we would automatically call them soul-mates; we sense this because *Miss Congeniality 2* has charted the journey of their growing relationship, and we sense this because this is a Hollywood film that requires romantic closure. This is the happy-ever-after story that the first film failed to sustain.

Significantly then, whereas in *Miss Congeniality* the romance between Gracie and Eric appeared 'tacked on', a nod to the mainstream convention of heteronormative romantic union, in *Miss Congeniality 2*, Gracie and Sam's budding love affair is at the very heart of the narrative. In the media, critics voiced their surprise at the film's lack of a male

9.3: Bosom buddies: Gracie and 'partner' Sam in *Miss Congeniality 2*.

lead; 'What we have here is a comedy . . . a major studio release . . . starring prototypical girl next door Sandra Bullock . . . where Bullock's unlucky-in-love character . . . does *not* end up with the guy' (Henerson, 2005). This comment highlights questions of the sequel's generic status and the atypicality of a Hollywood blockbuster without a heterosexual romance at its core. It is this absence of a male romantic hero that accounts for the difference in generic labelling in the move from the first to the second film. Whereas *Miss Congeniality* is universally labelled as a rom-com, as noted above, its sequel is widely thought of as a buddy movie. For example, in a review for *Sight and Sound*, Anna Smith calls *Miss Congeniality 2* 'a slapstick crime-fighting buddy comedy' (2005: 6). While Smith chooses to focus on Gracie and Sam's similarity to the male odd couple, she goes on to acknowledge their similarity to romantic leads, commenting on the film's 'lesbian undertones' and plot path (ibid.). However, in my view, and as argued in this essay, these are not mere undertones, they are in fact overtones that demand that in common with the first film, *Miss Congeniality 2* should be classified as a queer rom-com.

In this chapter, I have argued that *Miss Congeniality* and *Miss Congeniality 2* elicit a wide range of queer pleasures from their audience. Using close analysis of the films, I have offered queer readings at textual and subtextual levels: of Gracie as a queer-coded character who struggles to achieve a balance between her butch/masculine and femme/feminine characteristics; of the performative nature of gender and identity demonstrated by the central characters (Gracie, Sam, Vic and Joel); of the queerness of these stories that play comically with multiple disguises and change; and which offer the viewer the pleasure of sharing in an alternative romance. Queerness can be found not only at the level of character, story and plot, but also between the films as a pair, their generic status as contemporary rom-coms, and finally the romance between the text and the viewer in the practice of (queer) reading. In conclusion then, we might consider that all the relationships I have described are in some way queer, and that both films present us with moments of queer disruption that are characteristic of a genre in which gender divides are crossed and transgressive sexual desires are explored.

10 *What a Difference a Gay Makes*

Marriage in the 1990s Romantic Comedy

~ *Kyle Stevens* ~

LORD BYRON FAMOUSLY said, 'All tragedies end in death. All comedies end in marriage' (Byron, 1958: 109). This dichotomy suggests an intimate connection between life and marriage. Furthermore, from the vantage point of gay rights, it suggests the romantic comedy to be one of the most conservative of genres, since it has traditionally rooted itself in a celebration of the formation of the heterosexual couple and often paradigmatically privileged the institution of marriage as the narrative's clichéd and acceptable ending. It is striking, then, that throughout the 1990s the romantic comedy introduced a slew of representations of gay men into mainstream culture through television and film, most often in the form of characters who act as best friends to straight female protagonists, whilst remaining wildly popular with Anglo-American audiences. It will be my contention in this essay that this era's challenge to marriage as societal institution, which was being vociferously debated throughout the media and culture more broadly at this time, is mediated and explored in how these films confront marriage as a generic convention.[1]

Crucially, in the 1990s, the campaign for equal marriage rights for homosexuals was widely attended to in the mainstream media for the first time.[2] It emerged as a highly volatile issue with viable potential to impact on traditional definitions of marriage. On 12 March 1990, *Newsweek* broke ground by drawing public attention to matters in the homosexual community beyond AIDS with an article entitled, 'The Future of Gay America'. The article stated that, 'The No. 1 item on the political agenda remains AIDS. But gay leaders have also begun fighting for a slate of family rights including social security, medical benefits, inheritance, child custody and *even* gay marriage' (Salholz, 1990: 20, my emphasis). However, within just a few years (unfortunately in part a result of the spread of the AIDS epidemic to every community), the subject of gay marriage would be the most high-profile issue related to the gay and lesbian community. The *Newsweek* article describes gay marriage teleologically: 'The ultimate act of assimilation would be marriage, a right some gays have placed on their future agenda' (Salholz, 1990: 21). Nevertheless, noting a rapid change occurring, the article points out that, 'Seven U.S. cities, Los Angeles and Seattle among them, now have "domestic partnership" laws that grant gays a variety of spousal rights including insurance benefits, bereavement leaves and credit agreements' (ibid.).

By the mid-1990s, gay rights had become synonymous with equal marriage rights and a major debate was underway, with discussion of the possibility of domestic partner rights for gays and lesbians making it to the *New York Times* Metro section on 1 August 1993. In that same year, the Hawaiian Supreme Court ruled that barring same-sex marriage rights was unconstitutional (a ruling that was later summarily overturned by the governor). Usurping state power, federal legislation called the 'Defense of Marriage Act' was enacted in 1996. This measure denied recognition of legal marriages between same-sex partners, cementing second-class status to homosexual citizens by defining the word 'marriage' as 'only a legal union between one man and one woman as husband and wife, and the word "spouse" refers only to a person of the opposite sex who is a husband or a wife' (A. Sullivan, 1997: 203). Besides the menace such a bill posed to the guarantee for individual citizens to pursue life, liberty and happiness equally, it was the first Constitutional amendment to *remove* rights since the anti-alcohol law of Prohibition (which, significantly, was aimed at a drug, not an entire class of citizens).[3] My point here is not merely to encapsulate the extensive and complicated proceedings taken by both sides during the initial decade of this debate. Rather, it is to demonstrate that such defensive measures evince a belief that gay marriage posed a genuine threat to homosexuals' enduring status as inferior citizens.

The classic romantic comedy *The Philadelphia Story* (1940) follows the days leading up to Tracy's (Katherine Hepburn) wedding, conscientiously demonstrating the investment that early generic entries often placed in the institution of marriage. After realising (with his help) that her ex-husband Dexter (Cary Grant) is still the man for her, she almost erupts with happiness as she finally goes to be wed, exclaiming, 'You know how I feel? Like a human . . . like a human being!' In *Pursuits of Happiness*, Stanley Cavell expounds upon this legacy of the Anglo-American cinematic romantic comedy that imagines that marriage, and particularly the final wedding ritual, is not simply synonymous with love, but with becoming human. For Cavell, a strong value of the romantic comedy lies in playing out,

> the progress from narcissism and incestuous privacy to objectivity and the acknowledgment of otherness as the path and goal of human happiness; and since this happiness is expressed as marriage, we understand it as simultaneously an individual and a social achievement. Or, rather, we understand it as the final condition for individual and for social happiness, namely the achieving of one's adult self and the creation of the social. (1981: 102)

What Cavell describes is not simply another example of the personal as political. He interprets marriage as the creator of the social and the mature individual. It is all the more striking, then, that this genre, which designates subjectivity through the ritualised prospect of marriage, is the first in the mainstream to include openly gay and lesbian characters.

Following the resurgence of the romantic comedy in the 1980s, Frank Krutnik has detailed the decline of marriage's presence in the genre in the 1960s and 1970s. This move came after the focus on marriage in 1950s romantic comedies (typified by those entries starring Rock Hudson and Doris Day), in which marriage functioned as a contract, promising sex for the male and economic stability for the female. Krutnik argues that,

> Films never spring magically from their cultural context, but they represent instead much more complex activities of *negotiation*, addressing cultural transformations in a highly compromised and displaced manner. In the case of romantic comedy, it is particularly important to stress how specific films or cycles mediate between a body of conventionalized 'generic rules,' some of which have a lineage dating back at least to Plautus and Menander, and a shifting environment of sexual-cultural codifications. (1990: 57-8)

Krutnik goes on to suggest that marriage was not always the goal of the couple in romantic comedies, but a way of marking their coming together as an achievement: 'Marriage was not in itself a source of legitimation for heterosexual desire but instead tended to derive its legitimacy from the nature of the "special attraction" between the man and the woman, who seemed as if they were "made for each other" despite whatever obstacles lay between them' (1990: 58). The 1990s romantic comedies I highlight here often do regard marriage as their goal – and in no uncertain terms.[4] Engaging with their era's own 'shifting environment of sexual-cultural codifications' (ibid.), then, in these films, marriage is treated as the legitimator of heterosexual desire, and this treatment requires and utilises the presence of homosexual characters to ensure that marriage is, for the first time, marked as heterosexual marriage rather than simply 'marriage'.

This defensive move to present marriage as specifically heterosexual ironically opens up the possibility of other kinds of marriage or romantic relationships. Given the centrality marriage has had to the genre at different times and the cultural anxiety that gays and lesbians would redefine or undermine the institution, gay and lesbian characters posed a threat to the stability of conventional romantic comedy. This tension helps explain the genre's inclusion of gay and lesbian characters; it began adopting them if only to police them through the creation and reinforcement of stereotypes that diffused their sexuality and thus rendered any claim they might make to marriage rights a moot point. At the same time, films like *Four Weddings and a Funeral* (1994), *Miami Rhapsody* (1995), *Muriel's Wedding* (1995), *My Best Friend's Wedding* (1997), *As Good As It Gets* (1997), *The Wedding Singer* (1998), *Bridget Jones' Diary* (2001) and *The Wedding Planner* (2001) were less about creating the couple than about reconsidering the value and concept of marriage.[5] Rather than serving as the emblem of unification and narrative resolution, in these films weddings can be divisive. For example, in *Miami Rhapsody* it is only after heroine Gwen's boyfriend proposes to her that she learns how fraught and troubled the marriages of her parents and siblings really are. She increasingly sees marriage as an oppressive and unworkable institution and questions whether she actually wants to be married herself. She eventually works through her anxiety with the help of a man she initially believes to be gay. The apprehension that marriage might tear asunder rather than join together is strengthened by the presence of gay characters denied, even in fictional worlds, the possibility of marrying.

While theoretical attention has been given to 'serious' films that address homosexuality and feature gay characters, such as *Philadelphia* (1993) and *Boys Don't Cry* (1999), the gay best-friend character is mostly regarded as a fairly benign and commonplace, if generally stereotypical, representation. But this perceived beneficence results from the problematic equation of visibility with progress. In her extensive examination of representations of queerness in the media during the 1990s, Suzanna Danuta Walters devotes less than two pages to this character type. She describes them as 'incidentally queer', a 'hip accessory . . . used – to a certain extent – to add a certain up-to-date cachet of hipness to the film' (Danuta Walters, 2001: 154–5). Her claim implies that the inclusion of gay characters serves the same purpose for the films as they do for their diegetic protagonists: they are the narrative equivalent of a fashionable handbag. Danuta Walters writes that, 'the incidental queer often serves to unite heterosexual couples, or to provide solace to heterosexuals suffering from the slings and arrows of wayward affections' (2001: 155). But attributing such narrative agency and influence to these characters suggests that they are neither 'incidental' nor coincidental. It points to the possibility of understanding their presence beyond liberal tokenism. Walters observes that this figure is generally reserved for someone who embodies the 'image of gay men as charming, relational shopaholics that makes the confidant role work' (ibid.), but she neglects to account in any detail for this stereotype or its usefulness to the genre.

Although Walters uses the more inclusive 'queer', the films themselves label these characters 'gay'. Since the term 'homosexual' implies sexual desire (that is, desire with an object-choice) and this is denied to these characters, I will instead use 'gay' as a term to denote the construction of a specific identity that lacks a link to sexuality. Typically, the gay character's identity has been constructed and performed through multiple stereotype-defining behaviours, and I wish to argue here that in denying the homosexual male character sexual agency, the narrative ultimately denies his existence. Additionally, in this genre, to deny the possibility of marriage – the genre's fundamental affirmation – is to deny subjectivity. Primarily examining *Four Weddings and a Funeral*, *As Good As It Gets* and *My Best Friend's Wedding*, the driving question of this essay, then, is to ascertain why this stereotype of the gay man appears at this time in this genre.

~ *'Gaydar'* ~

While it is outside the scope of this essay to analyse in depth the entire group of romantic comedies that feature a gay protagonist (a sub-cycle of the genre specifically new to the 1990s), they nevertheless supply an interesting complement here. In films such as *The Wedding Banquet* (1993), *The Birdcage* (1996), *In and Out* (1997), *I Think I Do* (1997), *All Over the Guy* (2001), *Kissing Jessica Stein* (2001), and *Mambo Italiano* (2003), the narratives hinge on impending nuptials (either the protagonist's own or a family member's). It is always a looming wedding that forces the homosexual hero to confront his desires and definitions of love outside and separate from the institution of marriage. Complicating Byron's dictum, romantic comedies with homosexual heroes that end in marriage would constitute a tragedy.

Given the timeliness of this cycle, it is significant that Cherry Potter has argued that the battle of the sexes constitutes the romantic comedy's *raison d'être*. This is a view that seems at best reactionary when addressing films where gay characters and/or same-sex couples figure so prominently.[6] Potter contends that the significance of Simon's (Greg Kinnear) gayness in *As Good As It Gets* does not extend beyond gender performance, enabling her to claim that the 1990s romantic comedy still operates on the same tired battleground of the sexes as the genre historically did. There can be no doubt that in the 1990s the genre is troubled by questions of appropriate gender behaviour – but this applies to all the characters, not just the gay ones. Potter argues in her reading of *Four Weddings and a Funeral* that Charles (Hugh Grant) is representative of the 'New Man', possessed of a 'feminine charm . . . almost innocently attractive to the opposite sex, not least because of his apparent lack of guile, his feminine passivity' (2002: 257). She explains the appearance of the gay male character by claiming that he represents the 'contemporary tendency to split men into the good, feminine man and the bad, masculine man' (ibid.: 288). Potter conflates the new representations of sexual orientation with gendered behaviours and, moreover, fails to see the integration of non-traditional masculinities as anything but 'feminine'. In this way, by upholding a rigid gender binary that perpetuates gender stereotyping, she misconstrues these films' attempts to expand the range of behaviour acceptable for representations of straight men and neglects to recognise gayness as a specific designator of identity.

Female characters fare no better. While the genre's career women are ostensibly granted the choices feminism affords, these films still construe female characters' choice not to get married at any cost as a masculine quality. In *My Best Friend's Wedding*, Jules' (Julia Roberts) resistance to marriage is addressed again and again by the characters. As Kimmy (Cameron Diaz), who is dropping out of college to marry, succinctly puts it, 'You hate weddings; you never go. You're not up for anything conventional, or anything that's assumed to be a female priority, including marriage, or romance, or even . . . love.' Such a view has traditionally been a quality of the male hero in the genre, and accordingly, Jules is repeatedly masculinised. Besides her masculine nickname (her real name is Julianne, which, interestingly, George (Rupert Everett) uses when passing as her fiancé), even Michael's father tells her she 'should've been best man'.

Waging this battle of the sexes – or, rather, of gender performances – within characters as much as between them, the gay friend's performative fluidity often serves as comic relief. Arguably, the comedy lies in seeing a male body acting against normative cultural expectations. *My Best Friend's Wedding* reflexively exposes this source of humour in a series of scenes in which George 'passes' as Jules' fiancé. The spectator knows that George is her gay best friend (a fact made clear in the first scene of the film when she tells George that Michael (Dermot Mulroney) is 'just like [him], only straight'). Whether or not George is unwilling, or unable, to conceal gestures read by the spectator as gay is unclear. What is clear is that the humour of the ensuing scenes relies on the spectator enjoying the irony of characters failing to recognise that a charming man with an eye for a handbag is gay. By separating gayness and homosexuality, converting gayness into a clearly defined, visible set of behaviours and demonstrating the 'impossibility' of passing under the watch of their cinematic gaze, these films attempt to invalidate the potential threat the gay character might present the heteronormative spectator.

Perhaps more troubling is that such scenes position gay characters as the objects of the characters' – and spectator's – gaze. From Gareth's (Simon Callow) outlandish clothes in *Four Weddings* to the random, gay-coded karaoke singer who performs 'I Am Woman' in *My Best Friend's Wedding*, the gay friend's talent for acting out non-masculinity leads him to be regarded as spectacle. While passing as Jules' fiancé, George bursts into Dionne Warwick's 'Say a Little Prayer For You' in the middle of a crowded restaurant. The entire restaurant becomes enchanted and joins in. In contrast to George's flamboyance, Michael is practically somnambulant; when he wants to sing a song for Julianne, he must whisper it into her ear. Returning to Walters' assertions, the narrative mechanism of opposing the behaviours of gay and straight men is a double-edged sword. It precludes straight men from being 'relational', supportive, or even from participating in consumerism by liking to shop, even as it affords gay men 'aesthetic freedom' at the expense of being objects of the gaze (in other words, a freedom that connotes that the gay male can not only understand and experience aesthetic pleasure, but, through this understanding, can become an aesthetic object himself). Another method for delineating gay men from straight, and for reinforcing a traditionally male and heterosexual spectatorial position, lies in the films' suggestion that an eye for detecting gayness is a straight male prerogative. When George passes, it is only Michael who is suspicious of his fraudulence. Since the humour relies on the spectator's ability to do the same, the film not only aligns the female spectator with the straight male, it also rewards her for it.

Despite the apparent threat that representations of gayness and gender ambiguity pose to the classic model of spectatorship that assumes a default heterosexual male position, the narratives of these films also contrive to show gay characters enjoying precisely those behaviours traditionally reserved for the heterosexual male character. For example, *As Good As It Gets* encourages this identification as Simon is ludicrously distressed by the sexual advances of his male model, or when he is 'inspired' as he watches Carol (Helen Hunt) undress.[7] Once she realises she is being watched, rather than being disturbed by his voyeurism (which is rendered 'safe' by his status as a gay man), she lowers her towel, exposing herself to him so he can draw her (see Fig. 10.1). This play of spectatorial identification is complicated by the absence of an object of sexual desire for the gay character, which makes disavowing knowledge of his sexual orientation possible. It is not uncommon, then, for the spectator to be put in the (traditional Hollywood) spectatorial position of heterosexual male *through* the character of the gay man.

Furthermore, women are seen performing, and enjoying, the most traditional and obsequious kinds of femininity for these men. In fact, the gay best friend is allowed to take liberties with women in ways that men have rarely been allowed, even in the original cinematic screwball romantic comedies of the 1930s. For example, the spectator never sees Kimmy more ecstatic than when George (whom she thinks is straight)

10.1: The gay male gaze in *As Good As It Gets.*

slaps her ass upon meeting her in *My Best Friend's Wedding*. The gay male friend's lack of sexual desire (much less satisfaction) in these situations extends beyond offering an acceptable way of objectifying the woman as sexual object for a presumed straight male spectator as it is often the females who encourage this treatment. If gay males are indeed accessories for their straight female friends, it is their lack of desire – rendering them non-threatening – that is used to give pleasure to the female characters and allows for a particular fantasmatic for those spectators identifying with these onscreen women, where the male can be both attractive and passive.

~ Those who can't do, teach ~

In the seminal romantic comedy *It Happened One Night* (1934), Peter Warne (Clark Gable) tends to and tutors the object of his affection, Ellie Andrews (Claudette Colbert), steering her away from the wrong marriage and instructing her how to love properly. For this, she often calls him professor; she also marries him. Gay characters now frequently fulfil this role traditionally reserved for straight males: that of educator and moral centre. Cavell points out that, 'an essential goal of the narrative is the education of the woman, where her education turns out to mean her acknowledgment of her desire, and this in turn will be conceived of as her creation, her emergence, at any rate, as an autonomous human being' (1981: 84). In *My Best Friend's Wedding* and *As Good As It Gets,* George and Simon mould, assist and instruct their friends, guiding them to their ultimate romantic epiphanies. George helps Jules with more than fashion and skin care; he consistently tells her that Michael will choose Kimmy, and that she must learn to accept it. Beyond his soothsaying, when he arrives to console her after a breakdown, he coaches her to tell Michael 'the truth': 'Tell him you were afraid of love. Yeah, tell him you were afraid of love, of needing someone. We all are, sweetheart. I'm sorry about that.' Speaking universally, George is granted omniscience over other characters' actions. Similarly, Simon literally takes control of Carol's image as he poses and sketches her and opens up both Carol and Melvin to the possibility of love, eventually forcing Melvin to go and tell Carol the truth of his feelings. However, while enabling George and Simon to take on the superficially inclusive role of wise advisor, there is also a sense here that the films draw on another familiar cultural stereotype, by suggesting that gay love is inevitably tragic. The films arguably imply that it is because they are single gay men that they can take on this role, since they know from experience what it is to miss out on love or to have love wholly elude one and thus can recognise the spectre of this fate in those around them.

Perhaps the most powerful instance of the gay character as moral anchor is the speech Matthew (John Hannah) gives at Gareth's funeral in *Four Weddings and a Funeral*. Although the film does not reveal they are gay (much less a couple) until the funeral, Matthew's recitation of W.H. Auden's 'Funeral Blues' inspires Charles' most self-reflexive look at love and marriage, cementing his belief that they need not go hand in hand. After the funeral, Charles confesses his uncertainty about love and marriage in relation to Matthew and Gareth's relationship: 'Surely if that service shows anything, it shows that there is such a thing as a perfect match. If we can't be like Gareth and Matthew, maybe we should just let it go.' While at one level the film might appear progressive for valorising the love between these men, it is careful too to render it an abstract or nostalgic ideal through having Gareth die. Thus it refuses to pose it as a living relationship for other (straight) characters to aspire to at the film's end. Through gay death, *Four Weddings and a Funeral* reappropriates its model of gay love to revitalise heterosexual romance, an example of love outside marriage that allows Charles (and the narrative) to end happily when he proposes to Carrie (Andie MacDowell): 'Do you think . . . you might agree *not* to marry me? And do you think not being married to me might maybe be something you could consider doing for the rest of your life?'

It must be noted too that Matthew is excluded from the funeral ceremony proper. Before he begins, the priest introduces him in a side-angle close-up: 'Our service will begin in a few minutes, but first we have asked Matthew, Gareth's closest friend, to say a few words.' Matthew's exclusion from participation in institutionalised ritual underscores the gay character's lack of equal citizenship. Matthew begins his speech by reinforcing this inequity: 'Gareth used to prefer funerals to weddings. It's easier to get enthusiastic about a ceremony one had an outside chance of eventually being involved in.' One way of reading the existence of gay characters in marital narratives is to argue that gay characters' very presence reminds the heterosexual protagonists (and, presumably, the spectator) to embrace their capacity to marry because not everyone can; consider Bridget Jones' (Renée Zellweger) panic at becoming a spinster, since she sees the world as 'marrieds' or 'singletons'. Moreover, marriage will ensure you are not acknowledged (or mistaken) as gay. But the impulse to taxonomise this way does not adequately explain the presence of the gay friend as simultaneous moral advisor, social outsider, and possessor of a masculine gaze. Brian Henderson points out that in 'comedies of old love, the unspoken question is "Why did we stop fucking?"' and in the comedies of the 1970s the question is 'Why don't we fuck now?' (quoted in Neale, 1992: 285). In American culture of the 1990s, the possibility of sex is less fraught with obstacles, and though sex is not unimportant, for example, in *Notting Hill*, *My Best Friend's Wedding* and *Four Weddings and a Funeral*, the desire for 'the act' does not function as a problem that the narrative must resolve in order to end. Marriage is no longer the ticket to having sex since these characters have sex immediately, and repeatedly, without a hint of obligation. They do not ask whether or not to have sex, but worry instead about the prospect of having to marry. Charles asks the exemplary question: 'Why am I always at weddings, and never getting married?'

Like many protagonists in films that would follow *Four Weddings and a Funeral*, this question leads Charles to doubt the nature of romantic love itself, and to embark on a journey of learning to recognise and to declare love. Who better to answer such a question than one who is always at weddings and can never get married? Being outside the battle of the sexes as described here, the eunuch-style gay best friend is not subject to love's conundrums, and since sex is no longer an integral part of the equation, the sexless gay character can be safely introduced to the genre.

When homosexuality was the love that could not speak its name, the problem lay in talking about love while implying a sexual act (deviant or not). But, in these films, gayness connotes the love that cannot speak its name *aloud*, since it can be implied, as in Matthew's speech when he emotionally refers to Gareth as his 'friend', or in the photograph by George's answering machine of himself and another man. These moments flirt with the power of suggestion, effectively shifting the possibility of marriage away from the acceptability of a specific type of sex act (or acts), making the 'climax' of the 1990s romantic comedy the desire and ability to declare love publicly.[8] Moments of epiphany and passionate expression (depicted in chases, fights and other dramatic events borrowed from various genres) emerge as *the* dominant feature in each of these films. Bridget speeds down snowy roads to the song 'Ain't No Mountain High Enough' before making a very public declaration of her love for Mark (Colin Firth) in *Bridget Jones' Diary*. Charles makes his choice in front of an entire congregation. And in, *My Best Friend's Wedding*, despite the fact that Jules does not win her man, she does what she 'came here to do' and dramatically declaims her love for Michael. Such decisions are almost always influenced by the protagonist's friends, and often, specifically by the gay friend (perhaps fulfilling a vicarious function for them since they can not make such public declarations of love themselves within the terms of mainstream cinema). George finally enables Julianne to realise she's 'not the one' for Michael. In *As Good As It Gets*, Simon relentlessly helps Melvin realise what love is – and that he feels it for Carol – which enables the film's resolution. After agonising for the entire film about what he wants and what is right in endless conversations with friends, Charles finally achieves his ideal relationship resolutely outside of marriage – inspired by Matthew and Gareth.

The conclusion of *My Best Friend's Wedding* sees the newlyweds drive off in traditional style, complete with fireworks. Left behind, Jules sits despondently among the crowd of wedding guests. Her mobile phone rings; George has phoned to offer sage and comforting words about her future. Intent on convincing her she is not alone, he has miraculously shown up, knowing he would be needed. As she realises he must be present and searches the dancing crowd to find him, he describes himself as her ideal partner, further demonstrating his omniscience by speaking aloud her internal monologue: 'And although you correctly sense that he is gay, like most devastatingly handsome single men of his age are, you think what the hell. Life goes on. Maybe there won't be marriage. Maybe there won't be sex. But by God, there will be dancing!' Here, (stereotypically) allied with dancing and situated within heteronormative terms (what else *could* he be but legally 'single', even if in love and partnered?), gayness is metonymically placed outside marriage and sex. Moreover, this notion of gayness disallows even the desire to marry. And Jules is linked to him, connecting her position as a single woman, and therefore also outside marriage, to his identity as gay. Having both been rejected by marriage, the film fades on the couple, laughing and dancing, encouraging the spectator to accept this finale as a happy ending, albeit a non-traditional one.

Unlike the past model of romantic comedy that Krutnik described (in which, once romance was detected, a happy ending was in sight), whether or not these films individually end with a wedding is less important than the fact that the narrative's conclusion emerges out of uncertainty and scepticism. This situates love (and the desire to love) as a decision driven by the influence and presence of the gay best friend. But it is only the straight protagonists that enjoy the privilege of asking questions about their romantic futures. While it has never been a requirement for the romantic comedy to find partners for characters other than the leading couple, because of these films' historical context amidst the gay and lesbian movement to secure equal marital rights, this move takes on a more furtive connotation by suggesting that the gay friend character simply does not seek or want to be in love, much less to marry. At the start of this essay, I asked why this stereotype of the gay man appears in this genre at this time. In summary, then, it is arguably because his adoption allows the romantic comedy – perhaps traditionally the most resolutely affirmatively heteronormative of genres – to nullify the threatened social change posed by burgeoning gay marriage rights, rendering him either merely an asexual companion and/or agent of heterosexual union in the genre, even where marriage is not the overt end-goal.

The gay male friend character's lack of determinate gender and sexual desire, combined with the power allotted to him in the role of advisor classically reserved for straight males, provides an objectivity that affords these characters a privileged position from which to comment on and guide the gendered interactions of the primary couple. However, this position simultaneously denies him the subjectivity of his straight counterparts. Thus, the gay character is the victim of a paradox; his pedagogical power, acquired at the cost of subjectivity, means he teaches precisely the subject from which he is excluded. Situated outside the generically inherited battle of the sexes, he is also situated outside claims to institutional, generic – and ultimately cultural – affirmation.

11 *Homme-Com*

Engendering Change in Contemporary Romantic Comedy

Tamar Jeffers McDonald

QUESTION: which of these scenes is from a romantic comedy?

A man with irritable bowel syndrome goes on a first date. The woman chooses a restaurant with spicy food, which upsets his stomach. Balked from using the lavatory at the restaurant, the man, back at the woman's place, at last relieves himself messily in her bathroom, only to discover she has run out of toilet paper . . .

A man having sex begins to feel anxious. His partner insists on mutual climax, so he fakes it. Despite his orgasmic cry, the woman is suspicious, and questions him. He flees into the next room, tears off the empty condom and, as the woman enters, tries to fling it out the window. But the window is closed . . .

A man is preparing for his first partnered sexual experience. Erotically the woman massages his body, his legs, his feet. She bends her head and sensuously begins to lick his toes. Unfortunately the man is extremely ticklish. He tries to move his foot away, jerks his leg, and, involuntarily, kicks her in the face, causing a nosebleed . . .

ANSWER: they all are. What we might first find anomalous to our ideas about rom-coms in these three situations is their evident scatological and sexual emphasis. More fundamentally surprising is, I suggest, the fact that each synopsis begins with the words 'a man'. Surely contemporary rom-coms start, and end, with a woman, with her desires and dreams, her temporary frustrations and eventual fulfilment?

Certainly, the post-classical romantic comedy is usually associated with women: female concerns, female stars and female audiences are all implicit in the term 'chick flick', and a glance at the majority of rom-coms available in cinemas and for home viewing bears out the dominance of women within the narratives and marketing. Meg Ryan, Julia Roberts, Reese Witherspoon and Sandra Bullock have each built their careers on the success of various rom-com vehicles, although their success in escaping the confines of this genre and convincingly moving into roles outside the rom-com has been less uniform. New films continue to appear bearing the romantic comedy's hallmarks: female-centred narratives charting the rockiness of the road to true love, and including such well-used tropes as the initial mutual antipathy, the subsequent accord, the misunderstanding that breaks up the couple, the sacrifice or quest or embarrassing public gesture that stands as an apology and re-establishes the pair. Such tropes are variously discernible in late 1990s films such as *Clueless* (1995) and *10 Things I Hate About You* (1999), in *Two Weeks Notice* (2002) and *Laws of Attraction* (2004) from the early 2000s and more recent movies such as *Because I Said So* (2007) and *Music and Lyrics* (2007). All of these place the woman at the centre, aligning themselves with her worldview even if occasionally allowing the narrative to undermine her.

The films that own the scenes sketched above – *Along Came Polly* (2004), *40 Days and 40 Nights* (2002) and *The 40-Year-Old Virgin* (2005) – can be seen, however, as belonging to a relatively new offshoot of the genre. This contemporary grouping, which can be posited as beginning in the mid-1990s with *Swingers* (1996), shifts the emphasis in the narrative from the woman to the man, consciously opposing the currently dominant female-centred narrative through their presentation of texts focusing on male protagonists. These texts set out to explore and test the contours of the genre by repositioning the centre, rehearsing all the generic basics – dating rituals, feigned indifference, heartfelt passion – but making them new by considering them from a male point of view.

Does this collection of films, which might also include *The Tao of Steve* (2000), *Hitch* (2005), and *Wedding Crashers* (2005), really provide such an alternative take on the contemporary rom-com? While rehearsing the same old tropes as the now-traditional female-centred stories, this newer kind of rom-com for boys – what I will designate the 'homme-com' – does seem boldly different in its evident prioritising of the importance of the bodily, and particularly the sexual, elements within romance, the scatological and carnal motifs highlighted in the scenarios mentioned above.

William Paul (1994, 2002) has posited the increased popularity since the late 1970s/early 1980s of a strand of American film humour that he dubs 'Animal Comedy', occurring in films that employ 'gross-out' moments, such as *Animal House* (1978) and *Porky's* (1982). Paul Bonila, picking up on this theme, examines the elements of what he terms 'Hollywood Lowbrow': 'It often employs profane language and always employs farce based on scatological and sexual irruptions; it frequently depends on parodic frameworks or vignettes to sustain its episodic narratives and it attempts to provide fun . . .' (2005: 18).

Bonila sees such films as having a philosophical motive behind their attempts to gross out their viewers: their emphasis on the body, its urges and emissions, can be understood as an attempt to put increasingly alienated subjects back in touch with a corporeality subjugated to the demands of modern urban existence (2005: 20). The films of the Farrelly brothers can be seen as fitting both these paradigms, and may also be largely responsible for merging elements of slapstick, messiness and bathetic physical comedy with occasional tropes of the rom-com, amongst other generic plunderings, as in their box-office hits *Dumb and Dumber* (1994), *There's Something About Mary* (1998), *Me, Myself and Irene* (2000) and *Shallow Hal* (2001).

The homme-com seems to share some of Hollywood Lowbrow's insistence on the comedy derived from tumescence and engorgement, orgasm and ejaculate, and perhaps its motives can similarly be seen as intending to return the purely physical to understandings of romantic love. This new emphasis on the importance of sex and the body in all its messiness seems to offer a conscious rebuke to the standard form of the contemporary rom-com, which has been habitually downplaying the importance of sex for over a decade now. This essay will consider the rise of the homme-com and its increased emphasis on the sexual act. Examining the re-gendering of the genre's narrative alongside this new prioritising of the comic potential of the body, its drives and desires, the essay enquires whether this prioritisation is inevitably radical in either intent or achievement.

~ You've got stale: the contemporary Hollywood rom-com ~

Before moving to examine the new homme-com and what it seeks to reintroduce to the genre, it is necessary to revisit the contexts from which such films arose, an excursion that illuminates the current dominant form of the rom-com, now associated with women.

As I have noted elsewhere (Jeffers McDonald, 2007), the Hollywood rom-com has moved through several cycles and evolutions since the coming of sound in the 1930s brought the screwball comedy and the rom-com tropes now familiar to us – the 'meet-cute', the initially antagonistic couple, the inevitable last-minute volte-face and reconciliation – to cinema screens. The particular form of the genre prevalent from the mid-1950s for about a decade – the so-called 'sex comedy' where sex was the terrain being fought over by the female and male protagonists – has been assumed to appeal more to female audience members because of the valorisation of female pre-marital chastity. Both Al Capp (1962) and Alexander Walker (1966 [1968]), for example, assume that female audience members are responsible for the success of the Doris Day romantic comedy vehicle. Close reading of the most popular films of the time, including *Pillow Talk* (1959), however, reveals that the assumption that the films display a battle over sex, with men desiring and women withholding it, is inaccurate: actually both male and female protagonists want sex, but women want respect too.

Pillow Talk presents its chic career woman heroine Jan (Doris Day) as equally desirous of, and equally prepared to use scheming to get, sexual union with the playboy hero (played by Rock Hudson). Where the characters differ is in the lengths they will go to get sex: he will lie about his identity and desires, she will not. This, rather than her horror at learning his carnal plans, is what triggers the temporary break-up of their relationship. The early 1960s sex comedies can thus be seen intimating that sex is important to both genders, a fact picked up and focused on by the next evolution of the genre, the radical rom-coms of the 1970s. Films of this decade, such as *The Goodbye Girl* (1977), *An Unmarried Woman* (1978) and *Annie Hall* (1977) constantly stress that sexual fulfilment and pleasure, long acknowledged as significant to men, are vitally important to women also. These films show women asking for sex, enjoying sex, sometimes avoiding sex, but doing so at the dictates of their own bodies and desires, and not to please or appease their partners.

Despite the obvious impact of the feminist movement on these 1970s films and their assertion of sexuality's consequence to women, these texts were not contemporaneously perceived as being meant for female viewers only. *Variety* reviews of the time do not assume that *Annie*

Hall, for example, will find a natural audience in women; similarly 'gentleman's magazine' *Esquire* saw no anomaly in interviewing Woody Allen in depth about *Annie Hall* (F. Rich, 1972).

Unlike the radical rom-com, the films of the late 1980s and 1990s, which established the form of romantic comedy that still dominates today, were, however, both firmly centred on and associated with the female and forsook the emphasis on the importance of sex that had formerly been so prevalent. The insistence on gendering the genre's narratives, stars and audiences as all female inevitably couples the avoidance of sex with the female also. In this way, the most recent evolution of the rom-com – what I call the Ephronesque turn, as a way of noting Nora Ephron's influence as the writer of *When Harry Met Sally* (1989), writer-director of *Sleepless In Seattle* (1993) and *You've Got Mail* (1998) and inspiration of many others – is responsible for abandoning the egalitarian standpoint on sex established by the radical rom-coms and returning the genre to the putative 1950s 'double standard', when men wanted sex and women were exhorted to withhold it from them.

Visually, the Ephronesque films recycle elements from the radical rom-com: the almost inevitable location of love in New York City is there, as in the 1970s films (see Deborah Jermyn, Chapter 1 in this collection). But where the later products of the genre differ is in the ideology behind these choices of locale. The radical rom-coms were committed to showing a more modern and thus realistic view of love, including its transience. Situating their love stories in the city, where most of the audiences for the films lived, was thus, in the 1970s, another way of acknowledging their new realism: if love could occur in this hyper-alienating environment, there was hope for us all. The Ephronesque film maintains this focus on the urban setting but avoids the previous underlying objective: now love may seem difficult to achieve but will inevitably easily conquer distance, antipathy, time, even death.[1]

While, then, the current Ephronesque form is happy to plunder the 1970s films for inspiration, its most radical difference is to have abandoned the older form's commitment to affirming the importance of sex to both genders. This de-emphasis of sexual matters has extended across the current form of the genre since the late 1980s: if sex happens, it happens offscreen, but mostly it just does not happen. Sex is currently frequently portrayed in rom-coms as an immature pastime, a phase one goes through, which explains its greater prevalence in comedies aimed at teenage markets (such as the *American Pie* films). In *A Lot Like Love*

(2004), for example, the teen protagonists meet in an airport and almost immediately have sex on a plane; only later do they gradually fall in love. Giving in to the promptings of physical desire is thus associated with teenagers, with immaturity and relationship problems, while love and stability are associated with *not* having sex.

You've Got Mail epitomises many of the current problems of the genre, but none so much perhaps as the avoidance of sex. The female and male leads of the film, destined to be a couple by the conclusion, both have other partners to begin with, but neither pair is ever seen kissing in a manner other than desultory; although the couples go to bed together, it seems that in *You've Got Mail* all they do in bed is sleep, as matched scenes indicate. While this serves, alongside other hints, to bear out that Joe (Tom Hanks) and Kathleen (Meg Ryan) are destined for each other and not meant for their current, wrong, partners, it also establishes a frigidity the film cannot overcome. For if the wrong partners' wrongness extends to their lack of sexual compatibility with Joe and Kathleen, thus explaining why nothing is going on in the bedroom, the new couple must by contrast evince a passionate intensity in their relationship to underline why it is meant to succeed. But the film does not attempt this. The only intensity permitted Joe and Kathleen is their initial mutual dislike as business rivals. Once Joe has realised that Kathleen is also 'Shopgirl', his email pen-pal, he begins to be a kinder, nicer Joe to her and the energy of their encounters is instantly dissipated. The film indeed seems so uncertain of the appropriateness or desirability of physical contact that the couple's clinch is held off until the very,

11.1: The last image of *You've Got Mail.*

very last moment, when all secrets are aired and forgiven. Even then, the presence of Joe's dog in the scene makes the final picture less one of a passionately attracted couple and more one of a happily reunited family (see Fig. 11.1.

By de-emphasising sex as a necessary part of romance, and focusing on women as the 'natural' heroines of and audiences for, such sexless rom-coms, these films have implied the unimportance of sexual fulfilment for women. They have also established the contemporary form of the rom-com as such a sex-free zone that they have inevitably created a space for the reintroduction of such themes. Hollywood, like nature, abhors a vacuum, and so the homme-com was born.

While these male-centred films can be seen, as I discuss below, as challenging both that the rom-com is necessarily about women and that sex has no part in films of the genre, do homme-coms, however, maintain the idea that sex is a generally or exclusively male concern?

~ *The homme-com: romantic comedy for boys?* ~

One of the most noteworthy recent developments in the generally static rom-com genre has thus been the emergence of a male-slanted text. *Swingers* set the standard in 1996: recently dumped Mike (Jon Favreau) moves to Los Angeles and is taken around town by his woman-mad friend Trent (Vince Vaughn). Mike is told that what he has been doing wrong is treating women like people. Trent educates him, teaching him the rules of being irresistible, such as, for example, asking for a woman's phone number and then not calling until at least two full days have elapsed. By the end of the film, however, it is Mike and not Trent who has met a woman who is interested in him, and the film concludes with her ringing him.

Adopting the perspective of the male instead of the female half of the couple, *Swingers* enjoys revealing that its central male characters worry about relationships, dating rules, makeout conventions, what to say and wear, just as women have been doing in rom-coms for so long. They also spend more time with their friends discussing how to get a woman than with any women they get, paralleling the trope of the supportive group of friends again found so often in the Ephronesque rom-com. The film therefore sets out to show that, while the common assumption that men think about sex a lot of the time is founded in truth, they are also searching for real love just like women, the traditionally assumed audience and focus of the genre.

While *Swingers* reworks the common elements of the rom-com but places a man at the centre, later films in the sub-grouping of male-focused films have tended to add another ingredient to the recipe: the gross-out moment. This is an eruption of extreme and usually uncontrollable physicality into the narrative, and is the element that links films such as these new homme-coms with other contemporary comedies that, as noted, have been categorised as 'Animal Comedy' (Paul, 1994) or 'Hollywood lowbrow' (Bonila, 2005). A handful of moments from the homme-coms illustrates the persistence of excrement, urine and ejaculate as recurring tropes. *Along Came Polly* features the hero's attack of irritable bowel syndrome recounted above (see Fig. 11.2).

Explosive diarrhoea features again in *Wedding Crashers*, when it figures as the punishment of an arrogant character who has angered the central male duo John and Jeremy (Owen Wilson and Vince Vaughn). *The 40-Year-Old Virgin* includes scenes of visible physicality prompted by erections, urination, masturbation and, most difficult to watch, depilation.

I argue that the homme-com consciously blends this type of gross-out moment with the romance plot of the standard rom-com in order to get something new, male-centred and assumed to appeal to male audiences. It might also be suggested that such films are attempting to appeal to younger audiences too. While the Ephronesque rom-com is

11.2: Reuben's irritable bowel syndrome makes itself conspicuous on a date.

marketed to couples and to single women aspiring to be in a couple, the presence of messy slapstick moments and incidents of body humour in such films imply an immaturity of outlook that might profitably be coupled with literal chronological immaturity in audiences. Whatever the age of the audience, however, the comedy generated by the homme-com is likely to provoke mixed responses. By merging scatological and sexual foci with rom-com elements, the homme-com as end-product becomes an uneasy blend of tropes and techniques. Scenes intended to provoke the groan and laugh-out-loud response derived from gross-out sit next to more staid romantic moments that elicit quieter reactions: it is almost as if the sub-grouping's films have become schizoid in trying to juggle bodily excesses and excretions with tender emotional moments, to appeal to both guts and hearts.

One scene from *Along Came Polly*, which particularly seems to suffer from this split personality, can exemplify this problem. Recently jilted Reuben (Ben Stiller) is dragged to a party by his best friend Sandy (Philip Seymour Hoffman) and there re-encounters Polly (Jennifer Aniston), a girl he had known at high school. Polly and Reuben start flirting and Reuben is about to ask for her number when Sandy, who had wandered off, reappears and says they have to leave:

Sandy: Hey Reuben, I'm in a situation here. We have to leave *now*.
Reuben: Well, no, can't we stay a couple more minutes?
Sandy: Dude, no, this is serious. I just sharted.
Reuben: I don't know what that means.
Sandy: I tried to fart, and a little shit came out, I just sharted. S'alright let's go.
Reuben: You are the most disgusting person I have ever met in my life.

Sandy's confession provokes a mixture of responses. His use of the appropriate neologism 'sharting' is funny because the creativity involved in inventing the term somehow suggests it has been a necessary adjunct to his regular vocabulary. The embarrassment of the incident's timing, at a public and swanky event and its inherent messiness (Sandy walks to the lift in tell-tale stiff-legged way) all combine to produce a humorous scene, a moment of evident gross-out body comedy.

When Reuben dismisses his friend as 'the most disgusting person', two things are happening: Reuben is setting himself up to be the butt of the rebarbative moment of similar messiness later, and the film is attempting to disavow its own obsession with excrement. But Sandy seems to be in the film to act as an id to Reuben's super-ego, that is to say, to embody the bodily urgencies Reuben's overly uptight persona would happily forget. While the film itself attempts to produce straightforward moments of traditional romantic comedy – Rueben and Polly agree they are incompatible and should part, only to be found, in the next shot, passionately kissing – it also sabotages these attempts by inevitably linking them with body comedy, as when, following on from this kiss, Reuben is so over-aroused he does not even make his self-set target of five minutes of sex before orgasm.

Despite its uneasiness of tone, however, *Along Came Polly* does clearly attempt to revive the policy, begun in the radical romantic comedies of the 1970s but firmly eradicated since the rise of the Ephronesque rom-com, of using the sex scene as a locus of humour. Films like *Annie Hall* were aware of the importance of fulfilling sex to the success of the couple, and indeed to the well-being of both its members. Enabled by new ratings systems that no longer forbade the representation of the sex act itself, the camera in the radical rom-coms does not discreetly look away or permit a fade-out when the couple goes into a clinch: it watches. Thus the viewer learns in *Annie Hall* that Alvy uses the glow shed by a red light bulb in his seduction routine, and that Annie is often too uptight to have sex unless mellowed first by some marijuana. Not only are such moments of sex for comic value not included in the current dominant form of the female-centred rom-com, sex itself, as mentioned above, is hardly ever an occurrence and, when it is included, rarely shown. When the couple go into a clinch in *How to Lose a Guy in 10 Days* (2003), *Music and Lyrics*, and *Because I Said So*, for example, the camera watches them kiss but then discreetly pans away as they move to consummation. The sex scene is thus *unseen*: and it is certainly not made the matter for comedy.[2] In each of these cases the couple's intimacy is included in the narrative as the prelude for deeper feelings of betrayal when the (generically inevitable) break-up comes, rather than staged for the viewer as a comic occasion.

Not all male-centred rom-coms feature the quest for no-strings sex, however: from *Swingers* onwards there has been a trope in such films to position a lascivious lead in opposition to a more romantically inclined buddy. Thus Trent contrasts with Mike in *Swingers, Along Came Polly*'s Sandy diverges from Reuben, and Andy's posse of randy male workmates in *The 40-Year-Old Virgin* oppose his chaste outlook.

Despite this initial dichotomy in available male positions – priapic versus pro-monogamous – the end result is the same, however. While the homme-com hero sets out to find true love, and the Lothario wants yet another roll in the hay, they both inevitably end up in monogamous relationships by the end reel. Starting their narratives with very different desires and goals, the men of these male-driven texts finish by realising the importance of the stable union. The contemporary female-centred rom-coms also conclude with the would-be permanent establishment of the heterosexual couple; narrative closure for this genre seems, at the moment, predicated on monogamy.

This insistence on closure-through-coupling sits comfortably, on the whole, with the traditional rom-com and those examples of the homme-com that present the romantic hero, but much less so with those films that begin by celebrating the ability of their central males to lead hordes of women into bed. Indeed, *The Tao of Steve* and *Wedding Crashers* go beyond suggesting their heroes lead their victims and openly admit they con them. John and Jeremy from the latter film use weddings as their hunting grounds: they crash weddings at which they know no one and manipulate the romantic charge associated with such events (ironically celebrating monogamy) in order to bed bridesmaid after bridesmaid. The film makes it clear that the pair are seeking not soul-mates but easy prey; by skilful editing that matches the men attending successive events and repeatedly performing the same sequence of actions (arriving and announcing aliases; toasting the bride and groom; cutting the cake; dancing), the film conveys the habitual and calculating nature of their behaviour. John and Jeremy prey on the romantic tendencies of single women, inspired by the weddings to yearn for their own, by performing actions that are calculated to convince the women they are nice guys. A montage shows the men achieving their goals: having succeeding in attracting the attentions of their prey, each man twirls his partner in a dance move that cuts directly to the woman falling back, topless, onto a bed. The successful performance of this routine earns them the desired easy sex.

Dex (Donal Logue), the hero of *The Tao of Steve*, has a different approach: he doesn't approach. The film enjoys revealing why Dex, who is obviously overweight, indolent and selfish, still manages to get the girls; he operates by a code of cool that involves really listening to women, being their friends and not making a pass. Women, Dex says, especially good-looking ones, are so used to being pounced on by men that not pouncing makes them anxious. They then have to seduce Dex to make sure that they are still desirable.

While these films show the men enjoying the attentions of many women, they still each end up with just one at the film's end. The priapic excess that rules for most of the film must, seemingly, be abandoned in order for the resolution of the plot to be attained. The narratives then have to work quite hard (and at times to unconvincing results) to explain why the men should decide to give up their promiscuous and immature ways, in order to have meaningful sex with just one woman. As noted above, this is the inevitable end of the romantic homme-com too, but there such conclusions do not run against the grain of the main action in quite the same way. In *The 40-Year-Old Virgin*, Andy has been seeking one woman to love and have sex with throughout the narrative; it is his pack of male friends that insist on ending his uninitiate status. As the camera pans around Andy's wedding ceremony, it takes care to pick out all these same friends now ensconced in couples or secure family units with children. Despite 90 per cent of the film's 116-minute running time being given over to these men's lusty and repeated attempts to get Andy some casual sex, in the final ten minutes Andy's wedding seems to confer sensible monogamous relationships upon all.[3]

While *Wedding Crashers*' protagonists are on a quest for no-strings sex, rather than for true love and understanding, as Andy is, this film's ending is no less neat and coupled. Indeed, given the amount of running time given to the men's machinations in pursuit of their numerous, largely undifferentiated, prey, it actually requires some torsion of credibility to achieve the alteration of John and Jeremy from cynical Lotharios to devoted monogamists. True, John has been established as the more dreamy and less insatiable hunter all along, as befits Owen Wilson's relaxed and mellow star persona. Jeremy, however, is much more stridently exploitative, again tying in with the established characteristics of the star playing him, Vince Vaughn. The viewer observes John tiring of his bachelor existence, so it is no real surprise to find him falling for one girl, Clare (Rachel McAdam), but the film seems to acknowledge its own strain when Jeremy too falls in love, with Clare's sister, Gloria (Isla Fisher), who is even kinkier and more sex-mad than he is. The film ends with the four lovers/friends/relations reconciled – at, of course, yet another wedding – but the wrench in the narrative remains. The men's plot trajectory has moved from their desiring casual sex with endlessly replaceable females, to their wanting monogamous sex with just one perfect woman, in other words, to a perceived maturation of desires. While the beginning and ending points of such films could therefore be seen as prompting contradictory impulses – bedding as many women as possible versus settled domesticity with just one – the films' attempt to reconcile these oppositions by aligning them with the characters' development, so that as the men grow wiser they seem 'naturally' to grow more monogamous.

~ Conclusion ~

Can we thus convincingly say that the homme-com offers film audiences an alternative take on the contemporary rom-com? Narrative closure within this new grouping of films is only achieved by a capitulation to monogamy, the same outcome promoted by the dominant form of the genre, the very films the boy rom-com appears to be contesting. Across both the sexier and more romantic strains of the male-centred rom-com, an amelioration of hedonism seems inevitable: again and again the heroes, the winners, are the men who give up their randy, irresponsible, immature ways, to have meaningful sex with one woman. The emphasis on the importance of sex remains, but the accent on plurality or seriality of partner, of experience, is eroded. We might therefore deny that there is a transformative urge at work within the male-centred comedy, positing instead that the increased emphasis on the showing of and dealing with sex is excused, recuperated, by the films' conservative conclusions, which endorse heterosexual monogamy as much as their sex-averse Ephronesque competitors.

Finally, I want to focus on the one key underlying point about these films that seem to form a new sub-group – that they are meant to appeal to men. If, as this essay has demonstrated, the homme-com seeks to reinject sex into the genre, and the homme-com is aimed at attracting a male audience, it logically follows that sex is being assumed to be a male interest, prerogative and goal. Male audience members may like to take issue with the fact that they are assumed to find toilet humour funny, to like slapstick and mess, to be obsessed with sex. Women viewers may in turn object to the notion that such topics are not fitting subject matter for them either to laugh at or obsess over.

In this way, the new-seeming inflection of the rom-com genre that targets and prioritises the male may be seen to be just as conservative as the current sexless rom-coms. Both forms of the genre assume men want sex, and women withhold it from them, urging them to grow up and settle down. This inevitably recalls the double standard used to mandate men's premarital sexual experience and refuse women's rights to or desires for the same. Although the reintroduction of sexual topics to the rom-com is, arguably, necessary for its continued survival as a genre, it seems to me dangerous to allow the double standard to creep back into popular assumption, after the feminist movement and other political and cultural manifestations of the 1970s, including the radical rom-com, all did their best to banish it. This is what will happen, however, if we assign interest in sexual topics solely to men and thus exile the body and its urges and emissions to a sub-genre 'meant for' male audiences.

Director Judd Apatow has followed up his 2005 box-office hit, *The 40-Year-Old Virgin*, with *Knocked Up* (2007). This contains a scene between the married protagonists in which the man asks his wife, 'Shall we have sex tonight?' Her answer is a resounding negative – 'Yuurghhh!' – worsened rather than tempered when she expands, 'I'm just really constipated right now.' Here we see components of body humour in conflict not just with the romantic but with the sexual, as if the earthy and gross-out elements of these films have begun to war with each other. Significantly, however, it is again the man who wants and the woman who withholds sex. While the returned emphasis on the body and on sexual urges that the male-centred rom-coms introduce may, then, be welcomed as returning the genre to some of the realism offered by the 1970s radical rom-coms, if this is inevitably associated with male urges and with female restraint, this new turn within the genre offers no more validation of women's rights to sexual desire and fulfilment than the Ephronesque comedies such films ostensibly oppose.

12 *Lost in Transition*

Problems of Modern (Heterosexual) Romance and the
Catatonic Male Hero in the Post-Feminist Age

~ Janet McCabe ~

WHEN I SAW the Call for Papers for this collection on contemporary romantic comedies I was gripped by the possibilities of writing about Bill Murray as a new kind of romantic hero for the post-feminist age. Not your conventional lead, I grant you, but there is something undeniably magnetic about him. Long gone are the days of his swaggering sexual confidence when he literally swept damsels off their feet. Okay, so Sigourney Weaver was under the sway of demonic forces at the time. But let's not split hairs. The ageing Murray protagonist may not be so cocksure, but he remains for me at least a romantic kinda guy. Not sentimental, not schmaltzy. Just romantic. Or so I thought.

Feedback arrived. Interesting proposition. But the films featuring Murray I had selected – *Rushmore* (1998), *The Royal Tenenbaums* (2001), *Lost in Translation* (2003) and *Broken Flowers* (2005) – were not obvious contenders for the rom-com category. Strange hybrids, I know, but still. Had I become so cynical about the possibility of depicting true love in contemporary film that I misread these movies? Or had these small independent films given up on the delicious promise of the type of love that dismantles? Had they, in fact, lost heart in 'perpetuating a myth of romance as *the* purpose of life' (M.L. Johnson, 2002: 16), resulting in ageing heroes standing impassive as women they clearly adore walk away from them? And, am I alone in finding Murray's lamentable attempts to woo the ladies hilariously funny – and desperately romantic?

What happened?

~ Feminism, nervous comedies and the melodramatic male ~

The year 1978 saw Brian Henderson predict 'the death of romantic comedy' (19). Wistfully nostalgic about romance as it may be, the genre had by the late-1970s run its course he argued. His pessimism was signalled by films like *Semi-Tough* (1977), in which romantic love had become so parodied, so analysed, that it could no longer survive. Henderson related the difficulties of giving representation to love in our contemporary culture to the 'discovery' of the new self. He concluded that romance might help us find ourselves but not each other.

But love somehow survived.

For, at the very moment that Henderson lamented the demise of the rom-com, a new cycle appeared, independent films like *Annie Hall* (1977) and *Manhattan* (1979), which Frank Krutnik called the 'nervous romance' (1990: 57–72). Only finding love was not what it used to be, as these films made visible. Described by Krutnik as being about pushing towards a melodramatic resolution, mixing nostalgia for 'simpler' times with a scepticism about the utopian possibilities of the heterosexual couple, these films emerged from, and reproduced new gendered ideals of, a post-feminist, post-sexual revolution, post-counterculture world that endorsed non-monogamous and non-heterosexual choices and lifestyles. In turn, they inexorably undermined 'previously forged bonds between love and marriage, eroticism and romance, pleasure and procreation' (Krutnik, 1998: 16). Loving in the modern world was no easy matter.

Courting the ladies had become a difficult business in the post-feminist era. By the time Annie Hall (Diane Keaton) chastised Alvy Singer (Allen) for suggesting that not *every* bad mood she had could be put down to the vicissitudes of her menstrual cycle, it had become apparent that contemporary film, and independent movies in particular, were alert to a questioning of traditional gender roles and gendered assumptions, debates principally initiated by second-wave feminism. Letting Annie exhaustively rehearse complaints about Alvy's failings as a paramour – his obsession with death, with sex, with, well, himself – produced much humour as it revealed certain new truths about contemporary dating rituals and gender relations. Incessant talk, either between protagonists or presented through filmic devices like split screen, subtitles or voiceover, about each twist and minute turn of *the* relationship gave a shape to the new sexual politics. Women had much to say. And men had a lot to learn.

Kathleen Rowe, however, cautions us against the new post-classical rom-com heroes willing to listen to their women. Sensitive guys, or guys who learn sensitivity in the course of the film, like Nicholas Cage (*Moonstruck* (1987)), Billy Crystal (*When Harry Met Sally* (1989)), Richard Gere (*Pretty Woman* (1990)), Al Pacino (*Frankie and Johnny* (1991)) and Tom Hanks (*Sleepless in Seattle* (1993), *You've Got Mail* (1998)) appear, at first glance, to be 'liberated from a repressive masculinity classical romantic comedy valued' (1995b: 196). Drawing on what Juliana Schiesari describes as the '*homo melancholicus*, the melancholic male', as someone who 'stands both in reaction to and in complicity with patriarchy' (ibid.), Rowe claims that post-classical rom-com males appropriate 'femininity, feminized genres, and feminism . . . to prop up their own authority, which they then invoke to "instruct" women about relationships, romance, and femininity itself' (ibid.: 196, 197). Somehow (or so it seemed) feminism had become *all* about the man in the post-classical rom-com. It became his hermeneutic narrative function to incite a discourse about 'difficult' or emotionally damaged women over which he must keep constant vigilance. In the process of defining her as wounded and/or inexperienced in the ways of the adult world he could 'demonstrate . . . greater wisdom, charm, or sensitivity' (ibid.).

Bill Murray has, however, never been viewed as a modern lover in quite the same way as these reconstructed new men suffering for love. His career was rooted in countercultural dissent and misrule, with his breakthrough coming in 1977 as one of the *Saturday Night Live* team. Belonging to a generation of comedians, along with John Belushi, Dan Aykroyd and Harold Ramis, specialising in improvised comedy and scripted satire, his deadpan performance style was saturated in anti-authoritarianism. Murray went mainstream in the 1980s, bringing this anti-establishment dissension with him, playing droll men with little interest in instructing dates about either relationships or romance. He was after just one thing – getting laid. From dubious scientist Dr Peter Venkman exploiting his faculty position to chase female students in *Ghostbusters* (1984) to utterly unpleasant weatherman Phil Connors taking advantage of eternity to put all-new cheap moves on his producer Rita (Andie MacDowell) in *Groundhog Day* (1993), no one could do 'Insincere Guy quite as compellingly as Murray' (Schruers, 2003: 83). Phil may refashion himself as the ideal man through a series of selfless acts, but given past generic experience one cannot help wondering about his sincerity to change. Murray, after all, has a proven track record of playing the rakish Casanova with the Telfon charm. He may not be convinced about what he does, but he knows that it is the right thing to do if he ever wants to get the girl – and leave Punxsutawney, Pennsylvania.

But lately Murray has gone romantic. No longer the straight-faced, smart-mouthed clown, he has taken those generic traits and pitched up in independent films only to fall in love. As steel tycoon Herman J. Blume in *Rushmore* he becomes embroiled in an acrimonious dispute with precocious 15-year-old Max Fischer (Jason Schwartzman) as the two compete for the affections of widowed first-grade teacher Rosemary Cross (Olivia Williams). Blume may emerge as equally self-centred and immature as the teenager, but the older married man with adolescent children is also much more complicated and contradictory than his younger rival. He is calculatingly cruel yet emotionally fragile, chaste but desiring intimacy, desperate for love while remaining impotent in its pursuit; he embodies male achievement even as he finds its rewards less than satisfactory. With years of more experience getting in his way, Blume (who really should know better), suffering – and losing – in love, as he hopelessly yearns for the younger woman, projects a far more troubled and troubling male ego than previously seen at a time when 'authoritative norms of conventional masculinity were everywhere in flux' (Wiegman, 2002: 31).

~ Longing for love: approved (media) scripts of heterosexual romance and the limits of discourse ~

Nothing quite troubles post-feminist scholarship more than our continued cultural investment in the scripted fantasy of heterosexual romance conditioning our desires, our fantasies, our expectations of finding *the* one, our need to be undone by love. Feminist criticism has long sought to deconstruct the myth of heterosexual romance (Modleski, 1991; 1994; 1999; Radway, 1984), but tales – fables, songs, fairytales, poems, movies – of being utterly dismantled by love continue to exert a considerable mental hold over most of us, imbibing us into the norm experienced as erotic pleasure and personal fulfilment. We have learnt how to critique heterosexist-based romance, to know that it is restricted (and restricting) and to aspire to theorise differently. But we remain at the same time absolutely beguiled, incapable of ever quite relinquishing the belief that being loved will somehow complete us.

As cynical as he is, lost in the routine of marriage and monogamy, Herman J. Blume takes another chance on the delicious promise of love as he devotes his energy to romancing Rosemary Cross. Made visible in the *mise-en-scène* is a lyrical romantic idyll, a leisurely world of courtly love, in fact. In his performance of the romantic lead he *is* remade: suave, attentive, chivalrous, with impeccable manners. He escorts Rosemary on a formal date, gallantly leading her from her front door and into his waiting Rolls Royce; the couple hold hands; they walk through a rose garden gazing deeply into each other's eyes; they share a candlelit dinner. With the promise offered by the first date – the frisson of the first touch, the quiver of the first kiss, the desire to be unravelled by love, to be *the* one – Blume cannot help but fall madly in love.

But it is not to be.

Visiting the local country club with his family, Blume returns to marital routine and observed social niceties. Warily he climbs up to the top diving board. Looking down he spies the wife who despises him, the roughneck sons who quietly appal him and the community that he has worked hard to belong to scrutinising him. Blume up there on the diving board, burdened with having to prove his masculine prowess, unfulfilled by the heterosexual promise of marriage and children, is someone on the brink, desperate to jump in and enjoy the utter exhilaration of just falling. Few comic actors unerringly critique 'the self-deluded and self-important' (Schruers, 2003: 83) better than Murray, but at this moment Blume embodies a poignant disillusionment – an un-sayability. In part his silent frustration speaks about what Merri Lisa Johnson calls 'the inevitably disappointing expectations of romantic mythology [and] the disciplinary force of the traditional marriage contract' (2004: 22). It also makes visible what the rom-com hero can never say. And here lies the rub: a male hero struggling to express desire, to react differently even, beyond heteronormative cultural performances that praise particular models of male achievement and heterosexual masculinity, because he is speaking *in* and *through* a representation that has limited language to offer something different, to utter something new.

Recent feminist masculinity studies (Gardiner, 2002; Wiegman, 2002: 31–59) take the position that it is feasible, essential in fact, to interrogate the ways men are restricted and frustrated by the culturally sanctioned models of masculinity without reducing them to victims. None of the men played by Murray are victims but they are nonetheless constricted and let down by the dominant myths of what a man should be. Each is professionally successful, economically secure, sexually and racially privileged but ultimately they remain unfulfilled. Crisis comes when they find themselves in love, when these strait-laced, self-contained men, in sore need of unravelling, actually start to unravel. Moved in ways they find unfathomable, undone in ways they cannot comprehend, these men are asked to respond through a restrictive representational script – and it is in and through these often small but troubling moments that hilarity occurs.

Going independent has helped. Produced in and through an internal formal logic that seeks to challenge norms and defy established convention, these complex and nuanced comic male characters dealing with the romantic binds they find themselves in offer a contrapuntal performance. Reading the performance in this manner involves a form of 'reading back' (Said, 1993) from the independent perspective, to show how the underlying but pervasive presence of deep-rooted cultural attitudes toward love and romance structure the (generic) text. We begin to read, contrapuntally, with a simultaneous awareness both of our entrenched investment in fantasies of heterosexual romance and of a worldliness that questions and troubles those culturally approved scripts.

Nowhere does Murray capture that complex male ambivalence better than in his deadpan delivery. Long part of his comic persona, his style has, in recent times, been transformed from defiant arrogance and 'sarcastic hyperawareness' (Schruers, 2003: 83) into bewilderment, deep dissatisfaction and boredom, coming from a worldliness borne of bitter (generic) experience. For example, Murray turns in one of his most minimal and muted performances (quite literally at times) as eccentric Raleigh St Clair in *The Royal Tenenbaums*. Raleigh is married to the much younger, beautifully mysterious and former playwright prodigy, Margot Tenenbaum (Gwyneth Paltrow). In his professional life he may be a gifted writer and accomplished neurologist, but in love he falls into an almost catatonic state, unable to take initiative, or to say or do the right thing when it really matters. His relationship with Margot is conducted almost entirely through a locked bathroom door where she lies in the bath smoking and watching television.

Eventually Margot contrives to move back home with her mother Etheline Tenenbaum (Anjelica Huston). A taxi arrives to collect her. Raleigh dashes out. It is a moment that recasts the classic, and temporary, break-up scene, when the heroine dramatically leaving serves the narrative function to galvanise the hero's resolve to win her back. Sombre overcast skies replace torrential rain; awkward postures are evident rather than hysterical tears; a hesitant, motionless and crumpled middle-aged man substitutes for the vigorous lover giving chase to a moving vehicle. No temporary insanity here: just hesitation and dithering. Later he takes afternoon tea with his estranged wife. But there is no heart-stopping declaration of love, no breathtaking reconciliation, only melancholia and restrained civility over tea and butter biscuits in a drab winter garden. Margot tells Raleigh that she will never return. 'I want to die,' he says flatly. Dramatic words, but the precise framing, tight and almost claustrophobic, lingering uncomfortably for a little too long, formally grounds his realisation that nothing he says will bring her back, nothing he can do will stop her from leaving him. Yet such formal stiffness also makes visible an intimate portrait of this couple – highly intelligent, extremely protective of their emotions and decidedly sceptical of the possibility of ever being truly happy in love.

Suspecting his wife of cheating, Raleigh hires a private detective (Don McKinnon), who uncovers affairs and a secret bohemian life Margot lives unbeknownst to him. Raleigh remains impassive, his only reaction, 'She smokes.' Hilariously funny, but did he not hear what the detective said? She has made a cuckold out of him. Far from trying to win her back, fighting for her love, he lies immobile on the couch. Not even playing word games with, or experimenting on, his psychological subject Dudley Heinsbergen (Stephen Lea Sheppard) can draw him out of his melancholia. In the scramble to find the right one, the male ego is taking quite a battering. Independent films have no sentiment when it comes to treating men badly, as it changes the rules and fails to resolve the question of what happens to a man after he is unmanned by love. Like Herman J. Blume before him, Raleigh is undone less by revelations of infidelities and betrayals than from learning that he is considered mediocre – a middling man simply not considered as a long-term partner. For all his heterosexual male privilege – class, racial, intellectual, Raleigh St Clair is just not, well, enough for her.

But can Raleigh ever be *the* one for Margot?

Representational paradigms have shifted in recent years, and transformations in images of modern women in love are, once again, upsetting established ideas and putting pressure on values and knowledges defining heterosexual relationships, romantic love, marriage and monogamy. Where once those who resisted male charms were viewed with deep suspicion, representations of contemporary womanhood displaying a new self- and sexual confidence in their relationships with men are altering gendered scripts and putting into discourse a new sexual politics. Margot Tenenbaum is, for example, produced in and through a representational logic, and one sanctioned by independent film production, that expects her to trouble, to disrupt norms and challenge our thinking about gendered expectations. She is a woman who experiences sex entirely on her own terms and that does not necessarily equate with long-term monogamy. Third-wave feminists make the point that it is crucial for us to examine the ways women are 'advocating acceptance of our darker drives, and indulging in fascination with imagery that queers gender, decenters heterosexuality, and valorizes the erotic' (M.L. Johnson, 2007: 15-16). Such liberated portrayals are complex (and beyond the scope of this essay), but women like Margot are putting pressure on the category of heteronormative masculinity in new and surprising ways as they sample what they might or might not want from relationships – her one-day marriage to a Rastafarian, her lesbian lover from the Rive Gauche in Paris, her indulgence in anonymous sex with strangers, her long-term affair with Eli Cash (Owen Wilson). In choosing intimacy with her adopted brother, Margot opts for something less defined as she sits with Richie (Luke Wilson) in his tent listening to 'She Smiled Sweetly' and 'Ruby Tuesday' on an old record player.

Far from resolving the rom-com narrative, ending with 'happy ever after' and the promise of a lifelong monogamous commitment, Margot's experimenting with possibilities and choice opens up discussion and encourages us to think differently about what we want out of a romantic relationship – or even marriage. This may involve Raleigh remaining in her life. At the funeral of Royal Tenenbaum (Gene Hackman), Margot may drape her arms around Richie, but Raleigh, standing with Dudley under an umbrella, remains next to her. I have no idea how these relationships, without rules or any names, can be prolonged, and, as the film ends here, I guess it doesn't either. But the film hints at a relationship revolution (in the same way as *Some*

Like It Hot (1959) when it finished with Osgood Fielding III (Joe E. Brown) accepting 'Daphne' (Jack Lemmon) as a man and still wanting him anyway), pushes toward a generic revolt, in the dynamics passing between them.

But such representational paradoxes are only possible because independent movies, offering an alternative to the master narrative of dominant film culture, license them. Independents – directors like Jim Jarmusch and Wes Anderson, those working within a different media logic from mainstream Hollywood – have long made a virtue out of their autonomy from the constraints and restrictions determining the major studios. Arguably the complex wounded male characters featured in these small films are produced in and through an institutional discourse conscious of resisting established representations, adopting 'difficult' characters to show that they are being daring and subversive, and highlighting the contribution they believe they are making to contemporary (media) culture. Away from the mainstream, where the rom-com narrative demands obedience – and let's not forget that Phil Connors had to go back and repeat the romance plot until he got it right (see Paul Sutton's essay, Chapter 3 in this volume) – the independent film narrative works hard to complicate rather than resolve affairs of the heart. Its form destabilises narrative convention, upsets generic rules, and self-consciously demonstrates that it knows that it is being challenging and seditious as it searches out the new.

But let us be cautious.

For, as Tania Modleski puts it, 'we exist inside ideology, [we] are all victims, down to the very depths of our psyches, of political and cultural domination' (1991: 45). Independents do not function outside our culture; they are in fact always 'inside' cultural discourse and subject to its rules, prohibitions and controls governing norms representing gender and sexuality. Pushing representation to the limits, giving us images of complicated, contradictory men, 'smacks of revolt' (Foucault, 1998: 7), but we must, at the same time, maintain a keen sense of the meticulous rules governing media forms. Analysing two recent Bill Murray films – *Lost in Translation* and *Broken Flowers* – I contend that the contrapuntal performances given by him self-consciously critique the sexually potent romantic hero in the post-feminist age, and subtly rewrite the rules of rom-com, but in so doing it also makes visible the difficulties involved in doing different and strains the limits of media representational forms firmly rooted to age-old heterosexist-based fantasies of romance, marriage and monogamy.

~ *Tokyo Drifters: absent wives and the forlorn matinee idol in* Lost in Translation ~

Lost in Translation opens with Bob Harris (Murray), an ageing Hollywood action hero, travelling through Tokyo at night. He snoozes restlessly as his limo makes its way through the city, neon signs stretching endlessly past, to the luxurious Park Hyatt Tokyo hotel. Suddenly, something grabs his attention. He stares out more intently and we see, from his point of view, his own image, handsome and debonair, on a huge billboard, shot in black and white, and complete with enigmatic Japanese script. Harris, jet-lagged and disoriented, rubs his eyes, almost in disbelief, as if he cannot quite believe what he sees. *Lost in Translation*, in its opening sequence, functions to establish a counterpoint between the imperialism of Hollywood film culture and the independent perspective, a 'counter-narrative' that persistently penetrates beneath the surface of this film text to elaborate the ubiquitous presence of dominant fantasies of romance, courtship and marriage in our culture. It is the film's very condition of exile – characters away from home, cast into unfamiliar territory; a film made independently of the Hollywood majors, of its generic conventions and formal rules – that enables it to represent romance as simultaneously both about utopian promise and world-weary (generic) disillusionment.

Harris, we soon learn, is in Tokyo to film a commercial for Suntory whisky. Early scenes find him on set. Wearing a tuxedo, and lounging in a red leather-bound chair with a glass of Suntory whisky, he embodies the drink's smooth sophistication. As the director puts him through his paces, he imitates the swinging über-cool moves of Frank Sinatra or the minimal facial gestures with those cantilever eyebrows associated with Roger Moore. He understands only too well the approved scripts of male attractiveness as a series of illusory surfaces that he can use to construct and perform the sombre matinee idol. Humour is mined from the weariness Harris conveys through his body and particularly his face, and is further made sense of through generic echoes of past Murray performances, as he shifts from boredom to imitation, and rifts with various elements of performance. He acts out a myth of masculinity that he knows is only an absurd performance but nonetheless has rewarded him with a career, fame and recognition (of sorts).

Romantic fiction has long promoted the heterosexual ideal man as one of decisive action and physical prowess. As a Hollywood leading man

Harris has, we are told (and verified by an American businessman who recognises him in the hotel bar), successfully performed the accepted cultural fiction of the virile action hero; a man physically in control – of his body, of his women, of his destiny. Away from the photo-shoot, and literally off camera (we only see Harris watching one of his movies), Harris is lost without a role – uneasy within his body and uncomfortable with intimacy. Whereas the fast-paced, special-effects-driven world of Hollywood action harnesses his insolent slouch and shambling gait into self-confidence, in the comedic one of this independent film, with its austere visuals and sparse dialogue, Harris cuts a rather more ludicrous figure. Sight gags reveal Harris struggling with his surroundings. His tall, straggling frame towers above his smaller Japanese hosts when he enters the lift; he finds the beds too short, shower heads too low, and razors too tiny for him; his frenzied encounter with an exercise machine makes a mockery of his hard-man status as an action hero. And let us not forget his encounter with the 'premium fantasy' prostitute, mired as it is in miscommunication and physical comedy. It is pure farce, as the woman implores Harris to 'lip' her stockings. But the more she attempts to initiate some masochistic rape fantasy for his sexual pleasures, the more irritated, bored and motionless Harris becomes. Artificial and contrived, the fantasy abruptly ends with the couple falling off the bed as he tries to restrain her histrionic body caught in performing resistance and pleasure. He rolls his eyes but does precisely nothing as they crumple into a heap on the floor.

Harris, however, becomes reanimated playing the handsome stranger for Charlotte (Scarlett Johansson), the neglected young wife of a self-obsessed photographer (Giovanni Ribisi). Harris first sees Charlotte in the lift when she shyly returns his smile. But it takes another half-an-hour of movie time before furtive glances and meaningful smirks turn into conversation. No grand passion; only gentle quips and mild flirtation. Charlotte tells Harris he looked 'very dashing' when she first saw him in the bar, wearing a tuxedo. (No mention of the bulldog clips holding back his jacket to give him a better, more elegant, shape, but she saw them.) And she was particularly taken with his mascara. Able to see through the deception, the trickery, Charlotte shares Harris' desire for something more than this.

Against the artifice of the encounter with the prostitute, Harris embarks with Charlotte on a spontaneous adventure in the city at night, in which a gradual sense of freedom and lawlessness (quite literally at times) leads to romance. Reworking conventions of the classical 1930s screwball comedies, where the couple escape 'formality' and find love through madcap escapades, this contemporary relationship shares a similar cinematic vocabulary. *Lost in Translation* may demonstrate an acute awareness of how that fiction works, but it simultaneously indicates its complicity with a language and practice of romance embedded so deeply in our culture that it cannot be easily dislodged. Charlotte, for example, may be the highly intelligent, Yale philosophy graduate searching for a different kind of identity, but she remains the ingénue most prized by the rom-com. And it is to her that Harris is drawn.

In its contrapuntal structure, where Harris may motionlessly sit watching a stripper before critiquing her artistry, or engage in wacky antics taking Charlotte to hospital, or settling for casual sex with someone else, the film remains reliant on, and endorses, dominant myths of romance in its narrative and generic DNA as it uses them. Nowhere is this more evident than in the karaoke sequence. Here the vernacular and customs of romance may be reduced to postmodern irony, performative pastiche – Charlotte sporting an electric pink wig, Harris and his rendition of Roxy Music's 'More Than This' – but yet these elements continue at the same time to exert a considerable hold over the participants, and the audience. Wanting 'More Than This' the heterosexual romance has ripened so subtly that we barely noticed it happening. But, as Charlotte silently puts her head on Harris' shoulder as reward for his serenade, the melancholy of the gesture reveals the romance to be more like a crush, nothing more than expectation but not real. What right does she have to be so indignant, so incensed, when Harris later hooks up with the lead singer (Catherine Lambert) from the hotel's resident jazz group? Nothing will ever come of it, or of them even. But still. Ambivalence emerges from the intimacy that even surprises them, but also from how the text probes our investment in the fantasy of true love and finding *the* one as it at the same time perpetuates it.

Encircling the couple is absence – a distracted husband and a literally absent wife. In particular, Harris' wife Lydia emerges as an important structuring absence that puts pressure on the text, on the fulfilment of the romance in fact, as she proves a constant reminder of what he already has. Lydia, to a certain extent, represents the ghost of the traditional rom-com, of where the 'right' couple are destined – marriage; for she was at one time presumably *the* one. But her constant spousal intrusion also reminds Harris that he has achieved, however unsatisfactorily, lasting closure. The banality of her periodic appearances, albeit in virtual or aural form with a FedEx parcel containing carpet samples, a fax with a drawing of a shelving unit, a reminder of a birthday missed, is conveyed through Harris doing precisely nothing. Such a performance of nothingness may register resignation and marital routine, but it also makes visible that there is nothing within the traditional rom-com vocabulary beyond the promise of marriage and serial monogamy. (Even married couples in classic screwballs like *My Favorite Wife* (1940) and *His Girl Friday* (1940) had to divorce to find the exhilaration of potentially being a couple again.) But the long, unbroken take where Harris lies next to Charlotte on the bed, telling her about the perils of middle age and the love of his children, reverses the conventional moment when the couple consummate their relationship. Revealed in Harris' monologue, delivered in monotone, is, as Paul Julian Smith aptly puts it, 'that a hard-won middle-aged marriage is worth more than a fling with a girl half his age' (2004: 14).

Eventually the couple must part.

Independent films have never shown much interest in the right couple staying together. Ever since Annie Hall and Alvy Singer decided to go their separate ways on a flight back from Los Angeles, the message has been that couples may connect deeply and intensely but there is not necessarily a long-term future for them. Relationships are based on chance; the best we can hope for is to encounter romance and experience it before moving on with our lives. We should be happy in the now, rather than hopeful for some unseen future. *Lost in Translation* is no exception. But given its contrapuntal structure, with its deep-rooted investment in the traditional scripted fantasy of heterosexual romance piercing through the text, it cannot quite say it. Harris leaves Tokyo, happy to return home. But before he does he rings Charlotte. 'Goodbye,' he says into the answering machine, 'and enjoy the jacket you stole'. Mundane and quirky: in keeping with the independent spirit. But as he is driven to the airport he sees her on the street; he chases through the crowd, hugs her and whispers something in her ear. Despite the grand gesture (which Raleigh failed to make), there is no grand declaration of love uttered at the end. In what cannot be said the film may want us to fill in the silence, but it also reveals a wistful nostalgia for the possibility of what the classic rom-com promised.

~ *Saying it with Pink Roses: the perennial bachelor, broken promises and* Broken Flowers ~

> The past is gone. I know that. The future isn't here yet, whatever it may bring. All there is, is this. (Don Johnston, *Broken Flowers*)

Long has Murray been known for his pared-down, almost minimal performances, but, in his role as Don Johnston in *Broken Flowers*, this nothing-ness is taken to another level. Johnston receives in the mail a mysterious pink missive, sent from an anonymous ex-lover, telling him that he has a son who may (or may not) be coming to look for him. Urged on by his next-door neighbour Winston (Jeffrey Wright) to find out who sent the letter, he embarks on a road trip to visit his former loves. The past may catch up to disturb the present but it does little to drive Johnston out of his almost catatonic apathy.

Diane Negra (2006) notes the emergence of the perennial bachelor in post-classical rom-coms, those wacky guys languishing in arrested development, having too much fun to take their proper place in the social order. But away from the mainstream, the carefree bachelor morphs into an impotent and bewildered stranger unable to get off the couch. Whereas post-classical Hollywood has him driving off into the sunset to crash weddings with his paramour, there is no such easy resolution for our perennial bachelor who is past his prime. Contained in the independent film text is a worldliness rooted in harsh (generic) experience, as the longevity of Murray as a rom-com hero gets mapped onto Johnston's fatigue – and even his name Don Johnston, spelt with the 't', proves a running gag throughout the film. Just as Johnston sifts through the remnants of his former love life, Murray has long been working in the modern incarnation of the rom-com genre. In contrast to the new generation of rom-com stars like Matthew McConaughey, and Owen and Luke Wilson (who incidentally play the young men to whom Murray's characters often lose out in love), he has a world-weary disenchantment – he understands how the narrative finishes, knows how the generic form works. The opening of *Broken Flowers* starts (again) at the end with the song, 'There Is An End'. The lyrics, 'Spring brings the rain / With winter comes pain / Every season has an end', fade into Johnston's latest love Sherry (Julie Delpy) leaving. Like before, Murray's character attempts to stop her; but he is only going through the motions. He asks her what she wants; but she needs to figure that out on her own. Johnston returns to the sparseness of his lounge, the solitude of his couch.

In part, Johnston's condition is a result of belonging to the independent tradition. Reactive and directionless, he is drawn from those European art movies in which nothing much happens and protagonists may experience an intense encounter before moving on. It takes Johnston's African-American neighbour Winston to give him a narrative. He tells Johnston what to wear, how to behave and always to bring pink roses; he gives him an itinerary and a soundtrack to accompany it. But it is these experienced, older women, narrating back the past to him, who create the contemporary love story. Hearts have been broken, and there are few illusions left. Each has been, in subtle and not so subtle ways, disillusioned and emotionally broken by love.

As he drifts from one past love to another, Johnston is given the opportunity, an intimate glimpse even, to imagine what his life could have been if he had committed to one of these women – the single mum Laura (Sharon Stone) with the sexually precocious daughter aptly named Lolita (Alexis Dziena), the hippy Dora (Frances Conroy) who is now a respectable suburban wife, the trainee lawyer Carmen Marowski (Jessica Lange) who is now an animal communicator having a lesbian affair with her assistant (Chloë Sevigny), the bitter Penny (Tilda Swinton) who lives in the backwoods with her biker beau, and then there is the former lover who died. Of course he did not choose an intimate future with any one, but through these past relationships the film does question the whole notion of *the* one.

But still.

Romance keeps puncturing through the text. After Sherry leaves, and before he embarks on this road trip, Johnston sits alone in his lounge, motionless, while Marvin Gaye's voice pierces the silence; 'I want you to want me / But I want you to want me too / I want you / Just like I want you.' Sherry may have left, and he may have done little about her departure, but the aching possibility of wanting love, to be in love, remains.

Admittedly, I tend to laugh before Murray even opens his mouth, but his wistful performances in these independent films are keenly aware that less is more; a romance can be even more poignant with barely a kiss exchanged. These independents meditate on the idea of romance as inscribed right into the very inherited forms the films use even as they critique those forms. Ever since *Annie Hall* quite literally deconstructed the rom-com genre as Annie and Alvy's relationship disintegrated, independents have long made a virtue of their status to subvert, undermine or break away from dominant film culture. Self-reflexive and self-conscious, these films know too much, understand only too well how the romantic script works. To this end, independents work in parallel with the mainstream Hollywood rom-com, heckling from the margins, troubling the genre and precipitating a crisis. But still. Formal traces remain, and these films find it difficult to give up entirely on our romantic pleasures. Caught in this paradox is a rom-com hero like Murray, cynical maybe, but not quite prepared to relinquish the delicious promise of being dismantled by love.

13 A New Direction in Comedian Comedy?

Eternal Sunshine of the Spotless Mind, Punch-Drunk Love and the Post-Comedian Rom-Com

~ *Lesley Harbidge* ~

ON THEIR RELEASE, discourses surrounding Michel Gondry's *Eternal Sunshine of the Spotless Mind* (2004) and Paul Thomas Anderson's *Punch-Drunk Love* (2002) were similarly concerned with the films' flouting of expectations: expectations of star and expectations of genre. Here were two unique, surprising films that saw their lead actors, comedians Jim Carrey and Adam Sandler, playing remarkably against type; and, further, that seemed to somewhat eschew the preoccupations of the rom-com even while being understood as belonging to this generic terrain. Thus, Philip French's *Observer* review typically describes *Eternal Sunshine* as 'a romantic comedy with absurdist undertones' (2004a) while Elvis Mitchell (2004), in the *New York Times*, deemed it 'an angular and intelligent romantic comedy'. Similarly, of *Punch-Drunk Love*, *Empire*'s Angie Errigo wrote 'offbeat romantic comedy doesn't come quirkier than this' (2002).

What is clear from each of these reviews is that both films were perceived as misshapen and unexpected romantic comedies. Gondry's film, in fact, is a backward love story; a reworking of what Cavell has deemed the 'comedy of remarriage' (1981). After their relationship turns sour, the central protagonists Clementine (Kate Winslet) and Joel (Jim Carrey) resort to having their memories of one another erased. The film then charts their spiralling romantic fortunes and ineffectual attempts, not to get back together, but to remain apart. In terms of plot, Anderson's *Punch-Drunk Love* is the more conventional of the two rom-coms, revolving around the (on the surface) problematic union of socially maladroit Barry (Adam Sandler) and Lena (Emily Watson). Yet, while the protagonists *do* finally end up together, the overriding sense within this and Gondry's world (*Eternal Sunshine*, as I explain, features a truly ambiguous ending that is far from conventionally 'happy') is of the fragility of romance.

My central concern in this essay is that it is precisely through the simultaneous interrogation of the comedic personas of Carrey and Sandler *and* of the rom-com that *Eternal Sunshine* and *Punch-Drunk Love* might serve as significant milestones in the trajectory of the comedian comedy, a largely male-centred genre that has merited little discussion of late, and has certainly received no sustained interest since it was first brought to critical attention over 25 years ago.[1] At once unexpected Carrey/Sandler vehicles and dysfunctional rom-coms, they are symptomatic of the truly hybridised and self-conscious post-comedian rom-com: a new strain in contemporary Hollywood marrying and interrogating the frameworks of the comedian and romantic comedies. Specifically, it seems to be the concerns of the screwball, a genre closely aligned with the comedian comedy, that are being both harnessed and somewhat inverted here. The screwball's gender dynamics are replicated in that it is the females who are the initiators of each of the film's romances. Yet, the physical humour that is so central to the screwball is, for the most part, conspicuous by its absence. Carrey and Sandler, of course, are widely known for their exaggerated physical comic antics. However, these films work to reconceptualise that physicality, and, indeed, our expectations of its occurrence; in effect they recast and internalise it as the complex psychologies of Joel and Barry. In effectively decentring both comedy and romance, in finding themselves – particularly in the case of the Gondry film – preoccupied with, rather than compelled to observe the conventions of either,[2] these films certainly eschew the expected mechanics of the comedian and romantic comedies; yet, in doing so, they offer up a new and intriguing generic space for their mutual dysfunctionalities: the post-comedian rom-com.

~ Comedian comedy meets rom-com ~

Analyses of comedian comedy and of individual comedian comics (particularly Jerry Lewis (Krutnik, 1984; 1994; 1995); Jim Carrey (Drake, 2002); Steve Martin (McGale, 2003); and Adam Sandler (Michael, 2005)) have routinely employed the broad framework set out by Steve Seidman. Seidman maintains that the comedian's status as a well-known comic figure with a clearly defined extra-filmic persona serves to disrupt the verisimilitude of the fictional world, thereby generating the unique tension of the genre. Already and especially distinguishable, then (both Carrey and Sandler are known to us, of course, not just from other film comedies, but from stand-up, too), the comedian is less fictionally integrated than other characters: he has a special and privileged status that sets him apart from those around him and he is able to step outside and play with the rules of the film. Evidently, comedian comedy depends upon a specific relationship between the carnivalesque tendencies of the comic figure and the ameliorative tendencies of the narrative. Yet this relationship is a shifting one. Indeed, we may ask what becomes of this tension and, by extension, the genre in a climate of frequently unashamedly self-conscious and disruptive post-classical narratives, since these are surely a potential site of neutralisation for the comedian's divergence. One of Seidman's central observations is that comedian comedy constitutes a 'counter-tendency to the dominant mode of Hollywood fictional realism' (1981: 5). However, commentators have increasingly challenged this fundamental premise, not least because the notion of classical Hollywood narrative as a system that 'partakes in a closed structure that effaces marks of production and displaces itself as a product for consumption' (ibid.) has been disputed in recent years; moreover, the apparently unruly tendencies of the contemporary comedian comedy may no longer be entirely at odds with the concerns of the post-classical film, and, indeed, the post-classical rom-com, marked as they are by hybridity and self-referencing.

It may be this apparent negation of the comedian comedy's central drives that has prompted some critics to question its viability as a theoretical model, and for writers such as Jenkins and Brunovska Karnick to note that it has 'lost its distinctiveness since the early 1960s, reflecting the tendency towards hybridization within the postclassical Hollywood cinema' (1995: 161). Such 'hybridisation' is certainly symptomatic of the shifting preoccupations of the genre, as demonstrated by its recent conflation with the contemporary rom-com, itself an increasingly self-conscious genre. In fact, many comedian comics have worked within the rom-com genre, particularly in the latter part of their career. Comedian Ben Stiller seems to switch seamlessly between the two genres. Perhaps most famed for his roles in anarchistic comedies such as *Zoolander* (2001) and *Dodgeball: A True Underdog Story* (2004), he has also played the romantic lead in the more narrative-inclined rom-com *Duplex* (2003). Indeed, the rom-com may demand something of a maturing of the comedian comic. As such, my project here is to determine exactly how the genre manages the comedian's persona, as well as his distinctive performative talents.

Like any genre, the rom-com relies on a basic formula and reiterates expected narrative and ideological elements. Thus, most commonly, two people meet, various obstacles are thrown in their way, yet romance triumphs in the end and the genre is seen finally to celebrate the sanctity of the couple. This is, of course, an extremely simplified definition of the rom-com, and the genre has seen numerous variations upon its formula of late, such as changing gender pairings and male-centred narratives. It remains, though, that much derision has been directed at the rom-com, 'one of the most *generic* of genres' (Jeffers McDonald, 2007: 10), and stock usage of elements such as the meet-cute, the montage sequence illustrating the gradual bonding of the characters, scored to some sentimental or uplifting piece of music, as well as the happy ending, have commonly been seen as trite and cheesy, 'drearily predictable' (Zacharek, 1999).

Now, it is apparent that the contemporary rom-com has gone some way to insulating itself from such criticism with its increasing self-awareness. Thus, Jeffers McDonald opens her 2007 book *Romantic Comedy: Boy Meets Girl Meets Genre* with a discussion of Ephron's *Sleepless in Seattle* (1993), a film, she claims, 'wryly acknowledges both its own fictional status, and its place within a tradition of films about fate and love' (2007: 1). Issues of 'self-reflexivity and quotation' (ibid.: 2) have become of central concern to the contemporary rom-com and certainly fit with the mechanics of the comedian comedy. Such transparency is clearly paramount in a film like Marc Forster's *Stranger Than Fiction* (2006) starring another comedian comic, Will Ferrell, which is astutely aware of both the conventions of the rom-com and of storytelling more generally.[3] Perhaps of utmost importance, however, is that the Ephron and Forster films, as well as rom-coms like the defiantly titled *Love Actually* (2003), *Bridget Jones: The Edge of Reason* (2004) and *The Holiday* (2006), unashamedly uphold the unerring centrality of love, romance and fate. Indeed, it is in this sense that *Eternal Sunshine* and *Punch-Drunk Love* may offer up interesting sites of rom-com renegotiation. *Eternal Sunshine*, particularly, conveys romance as flawed and corrupt; the ending, where Joel and Clementine are compelled to repeat their past relationship in full knowledge that they will eventually resent one another, is subdued and resigned. On the surface, *Punch-Drunk Love* certainly offers a more conventional take on fate in the rom-com: Barry and Lena get together against all the odds. Yet, Anderson's film, I would argue, comes to fetishise romantic fate, revealing it, ultimately, as absurd and contrived.

Both Carrey and Sandler have played romantic leads in films other than the two I am discussing here. Yet, despite featuring romantic plots to some degree or other, the overriding sense in these films (Carrey's *The Mask* (1994), *Me, Myself and Irene* (2000) and *Bruce Almighty* (2003), and Sandler's *The Wedding Singer* (1998), *Anger Management* (2000) and *Mr. Deeds* (2002)) is that they are presentational forums; showcases for the actors' familiar anarchic, often crass personae.[4] With *Eternal Sunshine*, however, Gondry quite literally takes us inside Joel's mind to reveal his most personal memories, and, in fact, to invert the familiar Carrey persona. Like *The Truman Show* (1998) before it, and an increasing number of straight dramatic roles for Carrey (more recently Schumacher's *The Number 23* (2007)), *Eternal Sunshine* manages to obfuscate his larger-than-life persona, favouring, as does *Punch-Drunk Love*, a reticence and marked stillness that decentres the comedian comic. Stripped somewhat of their cartoonish facades, and reigned in by their respective 'no nonsense' directors, Joel and Barry are rather subdued characters. Both films evidently find their comedian comics in somewhat surreal worlds; yet, intriguingly, these are worlds where they are at their most naturalistic, reserved and, ultimately, romantically viable. Such rebalancing of the comedian comedy and consequent recasting of its central dynamic – Carrey and Sandler are, by and large, the still centres around which their dysfunctional romantic worlds turn, and not necessarily the frantic, bumbling misfits thrown into an otherwise 'normal' world – may serve to reinstate that all-important tension Seidman writes of, thus reinvigorating, reshaping and interrogating the comedian comedy.

Certainly, curiously transformative forces are at work in these films. On one level they are stylistically very disparate. Gondry's film utilises a gritty realism signalled primarily by the hand-held camera and pallid greyness of the *mise-en-scène*, while Anderson's sweeping technicolour and lavish brushstrokes evoke both the 1940s musical and 1950s romantic comedy. Yet they share something of an oppressive, claustrophobic atmosphere that impinges significantly upon the comedians. In short, both Carrey and Sandler are subservient here to the personal style and unique vision of their auteur-directors; both

Gondry and Anderson being known, of course, for their offbeat, edgy sensibilities and trademark experimentation with sound and narrative. Put simply, young directors Gondry and Anderson have their respective comedians on tight leashes: Carrey and Sandler no longer dominate the frame but are compromised, challenged and destabilised at the hands of these directors. Such calculated (mis)management, I suggest here, may, conversely, be liberating. In stripping Carrey and, particularly, Sandler of much of their baggage, in distancing them from our expectations, and, further, allowing the relationship/romance plots to somehow reinvigorate them, a new type of comedian comic, the post-comedian comic, emerges.

~ The post-comedian comic ~

Our initial meeting with Joel serves as a very economical illustration that this is a different Carrey vehicle. Gondry fades from black to an obtrusive close-up that reveals a conspicuously immobile Joel (we assume in bed), with his eyes closed. When he opens his eyes, his look is an odd, vacant one. It is a telling look that immediately suggests this particular Carrey character is somehow detached and unforthcoming; a different kind of Carrey figure, indeed. Carrey is almost physically unrecognisable as Joel: his voice, we soon hear, is gruff, whispery and sometimes inaudible, while Gondry's *cinema-verité* style is unforgiving on the usually vibrant Carrey. The predominance of blues and greys in the film's extremely limited colour palette cast Carrey as glum and sombre, and his skin pallid and coarse. He looks older, more wrinkled and weary. There is no trace of the buoyant, overacting Carrey, the physical plasticity, the mugging and flailing, the gleeful inhibition so often associated with him. Rather, we increasingly have the sense that Carrey is *under*-acting. He is certainly still loose limbed and sprawling, but this is a particularly naturalistic and restrained performance. Like Sandler as Barry, Carrey is markedly subdued as Joel, a brooding, introverted, unremarkable man with a constant air of apology and embarrassment. Even his apartment mirrors his blandness, with Patrick (Elijah Wood) later commenting that it is 'plain and uninspired'.

In his early exchanges with Clementine in the diner in Montauk and on the returning train, Joel is awkward and reticent. Clementine later tells him that he is 'kind of closed mouth', and she is right. He is inward and compulsive while Clementine is the opposite, a truly 'unruly woman' (Rowe, 1995b) who is much closer, in fact, to the familiar expressionistic and impulsive Carrey. Indeed, just as Joel constitutes an inversion of the Carrey persona, so, too, is Clementine an inversion of Winslet's delicate, English rose persona. Dressed in a bright orange pullover and sporting blue hair when we first meet her, she is loud, shifting and verging on the cartoonish at times. Like Lena – who is the one to pursue Barry, engineering their first meeting, date and kiss – at almost every turn, it seems, Clementine is the aggressor of this relationship. On the train (a clear metaphor for the anarchic journey she is set to take Joel on) Clementine's conversation is inane (she rambles on about her different hair colours) and her gestures are large, expressive and invasive. Constant chatter and movement, those traits usually attributed to Carrey, are displaced onto Clementine, rendering Joel's silence and stillness even more marked.

Thus, the opening shot is just the first of many the film uses to situate Joel as the largely still centre around which Gondry's complex world revolves. Framing is paramount, from the scene where Joel is rendered sandwiched between two other clients in the Lacuna waiting room, a sad figure clutching two black refuse bags of paraphernalia of his time with Clementine, to a subsequent scene where he is wired up to various devices as Stan (Mark Ruffalo) maps his memory in preparation for the later erasure process. The most sustained illustration of Joel's stillness, of course, occurs precisely during the significant section of the film where he lies, sedated in bed, while the largely inept team from Lacuna erase his memories of Clementine. In his new, just-out-of-the-packet pyjamas and crisp bedclothes, Joel cuts a sorry, detached figure as the technicians get progressively drunk and stoned around him. Here, Carrey's body, over which he usually has so much control, bounces involuntarily up and down with Stan and Mary's (Kirsten Dunst) every movement as they dance around him on the bed. Once again, those goofy antics usually attributed to Carrey are clearly being deflected, this time onto the Ruffalo and Dunst characters, and our expectations of Carrey's physicality are undercut.

A less sustained, but perhaps more telling moment of flouting expectations occurs early on in the film when Joel inexplicably ditches the train to work (we later find out he is compelled to go to Montauk to meet Clementine) and takes off back down the platform at speed. Though a series of shots reveal Carrey in familiar flailing movements as he rushes to catch the train on the opposite side and forces his problematic body in between its closing doors, these movements, within Gondry's altered world, are simply not comedic, or, more accurately, not allowed to be comedic. Gondry quite literally sets Carrey off on a different journey, committing him, and us, to a narrative of confounded expectations. Thus, when Joel discovers a significant dent down the side of his car and Gondry's intrusive, goading camera waits expectantly for a response, Joel registers little more than brief annoyance. Rather than providing an excuse for Carrey to freak out and display his usual contortion of limbs, Joel simply leaves a scribbled note on the windscreen of the next car reading 'Thank you!'. Gondry is teasing us (this scene takes place within the very first minutes of the film) and testing Carrey as Joel. In this sense, we might read Joel's mild annoyance as Carrey's, as his usual antics are being held in check. Indeed, Gondry has spoken of Carrey's frequent frustration during filming that he felt he was being 'stopped' from 'being funny' (Gondry, 2004).

Such restraining of Carrey is evident throughout, as is our sense, at times, that Carrey is bursting out of Joel. It is, in fact, precisely in keeping him in check for much of this film that Gondry brings Carrey's trademark persona into focus. The striking scene where he plays the young petulant Joel of his childhood past, hiding under the kitchen table and exhibiting familiar regressive behaviour, is anomalous and feels oddly like Carrey playing Carrey. Similarly, as a gleeful young Joel is bathed in an oversized sink, and Clementine says 'I've never seen you happier, baby-Joel,' we have perhaps never been more aware of the Carrey persona. There is a distance, here, with the boy-Joel not quite subsumed within Carrey as we might expect. It is fitting that these moments that most recall Carrey's familiar anarchic persona primarily occur in Joel's altered past when he tries to hide Clementine where she cannot be found by the team erasing his memory. This kind of behaviour may be allowed to exist in Joel's mind, but it is ill-fitting in Gondry's reality. Comedic performativity is smothered, curbed by directorial agency.

This is where the significance of the romance plot becomes paramount. For it is precisely in condemning Joel to a trajectory of complex relations with Clementine that the film works to unravel him. Thus, the voiceover of Joel of the beginning of the film tells us 'I'm not an impulsive person,' 'I'm incapable of making eye contact with a woman I don't know.' Yet the Joel of the apartment at the end impulsively urges Clementine to stay. In this penultimate scene *Eternal Sunshine*'s ultimate perversion of Hollywood romance and its trademark dark comedy come truly into fruition. In a central incongruity gag, the fledgling relationship between Joel and Clementine (they have just returned from their first night together on the frozen lake) is juxtaposed with its eventual collapse (they have returned to be confronted by their Lacuna tapes detailing one another's numerous vices). Present and past collide, and romance is conveyed as flawed and corrupt: the resentful Joel of the tape denounces Clementine's lack of education, her vocabulary, her hair ('It's all bullshit'), while the Joel of the apartment, who has just met Clementine, shakes his head and tells her sheepishly: 'I really like your hair. I really like your hair. I do.' As an offended Clementine goes to leave, against all the odds, then, Joel urges: 'Wait . . . I don't know, just wait . . . Just wait . . . I don't know. I want you to wait for, just a while.' While such a cautious delivery is hardly the stuff of grand declarations of love, this is quite possibly one of the most romantic moments in the film. Indeed, if Gondry's film posits the central question – would we, knowing that a relationship is ultimately doomed, repeat that relationship in order to experience the good times we shared? – *Eternal Sunshine* reticently but absolutely replies in the positive.[5] The film has certainly hinted at a hidden expressiveness within Joel with the drawings in his journal, yet it seems it has taken the influence of Clementine to unleash this impulsive side of him. Much like classic screwballs such as *Bringing Up Baby* (1938), the film reveals how pursuit by the female aggressor works to liberate the stuffy, reserved or reticent male partner. Despite, then, being somewhat kept in check by Gondry's diegesis, traces of the reckless Carrey are permitted to break through at the level of the relationship narrative.

A very different, and ultimately more complex and radical, reconfiguration of persona takes place in *Punch-Drunk Love*. In fact, Barry is, in many ways, a typical Sandler character. His rampant stupidity is certainly toned down, and he does not descend nearly as frequently as we might expect into moments of rage; but this is still the recognisable dim, childlike Sandler persona prone to bouts of anger. Thus, Anderson's is not a wholesale inversion of the Sandler persona as Gondry's is of Carrey. What is particularly significant is how Barry's actions are motivated and managed. This is essentially the same Sandler but, pitted against Anderson's suffocating diegesis – not to mention Barry's relentlessly overbearing sisters – everything begins to fall into place. Further, it is the romantic attentions of Lena that ultimately authenticate his actions: paired with her, Sandler's overarching demeanour fits, his otherwise wholly unacceptable antics are reasoned, and Sandler as Barry becomes sympathetic.

When we first encounter Barry he is at work, engaged in a monotonous telephone conversation and sitting at a small desk in the corner of a vast echoing warehouse, far away, we soon realise, from the exit. Anderson's widescreen and largely static camera effectively trap him within the cavernous space and denote the absurdity of Barry's isolation. Once again we are instantly faced with a character rendered completely detached, who does not dominate the frame as we might expect; and, once again, stillness predominates. Even as Anderson's trademark mobile camera takes off, the film world encroaches on Barry further. As he goes to move outside, his opening of the warehouse door is accompanied by the first of many harsh, grating spot effects. From hereon in, the film's powerful suffocation of him takes hold, and the true extent of Barry's outsider status begins to unravel. Anderson's world is thus seen to test Barry. But whereas Carrey as Joel is, for the most part, unyielding to Gondry's pressure, Sandler as Barry ultimately succumbs to the various forces operating upon him.

Indeed, it is Anderson's *sound* world that is particularly suffocating: Barry is goaded at every turn; by the eerie silence of the deserted industrial site at the beginning of the film; the loud, industrial sounds emanating from the warehouse and surroundings once the working day has begun; the cacophony of persistently jabbering, haranguing seven sisters; and by the experimental use of incessant drums and clicks scored by cult multi-instrumentalist Jon Brion. Significantly, Brion also scored *Eternal Sunshine*. Thus, a familiar sense of provocation occurs during Joel and Clementine's conversation on the train where increasingly dense instrumentation is utilised, not to fill the gaps in their continually aborted dialogue but to sound over their uneven conversation, further denoting Joel's awkwardness. On one level, the constantly discordant soundtrack in Anderson's film may serve to bring the audience into closer empathy with Barry as it is how he aurally experiences the world he feels is closing in on him. In this reading, Barry's largest obstacle in the search for love is himself: specifically his inappropriate and inept attempts to relate to those around him. Indeed, he often oversteps the mark in his relations with others, whether it is suggesting that a client call him at home or regaling the sex-line girl with completely unnecessary details about his work. Yet Anderson's awareness of and desire to play with the self-destructive Sandler persona is paramount. Various obstacles are constantly being thrown in his path and, though we know he is his own worst enemy, we feel his difficulties are greatly compounded by the unsympathetic world around him.

Barry is most under pressure, of course, when surrounded by all seven sisters, their spouses and children at the family birthday. In the climactic scene in the dining room Anderson typically backs him up against an imposing element of his *mise-en-scène* (a large display cabinet) and flanks him with a brother-in-law who looks on at him in bemusement and a sister who badgers him about his nervousness. Slowly inching closer towards Barry throughout, Anderson eventually traps him in shot, so much so that, even when the others have exited the frame, Barry appears strangely immobilised. As with his arrival at the house, where he attempts to enter and stalls three times, Barry tries to move, but is held back. So typically mobile is Anderson's camera that when it rests, as it does so noticeably in these examples, its stasis is dynamic and, further, provocative. When Barry finally moves, he is not followed. The subsequent, notably lengthy shot, like Gondry's of Joel as he discovers the dent in his car, is an expectant one: a wide shot of assorted family members preparing to sit down at the table – accompanied by the women's continual chatter about their brother's shortcomings – is conspicuous by Barry's absence. Goaded, it seems, from every conceivable angle, it is no surprise when breaking glass is heard and Anderson cuts to a wider reverse shot to reveal Barry repeatedly kicking at and shattering the sliding glass doors of the dining room. Here he is trapped once again by the film's tableau-like framing and *mise-en-scène* (Anderson sandwiches Sandler, with his back to us, between the broken panes and the assorted witnesses), and the momentary silence that ensues is just as suffocating as the previous cacophony of sounds.

Certainly, we are constantly being reminded of Barry's dysfunctional alignment with those around him. Yet, as in *Eternal Sunshine*, it is the romance plot that serves to change him: not to loosen him up, as in the case of Joel, but to further reign him in. I would argue that it is subsequent to meeting Lena that Barry's actions become explainable. Thus, his bursts of outrage at the brothers and the mattress company/sex-line boss are motivated by his desire to protect Lena. Further, when he is with her, the constant inquisition he is subjected to throughout the film ('Why are you wearing that suit?', 'What's all that pudding?', 'Whose is that piano? What is this pudding? Why is it here?') is replaced by Lena's unquestioning acceptance. Rather than alienate Lena as we might expect, Barry's peculiarities seem to intrigue her and, further, are even encouraged by her. In the film's central love scene, a bizarre exchange of dialogue between the two, initiated by Lena, serves to authenticate Barry's absurd ways:

Barry: I'm sorry – I forgot to shave.
Lena: Your face is so adorable, and your skin and your cheek. I want to bite it. I want to bite your cheek and chew on it. It's so fucking cute.
Barry: I'm looking at your face and I just want to smash it. I just want to fucking smash it with a sledgehammer and squeeze it. You're so pretty.
Lena: I want to chew your face and I want to scoop out your eyes. And I want to eat them. Chew them and suck on them.

Such an exchange is highly idiosyncratic, and at a great remove from the realism of Joel and Clementine's exchanges. While it still serves to distance Barry from the rest of the diegetic world, it works to unite him and Lena, to render them a perfect match for one another. With the final words of the film, Lena's 'Here we go', we have the sense that this is the beginning of their very own merry-go-round of romance. Barry and Lena, it is clear, exist in their own little romantic bubble.

Now, in a less self-conscious film, we might interpret their coming together as a simple reiteration of the centrality of romantic fate: that there is someone for everyone. But matters are much more complex, here, for those things that surely ought to be a deterrent to Lena, even within the throws of infatuation (Barry's social ineptitude, first and foremost), seem, inexplicably, to provide no significant obstacle to their romance. I would argue, then, that although it is the Gondry film that revolves around the absurd premise of memory erasure, it is the Anderson film that is ultimately most at a remove from realism. Thus, *Punch-Drunk Love* engages in some highly stylised, presentational moments of romance. When Barry and Lena first meet, a flare in the lens suggests an immediate, inexplicable magnetism between them; a sweeping orchestral score sounds as they leave the restaurant after their first date, and reaches a crescendo as they share their first kiss;

an iris in on their hands and an embrace in shadow, complete with a balletic leg lift for Lena, invoke those classical Hollywood markers of romance. So self-consciously staged and unmotivated are these moments, and so simplistic are love and romance ultimately revealed to be, that Anderson must surely be questioning their validity.

~ *Refocusing, reinvigorating* ~

Such juxtaposition of the comedian and surrounding world is, as I have suggested, entirely symptomatic of the comedian comedy genre. Yet it is clear that the tension Seidman identifies between the carnivalesque tendencies of the comic figure and the ameliorative tendencies of the narrative is being more than just reworked and inverted in these films. There is a calculated distance between Barry and those around him (he tells a brother-in-law after his outburst at the party that he doesn't 'know how other people are'), and, rather than him being at odds with the world, it appears as if the world is at odds with him. While both of these films, in fact, are clearly playing with their comedians, rather than having their comedians play with their worlds – these are undoubtedly Gondry and Anderson's playgrounds, and not Carrey and Sandler's – with Anderson's film especially we have the sense that he is rigorously interrogating the comic persona of Sandler and his place and resonance within the fiction. Though Seidman argues that it is the extra-fictional baggage the comedian brings to the film text that serves to dislodge him within the fiction, here it is the suffocating diegesis (in this sense, *Anderson's* baggage) that tests him, makes him different, renders him carnivalesque. Further, it is such mishandling of Sandler that serves to underscore the liberating possibilities afforded by the romance plot. Matched with Lena, Barry is ameliorated. No longer the inexplicably deranged 'spanner in the works' (Krutnik, 1995), Sandler as Barry is rendered genuine and understandable. Indeed, *Punch-Drunk Love* may encourage us to rethink our conception of the overarching Sandler persona. Through the lens of Anderson's complex, highly self-conscious world we may be able to see through it; reread it; recomprehend it; and bring it into focus as the masquerade of a lonely and unhinged, yet ultimately understandable and relatable lead. Persona, then, aided and abetted by the romance narrative, is what ultimately realigns the comedian comic within the fiction.

The overriding sense in both of these films is that Gondry and Anderson are refocusing; training their respective lenses on Carrey and Sandler and subtly adjusting their/our view. It is this that lends these films their overwhelmingly shifting, transitory feel. We may recall the early scene outside Barry's office where Anderson positions us behind Barry as he looks, inexplicably, down the empty street. As we begin to wonder what it is he is looking at, Anderson shifts focus, sharpening Barry's view, but blurring ours of Barry in the process. Indeed, this is the moment where Anderson runs with a different Sandler and may be akin to Gondry's literal change of track for Joel as he ditches the train to work for the one that will take him to Montauk and Clementine, and to a different trajectory for Carrey.

These films are ultimately operating on a more complex level than simply showcasing familiar comedians in unexpected and dysfunctional comedic/romantic roles. Rather, their manipulation of their respective comedians may serve to shed new light on the comedian and romantic comedies. The overriding emphasis on stillness, on pulling the brakes on the comic persona, and ultimately attributing him the kind of sensibility that might make him credible in a romantic setting may align *Eternal Sunshine of the Spotless Mind* and *Punch-Drunk Love* with other recent low-key comedian comedies such as Bill Murray's *Broken Flowers* (2005) (see McCabe, Chapter 12 in this collection) and Steve Carell's *Little Miss Sunshine* (2006), both of which seem to similarly restrain their respective comedians. Further, Gondry's film, particularly, clearly resonates with recent rom-coms such as *The Break-Up* (2006) and *The Last Kiss* (2006) which, in their admission that romance can be vicious, that no relationship proceeds as harmoniously as it does in the beginning, are intent on deglamourising romance. Less anarchic and less performer driven, the post-comedian rom-com signals the perfect partnership of the comedian comedy and the more transparent operations of the recent rom-com, suggesting that the love affair between these popular genres has only just begun.

14 'I Believe that if I Haven't Found my Prince Charming Already that I Will; or he Will Find me, if he Hasn't Already'

Jennifer Lopez, Romantic Comedy and Contemporary Stardom

~ *Alan Dodd and Martin Fradley*[1] ~

I think it's hard to find the right person. But I don't think I'll never find somebody. I'm an incurable romantic. (Jennifer Lopez, cited in Case and Martinez, 2002: 35)

We all know that the secret to a happy marriage is . . . Oh, who am I kidding?! (Jennifer Lopez (as herself), *Will and Grace*[2])

THESE CONFLICTING STATEMENTS serve as a useful synopsis of Jennifer Lynn Lopez's apparently contradictory position within the amorous generic terrain of romantic comedy. On the one hand, Lopez espouses her devout belief in the monogamous utopia of romantic love; on the other, the star makes a comically frank onscreen allusion to her notoriously problematic off-screen love life. Indeed, it is our contention that no other contemporary celebrity can match Lopez's ability to illustrate the concurrent trials and tribulations of romantic (im)possibility in the melodramatic narratives of her highly publicised private life. To this end, films such as *The Wedding Planner* (2001), *Maid in Manhattan* (2002), *Gigli* (2003), *Shall We Dance?* (2004) and *Monster-in-Law* (2005) are intriguing star vehicles that pivot upon a dense intertextual relay between the generic norms of the contemporary rom-com and the well-documented tragedy-cum-farce of Lopez's high-profile romantic dalliances and celebrity relationships. In turn, Lopez's synergistic metamorphoses between dancer, singer, actress, fashion designer, perfumer, restaurateur and gossip column favourite cultivate a saturation omnipresence that is illustrative of both the highly accelerated commercial logics of contemporary 'celebrification' and the absolute centrality of star personae to recent rom-coms.

Of course, this dialectic between the public and private lives of celebrities is central to their allure, and audience readings of Hollywood films are always already informed by the extra-textual paraphernalia of star biographies, celebrity magazines and so on. To this end, it is relatively easy to understand how the sanctioned voyeurism of prurient celebrity magazines colludes with star vehicles such as *She's the One* (1996), *Picture Perfect* (1997), *My Best Friend's Wedding* (1997), *The Object of My Affection* (1998), *Runaway Bride* (1999), *Notting Hill* (1999), *Along Came Polly* (2004) and *The Break-Up* (2006) deliberately to refract and reimagine the rocky extra-textual love lives of other female stars Julia Roberts and Jennifer Aniston. This interplay often seems particularly over-determined in the case of Lopez, however, wherein her troubled romantic life fuels the reflexive machinations of her romantic star vehicles. Indeed, Lopez's well-documented adventures in serial monogamy have become perhaps the cornerstone of her star image: her three marriages and relationships with hip-hop mogul Sean 'P. Diddy' Combs and actor Ben Affleck have to date attracted voluminous media attention that has arguably overshadowed her careers as either actress or pop starlet. Moreover, within the punitive moral economy that governs the contemporary celebrity sphere, romantic failure is the emotional pound of flesh extracted in exchange for Lopez's global success.

As a successful second-generation Latina immigrant, Lopez's stardom serves to epitomise the most utopian aspects of the USA's key national mythologies. Biographer Marissa Charles' (2004) hyperbolic and highly aspirational account of Lopez's self-determined upward social mobility is, therefore, illustrative in its rhetoric. Beginning with childhood dreams of stardom, Charles outlines Lopez's archetypal rags-to-riches story:

> Everything she set out to do, she has done ... Her story speaks to millions of young people around the world, because it is the American dream personified; the idea that that nation was founded upon. No matter who you are, where you come from or how much money you have, you can do anything you put your mind to ... In the end, [Lopez] got what she wanted. The movies, the fame, the cash, the clothes, the

jewellery, the adoration, the glamour, the glitz are all hers . . . (2004: 162–4)

However, absolutely central to the Lopez star image are the catastrophic romantic liaisons that are the structurally necessary underside of her professional successes. Other biographical accounts make this dichotomy explicit, suggesting that with the sudden onset of fame, Lopez found that 'striking a balance between professional success and personal happiness is an enormous challenge,' a challenge that poses a question that is central to the Lopez celebrity text: 'just how hard is [she] willing to work to have it all – and keep it?' (Tracy, 2000: 12). This rhetorical question is, we argue, fairly unambiguously couched within the popular discursive topography of what Sarah Projanksy (2001) dubs 'choice postfeminism', a seemingly benign cultural discourse that understands second-wave feminism as having succeeded in providing women with clear and self-evident lifestyle options regarding the relationship between marriage, motherhood and potential career trajectories. Lopez's glamorous embodiment of the introjective pleasures of commodity feminism also means that her image incorporates the key qualities of 'the sensuous, feminine, to-be-looked-at postfeminist woman' (ibid.: 80–1). This brand of celebratory post-feminist success is not without its pitfalls, however, and Lopez's celebrity is consciously structured within this contemporary 'everygirl' dilemma. 'When it comes to a balance between my professional and my personal life,' Lopez has remarked, 'it's a slow learning curve' (Samuel, 2006: 14).

~ *'I'm real': from* Out of Sight *to* The Wedding Planner ~

Lopez's first venture into romantic comedy's generic territory was the rom-com/crime thriller *Out of Sight* (1998). Lopez plays Federal Marshall Karen Sisco, a professionally and sexually confident female hero whose affair with her bank-robbing leading man (George Clooney) pivots upon the movie's neo-screwball dynamic and its comically sublimated sexual tensions. *Out of Sight* followed Lopez's Hollywood breakthrough in *Anaconda* (1997), a role that has earned critical approval for its subversion of Latina stereotypes. As both Mary Beltran (2004) and Yvonne Tasker (2006) point out, *Anaconda* and *Out of*

Sight ambivalently mobilise stereotypes about Latin ethnic 'toughness' to underscore the authenticity of Lopez's onscreen personae. Unlike *Anaconda*, however, *Out of Sight*'s comic dénouement – Karen gets her man, both professionally and romantically – adheres to generic conventions by ultimately valorising the heterosexual couple. This oscillation between professional 'toughness' and personal vulnerability also finds its way into her other quasi-action features *The Cell* (2000), *Angel Eyes* (2001) and *Enough* (2002). More importantly, it is this hard/soft dialectic that underpins the recuperative narrative trajectories of her rom-coms.

In the years after *Out of Sight* there were a number of major fluctuations in the nature of Lopez's fame. By the release of *The Wedding Planner* a myriad of images of the star had proliferated. An emergent and commercially successful career as a pop singer, a high-profile romance with hip-hop mogul Sean 'Puffy' Combs (followed by a spectacular break-up amidst rumours of firearm offences) and an apparently spontaneous second marriage to dancer-choreographer Cris Judd all combined to dramatically raise Lopez's celebrity profile between 1998 and 2001. These events effected a marked change in the nature of her celebrity, so much so that *The Wedding Planner*, as we detail below, is clearly suffused with, and overwritten by, the increasingly autonomous Lopez persona. Indeed, this was also the point at which she adopted the brand-name J.Lo. With her own clothing range, a best-selling perfume ('Glow' by J.Lo) and number one album (*J.Lo*), Lopez had become the figurehead of a substantial commercial empire. Viewing *The Wedding Planner* in the context of her saturation omnipresence in 2001 establishes a useful paradigm through which we can understand how the generic conventions of the rom-com are renegotiated in the light of Lopez's altering star image.

No feature of the rom-com synthesises the genre's core elements as conveniently as the wedding ceremony. For it is here, at the altar of the romantic imaginary, that the traditions of the past and the ideological flux of the present come together, where the internal turmoil of the most private, personal longings are declared, celebrated and legitimised in the public sphere, and where the problem of the eternal conflict between the sexes is heightened, investigated and then purposefully – nay, fetishistically – resolved. Indeed, from its very opening scenes, *The Wedding Planner* mobilises these generic motifs whilst simultaneously negotiating its lead actress's professionally commanding and emotionally controlled persona. Immediately establishing the costly, highly regimented and emotionally fraught nature of the proceedings, eponymous 'planner' Mary Fiore (Lopez) calmly and professionally diffuses a series of potential catastrophes from behind the scenes. Naturally, all of this quite deliberately invites comparisons with Lopez's real-life business ventures, the matrimonial industry functioning as a metaphor for her unified and commercially synergistic empire.

Just as Mary finds herself in control of every aspect of the weddings she is hired to organise, the commercial dispersal of Lopez's unified celebrity text manifests itself most obviously in the glamorous photographic images of the star approved for the publicity apparatus that mediates her public persona. Indeed, the extreme control Lopez maintains over her physical image finds its comedic counterpoint in *The Wedding Planner*, a film that frequently satisfies generic expectations by glorifying in the indignity of the body. From Katharine Hepburn's torn dress in *Bringing Up Baby* (1938) to Cameron Diaz mistaking Ben Stiller's semen for hair gel in *There's Something About Mary* (1998), women in romantic comedies are often the centrepiece of physical gags. Mary Fiore is no exception to this, often finding herself in spectacularly farcical situations that revel in the apparent loss of control over her high-maintenance appearance and professional demeanour. These comic set-pieces include the initial meeting between Mary and soon-to-be-client Steve Edison (Matthew McConaughey) in which the heel of her Gucci shoe gets caught in a subway grate, a battle with a runaway horse and an unexpected and suitably embarrassing public encounter with her ex-fiancé from whom Mary (unsuccessfully) tries to hide. In addition, the sight of Mary/Lopez crawling on the floor and attempting to conceal herself under a table is one of several visual gags that deliberately draws attention to Lopez's (in)famous posterior. These situations are not simply mechanically pre-scripted rom-com conventions, however; they also celebrate the possibility of a rupture between the ostentatious Lopez persona-cum-empire as represented in the press and that of the altogether more human Mary/Lopez as seen on screen.

This possibility is underlined by the transparent rhetorical homology that exists between Lopez as unattainable object of desire and Mary's status in the film. As awed minor characters speculate that this consummate organiser of fairytale weddings 'must lead *such* a romantic life', the viewer is offered a melancholy vision of Mary's lonely single life outside the performative realm of work: quietly preparing a meal for one, settling down to eat whilst watching *Antiques Roadshow* on television, going to bed early and alone. By providing a voyeuristic glimpse into the apparently 'real' life behind the glamorous, controlled masquerade of Mary's professional persona, *The Wedding Planner* offers a reflexive commentary upon what Lopez is 'really' like. The film's central conceit – that Mary has devoted herself to a career that successfully provides romantic wish fulfilment for her clients but never herself – is precisely the dilemma that Lopez has apparently struggled with. While Mary's sublimated romantic longings are lived out vicariously through her clients, so too do these romantic star vehicles reflexively fulfil a compensatory – even fetishistic – function for the 'real' Jennifer Lopez.

The Wedding Planner also synergises the relationship between Lopez's cinematic and musical personae by employing her single, 'Love Don't Cost a Thing', over the movie's closing credits. Ostensibly penned as a riposte to former beau Sean Combs, the problematic alignment of the song's anti-materialist sentiment with the film's polished glamour creates a text that is – inevitably – ideologically contradictory. Moreover, the R&B flavour of the track is symptomatic of the constant negotiations regarding her ambiguously racially coded onscreen personae. While she cultivates a sense of Americanness much of the time, the commercial aesthetic and cross-demographic appeal of Lopez's hybridised musical output seamlessly incorporates Latin-inflected rhythms and instrumentation as well as elements of (white) pop, (African-American) hip-hop, soul and R&B traditions. In much the same way, such racial indeterminacy in her musical output is continually, if ambivalently, foregrounded on screen. This fluid attitude to race and ethnicity is highlighted in *The Wedding Planner*'s centrepiece: a sexualised tango with McConaughey that, while synergistically pointing towards Lopez's off-screen pop career and Latin roots, nevertheless highlights the bizarre incongruity of Mary's *Italian* heritage.

Like many of Lopez's film roles, *The Wedding Planner* sets up an ambivalent tension between Mary's familial/ethnic background and her ambitions as an Americanised second-generation immigrant. While Mary's traditionalist father attempts to coax her into marrying Massimo (Justin Chambers), an enthusiastic Italian suitor who has held a torch for her since they were children, Mary instead wants to focus on her career. Thus, on the one hand *The Wedding Planner* seeks to rectify Mary's emotional repression and debilitating control freakery

('I've never met anyone before who alphabetises their credit cards,' Edison tells a transparently mortified Mary), whilst on the other the film struggles to coherently contain its racial/ethnic discourses. Mary/Lopez's post-feminist individualism and defiance of traditional immigrant conservatism conflates diegetic and biographical narratives: despite being handsome, loyal and infatuated, Massimo's unsuitability as a partner is signalled primarily by his weak grasp of English, a crude trope that underlines his only partly assimilated ethnicity. But just as the down-to-earth Mary is transparently differentiated from her neurotic middle-class clients, paediatrician Edison's attraction to her is also coded as being racially motivated. As the couple-to-be watch romantic musical *Flirtation Walk* (1934) screened under the stars in Golden Gate Park, Edison discards all his M&Ms except the brown ones. 'They have less artificial colourings,' he tells Mary, because 'chocolate's already brown' (See Fig 14.1).

The film's emphatic stress on the down-to-earth authenticity of Mary/ Lopez at this juncture is more than a little over-determined, particularly as the same rhetorical point about Mary/Lopez's 'authentic' brown- ness is reiterated in the movie's closing scene as the couple watch *Two Tickets to Broadway* (1951). Even allowing for the textual evasions of making Mary Italian-American, *The Wedding Planner*'s transparent investment in a dubiously essentialist conception of non-white identity both draws attention to Lopez's to-be-looked-at ethnic difference whilst simultaneously seeking to contain it.

14.1: Colour-coded candy: Mary (Lopez) and Steve (Matthew McConaughey) discuss the 'authenticity' of brown M&Ms in *The Wedding Planner*.

~ *Life is not a fairy tale?*: *Maid in Manhattan* ~

Maid in Manhattan continued the commercial integration of Lopez's many career strands. Contextually, the end of her second marriage and, subsequently, her hugely public affair with Ben Affleck dominated the tabloids and elevated Lopez to an even higher echelon of celebrity. As single mother and hotel maid, hard-working Marisa Ventura (Lopez) is romantically 'rescued' from her impoverished existence by wealthy Republican senator John Marshall (Ralph Fiennes) in what has been pithily described as '*Pretty Woman 2* for Latinas' (Knadler, 2005: 4). The implausibility of this scenario is, however, tempered by its acceptability within the self-conscious terms of contemporary rom-coms. Like the overt references to classical Hollywood romances in *The Wedding Planner* – a film that both acknowledges and then disavows the possibility that 'life is *not* a fairytale' – *Maid in Manhattan* is a post-liberationist exercise in 'harmless' nostalgia that explores the mythologies of classical Hollywood's romantic imaginary.

Of course, the title's deliberate pun emphasises that this is primarily a vehicle for Lopez who, as proud 'Nuyorican', was also made in Manhattan. It is hardly coincidental, then, that the film opens with Hollywood's standardised visual shorthand for the immigrant dream: a sweeping aerial shot of the Statue of Liberty and the lower Manhattan skyline (see Deborah Jermyn's essay, Chapter 1 in this collection). Yet as *Maid in Manhattan* topped the US box office Lopez also had a hugely successful single in the pop charts. The notorious lyrics of 'Jenny From the Block' – 'Don't be fooled by the rocks that I got / I'm still, I'm still Jenny from the block / Used to have a little, now I have a lot / No matter where I go, I know where I came from (from the Bronx!)' – espoused a heady combination of immigrant work ethic, entrepreneurial know-how, post-feminist economic autonomy and a 'bling' valorisation of conspicuous consumption. However, the striving, streetwise sentiment of the track contrasted sharply with a promotional video that presented Lopez lounging on yachts and in luxurious apartments with her square-jawed film star boyfriend. Although 'Jenny From the Block's' rags-to-riches narrative echoed both her star biography and the narrative trajectory of Marisa in *Maid in Manhattan*, the dispersal of Lopez's image across the entertainment landscape had become so conflicted that all semblance of 'ghetto' authenticity had become irrevocably problematised.

Stephen Knadler offers a detailed and perceptive critique of the assimilative fantasy that underpins *Maid in Manhattan*'s narrative structure, as one that values the traditional immigrant combination of humbleness and hard work. As an ethnic and economic 'outsider' in an over-privileged white social milieu, it is the consummate professionalism of Lopez's character that is again to the fore. Once more, the strain that the working life of Lopez's character puts on her personal relationships is key to *Maid in Manhattan*'s reflexively melodramatic narrative. As Charles suggests, media focus on Lopez's tangled romantic life between 2000 and 2004 – a period that featured two broken engagements and a short-lived marriage – helped fuel the perception that there was 'an inverse relationship between the successes in her professional life and the failures of her personal partnerships: the higher she would soar in the one, the deeper she would fall in the other' (2004: 126). This somewhat dystopian narrative trope is played out through Marisa's strained relationship with her son, Ty (Tyler Posey). When she is delayed at work before his school recital, stressed initially by his mother's unpunctual arrival and then by his absentee father's non-appearance, Ty falters and is unable to complete his well-rehearsed speech. That Ty's speech is about the flawed, contradictory personality of Richard Milhous Nixon – the ultimate recent US failed father – only emphasises the mournful conservatism as the heart of this ostensibly lighthearted romantic fable.

The parallels between character and star biography in *Maid in Manhattan* are, as ever, central to the Lopez text: like the daily journey cited in the title of Lopez's debut album *On the 6* – the aural document of her pre-fame years – Marisa travels by train from the predominantly non-white working-class enclave of the Bronx into midtown Manhattan to work. More significantly, *Maid in Manhattan* is far from obliquely self-referential in its critique of tabloid surveillance. Ever since becoming a fixture in the gossip columns the star has consistently maintained that there is a vast gulf between the 'real' Jennifer Lopez and the monstrous diva constructed by the media. As early as 2000, gently recuperative profiles appeared in the media in order to suture the more problematic fissures in her star image: a lengthy piece in *Empire* magazine disclosed that, in the flesh, Lopez 'bears scant relation to her tabloid reputation . . . Demure rather than sultry, self-possessed as opposed to arrogant . . . the overall effect is really quite charming' (Kennedy, 2000: 71). In addition, Lopez has regularly claimed in interviews that she is '*mis*interpreted and misjudged' by the popular press (Iley, 2005: 55).

Press intrusion and media misrepresentation are in turn homologically central themes in *Maid in Manhattan*. Senator Marshall, it transpires, is neither heartless right-wing populist nor the person salaciously represented in the tabloids. Indeed, like Lopez, Marshall is a victim of the panopticon of fame's judgemental scopic regime (Redmond, 2006). Marshall's predicament is thus effectively a synecdoche for Lopez's contemporaneous encounters with the media, something that becomes transparent when Marisa is misidentified by the paparazzi as Marshall's girlfriend, their unrelenting obsession with his private life clearly mirroring Lopez's own subjection to the intrusive media gaze.

Moreover, both Beltran (2002; 2004) and Knadler have critically interrogated the popular media focus on Lopez's infamous posterior in the late 1990s and early 2000s. For the latter, the insistent emphasis on the Latina star's 'jungle butt' serves primarily to trivialise and 'bleach out' any threatening elements of ethnic difference, whilst at the same time sustaining a fetishistic and reified aura of sexualised exoticism. Whilst Beltran also notes the assimilative processes at work in the construction of Lopez's image, her more ambivalent analysis of Lopez's emergent stardom in the late 1990s suggests that the star's wilful celebration of her non-normative (read: non-white) physique – her to-be-looked-at-Latina-ness – also has the potential to disrupt the status quo vis-à-vis hegemonic standards of physical normality. However, this assimilative shift towards the containment of Lopez's ethnicity is summarised by her responses when questioned about her body in interviews in 2002 and 2004. In the earlier interview, Lopez confidently and unapologetically states that she has 'a normal Latin woman's body':

> My mum raised me to be very proud of my race and how I looked. We never gazed at magazines and said, 'Oh God, that's how I should look'. My mother and aunts were all beautiful, voluptuous women, and it helped me to become comfortable with my own skin. (Case and Martinez, 2002: 34)

By 2004, however, Lopez's responses to similar questions are markedly more guarded, playing down her ethnicity and stressing her (implicitly 'white') everywoman characteristics. Informed by the journalist that Lopez's 'head-to-toe pink, shimmery make-up and relaxed friendliness don't conceal the don't-mess-with-me business attitude beneath', this description of her glamorous femininity coupled with confessions about 'universal' bodily insecurities serves to counterbalance Lopez's 'tough' business sense:

> *I'm like anybody else*, in that you have the body type you have, and you know what you have to do to get in form. *I'm only human* . . . sometimes I feel great about myself, at other times I think, 'I have work to do' . . . Also, when I don't work out, I have issues with my hips and thighs, *like most women*. (Steinherr, 2004: 153–4, emphasis added)

Maid in Manhattan seems to embody the competing logics of Lopez's fragmented celebrity text in both its comically auto-fetishistic focus on her celebrated *culo* and its appeal to an 'everywoman' fantasy. In one scene, Marisa tries on a wealthy guest's $5000 conspicuously all-white Dolce and Gabbana suit and is subsequently misperceived by Marshall as a fellow guest. Notwithstanding Knadler's entirely valid objection that Marisa/Lopez slipping casually into the size six trousers of an emaciated white socialite casually denies 'that there are any real bodily or class-based differences between Puerto Ricans from the Bronx and Daughters of the Revolution from the Hamptons' (2005: 6), the scene does make sense in terms of Lopez's high-fashion sense and extra-textual clothing range. Like the opera sequence in *Pretty Woman* (1990), then, Marisa's appropriation of designer apparel naturalises (implicitly white, middle-class) 'good taste' and reflexively emphasises Lopez's supposedly intuitive, sassy-classy *habitus*. As such, the vacuously wealthy socialites who make up the hotel's core clientele are clearly positioned as structuring others who allow *Maid in Manhattan* to disavow Lopez's narcissism whilst simultaneously celebrating her 'natural' beauty and exquisite taste. That *Maid in Manhattan*'s romantic narrative pivots on Marshall misidentifying Marisa-from-the-block as one of these effortlessly glamorous guests reiterates the over-determined and contradictory nature of Lopez's star image.

Walking with Marshall and her son in Central Park in another scene, Marisa sits down on a park bench only to inadvertently place her booty upon a magazine featuring Marshall's image on the cover (see Fig. 14.2). 'I nearly sat on your face,' apologises Marisa, a crude double entendre which nevertheless foreshadows her 'in your face' vocalisations about the impoverished New York housing projects that

14.2: An *ass*et to her profession, or 'bleaching out' ethnicity? Marisa (Lopez), Senator Marshall (Ralph Fiennes) and the white Dolce & Gabbana suit in *Maid in Manhattan*.

Marshall passes through on the election campaign trail. For all its inevitable political limitations and contradictions, *Maid in Manhattan* nonetheless ambivalently foregrounds Marisa's class and ethnic status through Lopez's bolshie characterisation and the confidently physical thrust of her star image. However, the commercial impetus of the film as a vehicle for Lopez and her ancillary empire is made transparent when, in true Cinderella fashion, a spectacular peach frock allows Marisa to once again class-pass (this time with Marshall's knowledge) on a grand public stage. Following a quasi-pornographic montage of conspicuous consumption that self-consciously echoes *Pretty Woman*'s Rodeo Drive sequence, Marisa is informed by a colleague that 'tonight the maid is a lie and *this* is what you really are.' Reflexively, of course, the beautiful glamour puss from the block *is* the 'reality' of Lopez's celebrity text, and *Maid in Manhattan*'s celebration of the pleasures and transformative potential of commodified femininity neatly assert the introjective possibilities of Lopez's affordable fashion range and best-selling fragrances.

~ *'I follow my heart, I make mistakes, and I just keep going':* Shall We Dance? ~

Excluding a brief cameo in *Jersey Girl* (2004), *Shall We Dance?* was Lopez's first feature film after the misjudged vanity project *Gigli*; more significantly, it was also her first major commercial outing since the public announcement of her split from fiancé Ben Affleck. Dubbed 'Bennifer' by wags in the tabloid press, Lopez and Affleck's two-year relationship was the subject of intense media focus, and in early 2004 – amidst tabloid stories about Affleck's supposed infidelity – the couple officially broke up, issuing a statement claiming their relationship was the victim of excessive media attention. After the abject critical and commercial failure of *Gigli* – a romantic crime caper featuring Lopez as a lesbian improbably converted to heterosexuality by the amorous prowess of co-star Affleck – *Shall We Dance?* was a relatively low-key recuperative performance that attempts to suture the gap between the generic pleasures of the rom-com and the painful schisms in Lopez's personal life.

Meanwhile, Lopez's fourth album, *Rebirth*, was released in early 2005. Interviews from the period saw the star offering commentary upon the personal upheaval of her *annus horribilus*, portraying 2004 as 'a tough, transitional year': 'It was a growing year. Things happened that haven't before and I believe they were meant for me. You don't learn things through happy times . . . it really is a rebirth for me, and I'm having tons of rebirths' (Iley, 2005: 56).

In an attempt to regain control of her image after the media overkill surrounding 'Bennifer', Lopez's promotion of *Shall We Dance?* was relatively low-key. In interviews she maintained a consistently guarded tone, stressing that she was no longer prepared to divulge details about her 'private' relationships. Lopez plays Paulina, an enigmatic and introverted dance instructor whose talents as a professional dancer have been sidelined following a traumatic break-up with her romantic and professional dance partner. John Clark (Richard Gere) is an overworked lawyer whose repetitive daily commute serves as a metaphor for his professional and personal anomie, a kind of bland middle-class death-in-life that also afflicts his similarly careerist wife, Beverley (Susan Sarandon). One night on his way home, John spots Paulina standing mournfully in the window of Miss Mitzi's Dance School and is enraptured by this melancholy glimpse into another, more exotic, world. As the narrative progresses, it becomes clear that *Shall We Dance?* is a gently comic melodrama about personal masks and repression wherein 'dancing' functions as a metaphor for the liberating expression of the authentic self: underneath Paulina/Lopez's cold, professional veneer hides a vulnerable, passionate soul; behind John's grey flannel suit there lurks vibrancy and repressed romantic vigour. The film's central thematic trope – the oppressive conformity of everyday life and the liberating, 'authentic' release that dance provides – serves as a negotiation of the post-'Bennifer' Lopez persona.

It is the liminal, transformative space of Miss Mitzi's which, in the tradition of the classical musical, permits the students freedom from the stifling restrictions of their everyday lives. Frequently imbued with warm reds and oranges (in contradistinction to the dominant greys of John's commuter train, for example), the *mise-en-scène* of the dance studio is the film's central expressive space, and it is this space in which Paulina is emotionally self-imprisoned. Indeed, *Shall We Dance?* is quite explicit in evoking the sublimation involved in Paulina's heartbroken withdrawal from heteromantic pursuits, something homologously underlined in contemporaneous interviews which stressed that Lopez 'uses a heavy workload to anaesthetise herself' (Iley, 2005: 56) from personal unhappiness. Most obviously, a centrepiece tango between Paulina and John allows Lopez to showcase her talents as a dancer whilst emphasising the necessarily unconsummated passion between the leads. Leaving them both panting and soaked in sweat, this choreographed coupling illustrates Paulina's earlier description of the rumba as 'a vertical expression of a horizontal wish':

> You have to hold her like the skin on her thigh is your reason for living. Let her go like your heart's being ripped from your chest. Pull her back like you're going to have your way with her right here on the dance floor. And then finish like she's ruined you for life.

That this speech is followed by a cut from Paulina's breathless features to a pasta pot boiling over in Beverley's kitchen only reiterates that the Latin energies embodied by Lopez (and subsequently introjected by her pupils) are the film's antidote to the stifling repressiveness of 'white' bourgeois normality. As John and Beverley's marriage is eventually reignited after the latter witnesses her husband dancing, Paulina abandons her voluntary withdrawal from the professional ballroom scene and, like the reborn Lopez, re-emerges ready for new professional challenges and, implicitly, a renewed zeal for heteromantic commitment.

~ *'I'm a girl, and absolutely, I believe in love':* (Marriage and) Monster-in-Law ~

As in *Shall We Dance?*, the genre's traditional emphasis on romantic fulfilment is marginalised in *Monster-in-Law* by other concerns, namely Charlie's (Lopez) comically strained relationship with her fiancé's mother – the film's eponymous monster – Viola Fields (Jane Fonda). Lopez plays the hard-working yet laid-back Charlie, employed as a receptionist in a doctor's surgery, as a caterer and dog walker as well as being an enthusiastic and talented amateur fashion designer. The hardly oblique references to Lopez's off-screen status as restaurateur and fashionista are thus interwoven with more nurturing roles, a deliberate mellowing of her image that seeks to negotiate her reputation as high-maintenance diva. Viola, by contrast, is highly strung, competitive and ambitious, a woman who has reached the pinnacle of her career in television journalism only to be casually replaced by a younger, prettier usurper and subsequently driven to an on-air breakdown by a vacuous, pneumatic pop starlet. We would argue that given Fonda's inextricable public association with second-wave feminism, Viola's 'monstrosity' serves primarily as a structuring other upon which the film can project the negative elements of Lopez's star image; however, just as Viola defines herself in total opposition to the highly sexualised post-feminism of the scantily-clad pop star, so too does *Monster-in-Law* make it clear that this kind of hypersexual performativity is equally far removed from the demure, authentically sensual femininity of Jennifer Lopez.

Viola is nevertheless broadly characterised, *à la* Lopez, as a narcissistic diva whose ambition and career-driven mentality has left a trail of failed relationships in her wake. As this was Fonda's belated return to mainstream filmmaking after a 15-year semi-retirement, it seems safe to assume that the (extra-)textual logic for her reappearance in *Monster-in-Law* was based primarily upon her own star image's intersection at the historical and ideological juncture between second-wave feminism and the emergence of a post-feminist culture. For if, as we have suggested, Lopez's roles in rom-coms are typically imbued with the neo-utopian discourses of post-feminist 'choice', then structurally Viola is the dysfunctional and fundamentally unhappy victim of second-wave feminism's supposedly anti-feminine imperatives.

With Lopez remarried by this point to long-time collaborator Marc Anthony, her characterisation is more confident in tone than that of

Paulina in *Shall We Dance?*, mirroring as it does contemporaneous press descriptions of Lopez as 'a woman who has crawled through an abyss and got out the other end stronger' (Iley, 2005: 56). Indeed, *Monster-in-Law* is less interested in amorous escapades than it is in renegotiating Lopez's star image through and against Fonda's dense celebrity text, a truism underlined by the casting of the comparatively unknown Michael Vartan as her husband-to-be. As with the populist dynamic of her previous rom-coms, the upper-class environs of Viola's home and social circle function as a suitably stifling and laughably pretentious bourgeois *mise-en-scène* that underlines Charlie/Lopez's quasi-proletarian ordinariness. Indeed, in a gesture towards accusations that she was guilty of commercially 'bleaching out' her Latina identity, a scene in which Viola lends Charlie a vintage dress serves as a revisionist corrective to the borrowed frock that allows her to effortlessly class-pass in *Maid in Manhattan*. This time, Lopez's body refuses to fit into the restrictive bourgeois world symbolised by the dress; more specifically, a shot of Charlie/Lopez struggling to pull the vintage gown over her most overdetermined physiological *ass*et both literally and figuratively demonstrates her difference from – that is, her inability to assimilate into – Viola's white social milieu (see Fig. 14.3). Indeed, Viola's quite deliberate strategy throughout the film is to humiliate Charlie precisely by reminding her of this ethnic difference: just as Viola repeatedly makes derogatory comments about Charlie's weight and body shape (even at one point asking if she's 'an illegal immigrant'), so too does

14.3: Mirror stage? Charlie (Lopez) conspicuously struggles to fit into the symbolic vintage dress in *Monster-in-Law*.

Viola's own monstrous mother-in-law casually describe Charlie/Lopez as 'an exotic Latina'.

Once again, then, Lopez's individualism and confidently assertive self-image is reflexively played out against the impositions of family. Whereas earlier romantic vehicles mobilised the trope of transcending the limited ambitions of first-generation immigrant parents, *Monster-in-Law* displaces familial antagonism onto Viola and the stultifying bourgeois world she metonymically represents. To this end, it is hardly insignificant that the film's emotional climax comes not with the couple's inevitable union, but with the reconciliation of Charlie and Viola in a truce that is grounded in terms of familial continuity and inclusivity. As Viola insists that – for all her determined efforts to the contrary – she wants the marriage to go ahead, Charlie gently demands that the one area of their lives that her mother-in-law must be involved in at all times is in the raising of her grandchildren. With Lopez's recent marriage and endless media speculation about her ever-ticking biological clock, *Monster-in-Law* confidently predicts domestic fecundity both diegetically and extra-textually. Charlie's trajectory towards marital bliss was also echoed in contemporaneous interviews with Lopez. Discussing her newfound love of domestic pleasures, the contented star portrays herself as a repentant career girl who has belatedly found her gendered place in the social order. 'I have made sacrifices for my career,' she claimed. 'Now I'm just loving doing normal stuff' (Iley, 2005: 56).

Couched in the quietly alluring rhetoric of domesticated marital harmony, Lopez's love of 'normal stuff' finds its echo in the heteronormative utopia of her rom-coms. It appears that the quixotic and hugely entertaining romantic minefield that makes up a key element of Jennifer Lopez's celebrity text is – for the time being – closed. Like the quotation that forms part of the title of this essay, however, it is difficult to shake off a nagging sense of the always already impermanent nature of Lopez's amorous arrangements. Yet, rather than being simply contradictory, Lopez's idealisation of enduring romance functions to humanise a persona that has often been depicted as aloof, demanding and self-interested. Just as it is difficult to shake off the conclusion that the construction of Lopez as an arrogant diva had more than a little to do with racist preconceptions that this outspoken Latina should know her place, so too does the post-feminist morality tale concerning the incompatibility of the star's career with her love life melodramatically punish Lopez's 'excessive' personal desires and ambitions. At the same time, it is this 'authentically' vulnerable flipside to her tough professional image that dominates her rom-coms. Lopez's phantasmatic existence within the performative matrix of media representation and the culture of celebrity offers only an ephemeral affective grasp of the amorous fabrications that make up 'authentic' desire. Like so many female stars, then, Lopez's gendered place within the romantic imaginary – the 'reel' of the contemporary rom-com – seems predicated upon the opaque veracity of her off-screen oscillation between bouts of heartbreak and passionately committed relationships. 'I'm a girl,' this text tells us, 'and absolutely, I believe in love. It's the only thing. It's why we sing, it's why we dress, it's why we wake up, go to sleep. It's everything' (Iley, 2005: 56).

15 *Le Divorce*

Romance, Separation and Reconciliation

~ *Hilary Radner* ~

FOLLOWING IN A Shakespearean tradition, the romantic comedy of classical Hollywood often emphasised the theme of education: 'An essential goal of the narrative is the Education of the woman,' remarks Stanley Cavell in his now canonical study of this genre (1981: 84). We might, then, ask whether feminism transformed the way popular cinema represents the way a woman is 'educated' into romance. A close reading of the 2003 *Le Divorce* demonstrates that contemporary film may both draw upon and transform the conventions of romantic comedy in response to changing social mores – in particular, that current narratives of education often strive to reconcile traditional concepts of femininity with new ideas about self-fulfilment associated with feminism.

~ *Education, romance and the girly film* ~

In 'girly' films – such as *Pretty Woman* (1990), *Sabrina* (1995), *Romy and Michele's High School Reunion* (1997), *Legally Blonde* (2001), *Maid in Manhattan* (2002), *Something's Gotta Give* (2003), *Le Divorce*, *13 Going on 30* (2004) – romance may provide a significant narrative structure, usually the defining narrative structure. Only a few of these films conform to the definition of romantic comedy, in the form of the screwball comedy, as described by scholars of classical Hollywood cinema (Schatz, 1981: 150-85). They have in common, however, the emphasis on a female protagonist and a concern with the problem of 'education' and its relation to the heterosexual couple. For Cavell, one of the primary functions of the screwball comedy is to represent the education of the heroine from girlhood into mature sagacity, which involves recognising the violence of men, of the human condition, as part of accepting the world as it is. The girly films cited above continue the tradition of Shakespearean romantic comedy in their focus on this process of maturation and on the female heroine, within a contemporary context that has been defined, at least in part, by the impact of second-wave feminism.

I will use the term 'girly film' to distinguish these narratives from the romantic comedy *tout court*. Charlotte Brunsdon (1997: 101) coined the term 'post-feminist girly film' to describe movies (initially appearing in the late 1980s, such as *Pretty Woman*) that, while not feminist per se, demonstrate the impact of feminist issues on popular culture. Here I use the term 'girly' more loosely to denote films that revolve around a feminine protagonist in a period that might be called 'after feminism'.[1] While not constituting a genre, in the strict definition of the term, this group of films represents a continuation of the woman's film of classical Hollywood as described by Jeanine Basinger (1993), while also manifesting the influence of second-wave feminism on popular culture.

One of the strategies whereby cinema has addressed the concerns of contemporary women, in the wake of movements such as sexual liberation and the women's movement, is by elaborating on traditional genres such as the romantic comedy to accommodate concomitant changes in social values and social mores. This renovation of film formulas has been accompanied by the proliferation of film guides or viewing handbooks for women, demonstrating the ways in which the girly film as a type of narrative develops in response to the notion that women, after feminism, are considered a relatively homogeneous (and powerful) demographic category in terms of tastes and concerns.[2] These handbooks often focus on romantic comedy, but also develop new categories for describing the permutation and hybridisation of traditional genres in response to what their authors understand as their constituents' viewing needs and issues. They are, then, part of a larger strategy to target women as a demographic category within popular culture, which includes repackaging old films and producing new formulas, creating both new genres and new spokeswomen for these genres.

~ The relationship film ~

A significant development in terms of elaborating on traditional genres is the emergence of the 'relationship film'. In one guide to films for women, *Chick Flicks: Movies Women Love*, the authors, Jo Berry and Angie Errigo, define the 'relationship film' in terms of relationships that are not 'romantic': 'those between mothers and their children, between sisters and other siblings, and those special friendships between women who aren't related but stick together through thick and thin' (2004: 316). Within this category, they claim that 'the movies that are truly chick flicks are those that feature gal pals. In these, girls and women are friends to the end, while men are sidelined and at best peripheral to the plot' (ibid.: 317). They further note that most of these films were made 'in the last twenty years' as a direct result of the rise of powerful women producers, often stars. While this may or may not be the case, this observation testifies to a general perception that second-wave feminism, insofar as it has afforded opportunities to at least some women, has had an effect on what is available on both the big screen and the small screen.

A number of girly films revolving around notions of education are categorised by Berry and Errigo as 'relationship films': notably *Le Divorce*, *I Capture the Castle* (2003) and *Hanging Up* (1999) among others. An equal number show up in other categories such as 'working girls' (*Legally Blonde*), or romantic dramas (*The Other Sister* (1999)). Most girly films, however, are classified as romantic comedies, including: *Pretty Woman*, *Maid in Manhattan*, *What Women Want* (2000) and *Something's Gotta Give*.

The authors devote the opening section to 'romantic comedies' or 'rom-coms', excluding films that appeal to men and focusing on what they call 'girly romantic comedies'. The girly romantic comedy features 'gorgeous men, to-die-for frocks, romantic kisses, and sometimes that ultimate move repellent for men, weddings' (Berry and Errigo, 2004: 8). Though films such as *Le Divorce* are classified as 'relationship films' by the authors, all the movies that I would categorise as girly films include romantic heroes, stylish clothing and usually weddings – though not necessarily in that order. More importantly, the traditional romantic comedy provides the structure that upholds the narrative, while allowing for evolution and permutation. Indeed, we usually find some variation of the formula 'girl meets boy, girl loses boy, girl finds boy'. The idea that the protagonist may or may not find fulfilment through a romantic relationship is almost always a significant issue in the narrative. Even though not all of these films fall clearly into the category of romantic comedy, all of them do owe a significant debt to this genre in terms of structure and emphasis. As Kristine Brunovska Karnick points out in her discussion of classical Hollywood, the distinction between melodrama and romantic comedy, for example, cannot be made in terms of subject matter. Tone, particularly verbal exchange, define the latter as a mode, rather than as a narrative per se (1995: 123-30). The girly film exploits this ambiguity in order to create hybrid genres that, as in the case of *Pretty Woman*, cross over between melodrama and romantic comedy as a means of responding to ongoing debates on romance and femininity (Rowe, 1995b: 197-200).

~ Reconciliation ~

Nonetheless, it is probably correct to say that it is 'comedy' rather than 'melodrama' that has come to define contemporary girly films for women. This trend holds true for television. Though *Sex and the City* (1998-2004) and *Desperate Housewives* (2004-) borrow structurally from soap operas, they also rely heavily on a comic mode and the impetus towards reconciliation that characterises comedy as a whole, and romantic comedy in particular (Schatz, 1981: 150-85). In other words, these narratives emphasise the need for union and community rather than underlining the importance of law, order and duty. The conclusion, like that of the musical comedy, will usually unite the characters in a final scene highlighting the importance of social and human connection as essential to the happy ending. Differences are smoothed over and resolved. Moral absolutism makes way for compromise and cooperation (which is a significant aspect of the heroine's education). This impetus towards 'reconciliation' is the single most important dimension of these films. In contrast, films such as *An Unmarried Woman* (1978), initially associated with second-wave feminism, often end with the woman alone, happy in her self-sufficiency. In the neo-romantic comedy (as in *13 Going on 30*), the girly heroine resolves her dilemma through a relationship - often, but not necessarily, a traditional heterosexual marriage (Rubinfeld, 2001). She is rarely, if ever, alone.

In spite of this emphasis on reconciliation, it would be a mistake to conclude that the girly film is essentially a conservative cultural form. Rather than returning to an earlier paradigm, the girly film supports and solidifies the developments in the women's position inaugurated in the 1960s and 1970s by the sexual revolution. What Barbara Ehrenreich refers to as 'the symbolic importance of female chastity' has disappeared in the girly film (1986: 2). The girly film represents the triumph of Helen Gurley Brown over Betty Freidan and Germaine Greer – or, perhaps even more significantly, the persistence of a certain kind of neo-liberal feminism exemplified in popular figures such as Oprah Winfrey – in which her right to her own fulfilment is the governing term of a woman's identity. The girly film seeks to recognise that right while reconciling the need for personal fulfilment with the acceptance of human relations as the defining moment in a woman's life. Though these films are not necessarily optimistic about the possibility of reconciliation, they underline a desire that extends beyond the individual in which fulfilment involves the recognition and extension of inter-subjective relations: of relations beyond the self.

This emphasis on reconciliation has led some film scholars to view the new romantic comedy, particularly in the form of the girly film, as a reactionary return to pre-feminist values (Holmlund, 2005: 116–15). While this perspective is not without legitimacy, it fails to take into account the ways in which girly films are concerned with how and why women might wish to maintain their identity as feminine within intimate culture – the private sphere of family, friends and romance – while accepting, even celebrating, independence and autonomy within the public sphere. Similarly, girly narratives seek to preserve the experience of femininity in the face of a public culture that is increasingly indifferent to gender in response to an economic imperative that de-personalises the employee. These films, then, rather than returning to values of an earlier generation, attempt to reconcile the past with the present. Though many are imbued with nostalgia, they look forward to a future in which, for example, motherhood and artistic fulfilment are not incompatible, constituting an attempt to forge something new that reconciles the political and economic developments of the last half of the twentieth century with notions of gendered identities that have remained more or less intact in spite of these changes.

~ Le Divorce: *a girly film* ~

Le Divorce offers an example that illustrates the primary characteristics of the girly film as a variant of the romantic comedy. Though classified as a relationship film, the narrative exhibits many of the defining attributes of the romantic comedy without corresponding to a traditional narrative pattern that focuses on a single heterosexual relationship, its trials and tribulations, moving towards the inevitable happy ending represented by marriage or its promise. More importantly, *Le Divorce* (by its title alone) suggests the difficulties that the romantic comedy as a genre has had in incorporating at least some of the ideals of second-wave feminism while preserving a stable notion of feminine identity defined in terms of intimate culture and the maternal bond. Very specifically, *Le Divorce* incorporates elements of the romantic comedy (such as the emphasis on heterosexual relations) with the woman's buddy film or gal pal film. In so doing, the movie underlines certain key thematic and formal elements of the girly film, in particular the strategy of doubling, the tensions between a femininity defined in terms of maternity and one defined in terms of self-fulfilment, and finally the relationship between consumer culture and femininity.

    Le Divorce highlights the location of Paris as a significant space in the imaginary geography of femininity, a common trope in the girly narrative. For example, in the 1995 remake of *Sabrina*, the protagonist is 'educated' into femininity through a visit to Paris. In *Sex and the City*, a girly epic, the protagonist's ill-fated move to Paris sends her back to New York, to her girlfriends, and her old flame. She, too, then learns from Paris.

    More central to the plot of *Le Divorce* (as opposed to its *mise-en-scène*), is the inability of the feminine subject to anticipate or control the seemingly random acts of male violence, including emotional violence, that provide the impetus to the plot – highlighting a stock figure of the romance, the unfathomable rogue male who breaks the heart of the female protagonist. In the girly film (as in the romantic comedy more generally), the masculine subject is foregrounded as necessary, often desired and desirable, but also unreliable and even dangerous.

    Like many other girly films, such as *Romy and Michele's High School Reunion*, *Le Divorce* does not focus on a single heroine. Rather, it recounts the story of two sisters, each of whom must discover her 'self'. The older sister Roxy (Naomi Watts) is married, a published if unremunerated poet, a mother of one child and expecting another. Her younger half-sister Isabel (Kate Hudson) is sent to assist her during the months of pregnancy. The arrival of Isabel coincides with the departure of Roxy's husband, Charles-Henri, an event that sets off the convoluted plot that includes his death. By the film's conclusion, Roxy will have already found a suitor in the form of her solicitor. Isabel, in contrast, emerges from her affair with Charles-Henri's uncle, Edgar, with the conviction that she must take life as it comes. 'Il faut prendre la vie comme elle vient,' she states, summing up her education.

~ Irrational men ~

Isabel and her education provides the focus of the film. Initially, she attempts to find a sense of self by journeying to Paris to join her sister. Here, she confronts the film's first act of violence (in this case, emotional violence): that of the husband who abandons his pregnant wife and child, without concern for their material or emotional welfare. Unlike the novel on which the film is based, which maintains an ironic distance from its characters, the film sentimentalises the plight of the abandoned mother, a sentimentality that progresses as she becomes more and more obviously pregnant (D. Johnson, 1998).

The use of sentimentality within what is basically a screwball plot (in which all the characters are prone to irrational behaviour, which lands them in improbable and ludicrous situations from which they must be extricated) is a strategy that recurs within the girly film, symptomatic of a general trend towards hybridity in film narrative. The mixing of genres contributes to the sense that the film's narrative is not quite up to the task of solving the problems that it poses, in this case the double demands of self-fulfilment and family as defining moments in the articulation of feminine identity. At the heart of the film is its inability to justify its plot in terms of cause and effect. In particular, the film can never explain or even justify Charles-Henri's actions, which seem finally senseless, as 'insane' as those of his murderer, the betrayed husband of his new lover, Magda. In the screwball comedy, this irrationality is shared by all characters, and is rarely fatal. Often, in fact, it plays a significant role in reconciling the couple. In *Le Divorce*, irrationality and unpredictability are far from benign, threatening the family both symbolically and literally, and culminating in the double murder of

Charles-Henri and Magda. The effect is that, far from accepting this violence, Roxy and Isabel reject the rogue male in favour of other more conciliatory and docile partners.

~ *Patron saint of young women* ~

Isabel's education is not, however, confined to affairs of the heart. A significant subplot centres on a painting that may or may not be a 'La Tour', belonging to the Walker family. A representation of Saint Ursula, the patron saint of all young women, the painting becomes a source of conflict in the subsequent discussions over the division of property between Roxy and Charles-Henri, emphasising his cruelty: he attempts to wrest the very image of her femininity from her and translate it into mere money. The couple's problems are resolved abruptly when Charles-Henri is murdered by the American husband of his new lover. This second act of male violence seemingly counterbalances the first because it allows the painting without further dispute to revert to the Walker family. The painting is sold at auction, securing the daughters' independence, returning to the family as a 'sign'. Their picture of Saint Ursula becomes the emblem of a charity organisation, in which the Walker sisters participate through their new wealth, bringing relief to women and girls. In part, then, through the ironies of technological reproduction, Saint Ursula's sanctity is at least partially restored. While recognising the loss of Saint Ursula as a loss of authenticity (Roxy in particular is distressed at losing the painting), the film is, nonetheless, also able to celebrate at least some of the positive consequences of this loss in view of the freedom it affords the two sisters and the women who are the object of their charity. The serendipity of the conclusion underlines the importance (for Isabel) of taking life as it comes, while pointing to the precariousness of the two sisters' position.

~ *Doubles* ~

Importantly, the film concerns itself with two heroines, united through their ties to Saint Ursula (a symbol of feminine solidarity), but separated by their differences. Though Isabel claims to have achieved a greater knowledge of self by the film's conclusion, it might be more accurate to say that she does not change as much as she comes to accept herself as different from Roxy. She accepts her girlishness as part of who she is, rather than something that she must outgrow. The centrality of the Saint Ursula figure, a girl forever young, but also patron of young girls, seems to highlight the importance of this girlishness to the survival of the family. Isabel is as crucial to the family and its survival, as is the more obvious family-oriented (yet still girlish) Roxy. When the Saint Ursula image becomes the icon for a charitable trust designed to help women, in particular by bringing them consumer items such as tampons and make-up, she seems to represent the crucial element of girlishness that all women must seek to preserve as well as the fragility of these qualities that seem threatened.

By doubling the protagonist (Isabel) with a shadow figure, in this case the sister, the film solves the problem of the contradictory expectations of maternity and sexual fulfilment. Roxy lives out the destiny of the 'mother', while Isabel pursues the single life, as an autonomous and largely undirected individual who seeks intellectual and personal fulfilment: forever girlish. Unlike Roxy, who finds herself through marriage, a self that she feels she may lose through divorce, Isabel finds herself through an affair with an older married man. She chooses to be a mistress rather than a wife. The doubling-up of the heroines underlines the ways in which, in the girly film, femininity is too large and too complex to be incarnated by a single figure.

The doubling of the sisters, who are so close that they share the same apple, suggests how identification and difference can serve the fantasy function of the girly film, in that both models of femininity are offered simultaneously to the female viewer. The doubling function reassures the viewer that contradiction can be overcome, while also challenging the reality of that contradiction as a contradiction. Certain significant differences between the novel and the film underline these tendencies that unite the two sisters as the full expression of femininity in its contradictions. Rather than contrasting with each other (in the novel one is fair and the other is dark), they are depicted as resembling each other, both blonde, which corresponds to dominant traditions of all Americanness (D. Johnson, 1998). Even though Naomi Watts, who plays Roxy, is Australian, she goes to great pains to 'Americanise' her accent. Kate Hudson brings a legendary dimension to her role; she is the daughter of Goldie Hawn, a cult actress and iconic blonde of the 1970s, noted for her comic roles – a proto-girly heroine. This legacy lends weight to Hudson's depiction of the California girl, the stereotypical ditsy blonde with a hippy-dippy aura originally incarnated by her mother in such films as *Shampoo* (1975). (The Walker family does indeed come from California.) Isabel signals the resiliency of this persona, and her ability to adapt and survive. Another notable girly heroine, Elle Wood in *Legally Blonde*, is also a California girl. Isabel, like Elle, is wholesome, unhampered by prudery yet untainted by prurience or perversity. The character of Roxy adds another dimension to the same blonde stereotype who is now able to assume the responsibilities of motherhood and to understand the intricacies of culture. As a poet, Roxy would have encountered the same prejudices as Elle does in *Legally Blonde*, having to fight for acceptance in the legal fraternity. The dolly-bird image that characterises many girly heroines points to the link between this type of narrative and the larger arena of popular feminine culture, in particularly consumer culture, which is naturalised in these films as a taken-for-granted dimension of the heroine's education, often represented through the fashion show or the makeover.[3]

~ Consumer culture and the new femininity ~

Typically, then, one strand of Isabel's education revolves around consumer culture. Consumer culture is represented in heavy-handed manner through the legendary Kelly handbag made by Hermès, which Isabel's lover offers her at the beginning of the affair. Through the good offices of her illicit and older lover, Isabel is initiated into the rites of femininity as performance. Here, he stands in erotically for the father, who cannot complete his daughter's sexual education and who (as in many girly films) remains a relatively minor figure. With the help of her father/lover, Isabel learns to clad herself in expensive undergarments, display her assets to advantage and to order correctly with discernment from French menus. The Kelly bag, however, which seems to signal Isabel's status as a woman of the world is, as often as not, a source of embarrassment. Isabel takes it everywhere, to a poetry reading and to the opera. It reveals, not her sophistication, but, rather, that her lover, a married man, has yet again had the bad taste to become involved with a young and entirely inappropriate woman. In the end, Isabel refuses the Kelly bag, and what it seems to signify in terms of accepting the old compromises of an outmoded femininity in which a woman's options were wife or mistress. Near the film's conclusion, Isabel, after lending the bag to her mother, retrieves it, puts the murderer's gun in it and throws the bag and the gun off the Eiffel Tower. The family is saved, but at a certain cost (the price of a Hermès bag); however, Isabel reassures us that the lessons of the bag have not been lost on her. She will take life as it comes – in opposition to Roxy, whose life as a mother is set. Isabel, however, retains her freedom, her independence and her femininity as a sexual being.

Kate Hudson's performance as Isabel highlights the notion of an identity that is not fixed but transformative, while retaining a certain permanence in its link to the family. Part of the film's pleasure is in tracking Kate Hudson as Isabel through her fashion transformations as California girl, Parisian seductress, back to student of life at the film's conclusion. The girlish style represented by Hudson (as a star) is one grounded in consumer non-durables, in change and ephemera as the essence of fashion and youth culture. A true girl remains in control of her own sexuality and appearance. She doesn't invest in fashion, in the old moneyed and stable elegance of the Hermès bag. She dresses for herself – but has the freedom to alter her look at will, to experiment with her sexuality as well as her clothes.

Hudson as Isabel represents a new femininity, predicated upon change, in which education is a state of mind, a lifestyle, rather than a goal. Her laissez-faire attitude is played against the extreme emotionalism (tears, suicide attempt, outbursts of anger) exhibited by the character Roxy as the example of a more traditional fragile and volatile femininity. Yet Roxy, for all her fragility, gets exactly what she wants, if not Charles-Henri, then another more than adequate potential husband. Reversing the traditional melodramatic plot, the tragically widowed wife re-enters the couple, while the comic heroine (Isabel) assumes that noble position of woman-alone, breaching the conventions of romance (Cavell, 1996). Ultimately, because of this proliferation of possibilities, the film does not convince us that it is able to reconcile the conflicting demands placed upon young women today. The fantasy of a double (two sisters who are so close that they can live with and for each other) enables a temporary resolution of the demands of motherhood and self-fulfilment, one that survives only as fantasy.

~ *Irreconcilable differences* ~

This process whereby a fantasy is fulfilled, but also signalled as a fantasy, is mirrored in the film's treatment of the family. The Walkers are reunited through the painting only to be separated again since the painting must be sold and the profits will be divided among family members. The film retains the optimism of the genre by suggesting the family's endless possibilities as a process of reconfiguration and reconstitution. The family is not stable; rather, it is represented as a shifting field of relations that, nonetheless, remains a vital grid of meaning capable of affirming the changing identities of its members. These optimistic fantasy elements, a set of virtual relations, in perpetual flux, usually associated with Isabel's story, are countered by the more violently emotional (and sentimental) events associated with Roxy, in particular her suicide attempt, a response to the reality of infidelity and the demise of the traditional family as she understood it.

This sentimentality of the film (associated with Roxy), in contrast with the irony of the novel, offsets the heroines' attempts to free themselves from the stereotypical expectations that they embody. A further effect of the film's sentimentalisation of the material presented by the novel is a romanticisation of French life – such that even the mercenary, self-serving French matriarch (Leslie Caron) and her philandering brother (Isabel's lover) seem glamorous. The satirical and often very critical depiction of French culture that characterises the novel is muted in the film, apparent only from time to time in the depiction of *la grande famille française* – replaced by a celebration of Frenchness and of Paris – as a space in which femininity is somehow set free, flying around like the Hermès bag with a gun inside. Though there is nothing ominous in the music or expression of the bag's fateful and happy journey, the metaphor of gun hidden inside an expensive handbag remains troubling, one of the many unresolved contradictions of the film that are passed off as mere stylistics devices. Indeed, there is a lyrical, fantasy quality to the bag's journey, which seems to float rather than fall, echoing other whimsical moments in the film, such as a brief montage sequence depicting French women's superior knowledge of the scarf and the many ways that it can be used to adorn the feminine woman. These lyrical interludes are at odds with the film's more melodramatic moments. Indeed, the bag's journey follows upon one of the film's dramatic climaxes, during which the family is held hostage on top of the Eiffel Tower. It is as if the film, like Isabel, cannot quite believe in its own melodramatic moments.

~ *Conclusion* ~

Finally, then, the film presents a fragmented and contradictory vision of femininity through the two women, Isabel and Roxy. Like the traditional rom-com, *Le Divorce* celebrates reconciliation; however, it also foregrounds separation, not only the separation of couples, but also of the sisters themselves, who must pursue their private destinies. Paradoxically, the film also values reconnection and the reconstitution of the family as 'movement' rather than 'stasis'. The failure of this film to resolve its contradictions underlines the problematics of what I call femininity after feminism, in which the contradictions between parity of the sexes in terms of fiscal and sexual opportunity and the preservation of difference as crucial to identity have yet to be resolved. How does a woman retain her identity as 'feminine' in a culture in which the pursuit of self-fulfilment is gender blind?

Berry and Errigo, though they include *Le Divorce* in their volume of *Movies Women Love* (indicating that this is a film that at least some women love) are not hugely enthusiastic, possibly because it does not offer a convincing dream of reconciliation. As a rule, Berry and Errigo do not share the concerns of critics and tend to expend little time on plausibility, character or plot, at least in the terms employed by film scholars. They report that the film 'has the feel of one of Merchant-Ivory's period dramas performed in modern clothes' (2004: 345), indicating perhaps that the film is too intellectual for their taste. From their perspective, the humorousness of the novel (which they enjoyed) is missing from the bulk of the film and the ending, which they found entertaining and light, is 'out of sync with the rest of the film' (ibid.: 345). Perhaps *Le Divorce* touches too many raw nerves and leaves too many loose ends. Divorce is increasingly one of the realities of contemporary life.[4] It is, however, remarriage and not divorce that lends itself to a narrative of reconciliation. Precisely because *Le Divorce* emphasises the difficulties of a concept of marriage defined through divorce, it fails to reconcile its contradictions. Why will Roxy's second marriage be any more successful than her first? Will Isabel ever settle down? These are questions that the film does not answer.

These lingering unanswered questions are, however, a prevalent facet of the girly film. In *Pretty Woman*, how will Vivian and Edward reconcile their very different backgrounds, for example? Indeed, the film's first ending (deemed too pessimistic for Hollywood) predicts a tragic end for Vivian (alone and back on the street), not unlike that of her predecessor, Violetta in *La Traviata*.[5] In *Maid in Manhattan*, Ralph and Marisa are 'still going strong' – but not yet married at the film's conclusion. In *13 Going on 30* (2004), the film offers us two endings. In the first, the heroine loses the hero to another woman. In the second, they marry. Is this second ending merely a fantasy? The film leaves that possibility open. Certainly one can point to ambiguous endings in earlier films, for example, that of *It Happened One Night* (1934). Are we really convinced that the spoiled heiress, played by Claudette Colbert, will live happily ever after with the alcoholic reporter played by Clark Gable? Perhaps not, yet as a rule, audiences are happy to lay aside their doubts – in part because the film devotes a great deal of its plot to demonstrating that in spite of their seeming differences, they come from the same stock. The ambiguity of the girly films is far more pronounced. Indeed, often girly films must resort to magic (as in the case of *What Women Want* and *13 Going on 30*) in order to make any headway whatsoever on the romantic front. *Le Divorce* may be slightly more overt in its ironic perspective on happy endings, and as such it points to a significant trait of the girly film as a narrative that seeks reconciliation while at the same time maintaining a certain scepticism. The enduring relations are, as often as not, outside the heterosexual couple – in *Le Divorce*, between Roxy, Isabel and the larger Walker family.

The lessons of *Le Divorce* are clear: 'Don't trust the boy. He may be fun – even useful under certain circumstances – but he's not reliable. The good news: he can easily be replaced, as necessary.' Perhaps the new hybridised romantic comedy is not quite as romantic as it seems – and herein lies the essence of its education.

~ *Notes*

~ *Chapter 1* ~

1   Many thanks to Georgina Blau, director of On Location Tours, for meeting with me to discuss film and TV tourism in New York.

2   In fact, characters in rom-coms are recurrently captured watching other rom-coms (e.g. Sara in *Hitch* is seen at home watching the 'You had me at hello' scene in *Jerry Maguire* (1996)). This motif underlines its place as one of the most overtly intertextual of genres, in sequences that serve to confront and foreground its awareness of its own generic heritage and conventions.

3   At the same time it would be wrong to let the romantic mythos of immigration to the USA at this time blind us to some of its harsh realities. As Emanuele Crialese's 2006 film *Nuovomondo* (*Golden Door*) vividly shows, many came to the USA fearful and driven by poverty to face loveless arranged marriages on arrival.

4   For a detailed examination of *Sex and the City*'s representation of New York (and its relationship with cinema) see Jermyn (forthcoming, 2009).

5   Hitch opened at number one in the US box office on Valentine's Day weekend 2005, achieving $45.3m in receipts (Billey, 2005: 2).

6   There is no explicit engagement, for example, with the experience of segregation or its negative repercussions. However, this is something that is nevertheless suggested by the silence of the wives in both these vignettes; while at one level it can be read as a comic touch, suggesting their bemused resignation to their husbands' storytelling, it might also be seen to imply their lack of spoken English. Women immigrants who become doubly isolated within both the home and within segregated communities, often have less opportunities than men to gain access to new language skills.

7   More recently the DVD of *How to Lose a Guy in 10 Days* (2003) makes the same point interactively; the Extras stress the authenticity of its location shooting with a feature called 'Mapping Out the Perfect Location' where one can explore locations used in the film by highlighting them on a screen map of New York.

8   Marisa's 'authentic' knowledge of New York here blurs with and exploits that of Lopez's, since the star herself hails from the Bronx (see also Alan

Dodd and Martin Fradley's essay on the J-Lo rom-com persona in Chapter 14 of this collection).

9   All photos in this chapter copyright the author.

~ Chapter 2 ~

1   I am not suggesting that Allen finds this juxtaposition entirely ironic. The oscillation between an identification with and a rejection of the romanticism of Tin Pan Alley songs gives his films a particular wistfulness. Nostalgia is always about longing for what was lost, even if it is a utopian fiction.

2   The 32-bar song form is the classic structure of the Tin Pan Alley songwriters, from Irving Berlin and Jerome Kern, through George Gershwin and Cole Porter, and on through Burt Bacharach. A song is a series of repeated 'choruses', each of which is composed of four 8-bar phrases arranged in AABA fashion. The B, or bridge section, of contrasting material is also called the 'middle eight' because in sheet music, the repetition of the initial A is usually not written out. In the latter half of the twentieth century, the dominant pop-song configuration came to be based on the alternation of a 'verse', with varied lyrics, and a hook-based 'chorus', the lyrics of which repeat (a variation on the stanza-refrain format of many folk songs). The contrasting bridge section usually occurs after the second chorus, and is still sometimes anachronistically referred to as the 'middle eight'.

3   A simple example would be a leap up to dissonance that falls back to a resolution on a relatively weak beat: Cole Porter's 'Do I Love You?', Irving Berlin's 'What'll I Do?' and Gerry Goffin and Carole King's 'Will You Love Me Tomorrow?' are classic examples of this gesture, and its use in 'Over the Rainbow' adds a tinge of adolescent longing to an otherwise lullaby-like tune.

4   See Gorbman (1987), Chapter 4 'Classical Hollywood Practice' for a good grounding on the subject of music and narrative function through the 'leitmotivic', or thematic, technique.

5   Peter Bogdanovich's early films owe a heavy debt to the romantic comedies of the 1930s and 1940s: *Paper Moon* (1973) follows the father-daughter romance format familiar from any number of Shirley Temple films, with a chorus of popular songs pouring from the radio. *What's Up, Doc?* (1972) bears strong resemblances to *A Song Is Born* (1948), which was itself a remake of *Ball of Fire* (1941), and is an unofficial remake of *Bringing up Baby* (1938). And the notorious flop *At Long Last Love* (1975) was an overt homage to the musicals of the 1930s.

6   'Comedy' as a broad category cannot even be said to have a style, although musical cues can be *comedic*; this is not radically different from the

converse 'drama', although there are perhaps more shades of dramatic music, and the genres tend to develop more distinctive styles.

7   There is a slight anachronism, as most of the songs are from the early 1980s, an era somewhat older that the 17 years pre-2006 mentioned in the film.

8   Burns points out the local specificity of choosing music by Eddie Money (Mahoney), a former Long Island police officer.   .

9   Still, Ani DiFranco, whose 'Worthy' also appears on the soundtrack, is a pioneering indie artist, one of the first to successfully distribute albums on her own label without the backing of a major company.

10   One of *The Groomsmen*, T.C. (John Leguizamo), comes out to his friends over the wedding weekend, and gay rom-coms like *The Wedding Banquet* (1993), *The Incredibly True Adventure of Two Girls in Love* (1995), and *Jeffrey* (1995) began to appear in the mid-1990s, many of them as independent films with jukebox scores (*Incredibly True Adventure* juxtaposes Randy's rock music with Evie's classical music in one of the most basic of classical thematic scoring tropes).

~ Chapter 3 ~

1   See Laplanche (1992) for a detailed discussion of this term.

2   Nat King Cole sings 'Almost Like Being in Love', written by Alan Jay Lerner and Frederick Loewe, a song that comes from *Brigadoon*, whose lyrics might be seen to limit the plausibility of Phil and Rita actually being in love.

3   The spectatorial paradigm proposed in this chapter develops directly from the Freudian concept of *Nachträglichkeit* or deferred action, which emerged out of his work on traumatic neuroses and the abandoned seduction theory. Furthermore, 'Afterwardsness', Laplanche's reworking of Freud's concept, and the cinema, both share a concern with temporality that informs my argument in this chapter.

4   For a more detailed account of afterwardsness in film see Sutton (2004).

5   See Millar (1997) and Gibbons (1999).

~ Chapter 4 ~

1   See Shary (2005) for a history of youth in American cinema.

2   It should be noted that the high-school experience depicted in this genre is specific to North America, but the popularity of these films internationally does suggest that the genre touches upon emotions and anxieties of teenage life and love that transcend cultural specificity.

3   This camera movement is reminiscent of James Cameron's similar use of camera movement to move into flashbacks in *Titanic* (1997), which Simon Brown argues invites the audience to 'turn from the now, and to believe

in the accessibility and power of the past, and, through the reification of their own memories, indulge themselves in this lost purity' (2003: 85).

4   Space does not allow for a queer reading of this film along the lines of Claire Hines' discussion of *Miss Congeniality 2* in Chapter 9 of this volume but such a reading would offer a further example of a revisionist high-school experience.

~ Chapter 5 ~

1   These themes are found in other popular Indian film texts, notably the mythological film. However, they are particularly central to the ideological nerve-centre of the rom-com.

2   The kiss between the two lovers was highly controversial at the time. Certain cinemas in India refused to show the film because of it. Up until this point convention had it that just as the two lovers were about to kiss the camera would either cut to another shot or an object would materialise to block out the act.

3   It is noteworthy that the comedic characters are separate from romantic characters, while in typical Western rom-coms the leads are both romantic and comedic heroes.

~ Chapter 7 ~

1   I would like to thank Geneviève Sellier for a stimulating 'brain-storming' about rom-com in a French context as well as Deborah Shaw and Hannah Taïeb Davis for their reading and comments.

2   I was surprised to find Jeunet's film at third position of the 100 best rom-coms on imdb.com, and even more to notice Klapich's *L'Auberge espagnole* at the 49th place, since I had never seen these films classified as rom-coms before (http://www.imdb.com/Sections/Genres/Romance/average-vote, accessed 11 February 2007).

3   Sellier (2004a) sees it as a way to avoid dealing with social issues.

4   Such a model is still active in contemporary French cinema, the most recent example being the box-office success *Quand j'étais chanteur* (2006) with Depardieu as an ageing has-been crooner having an affair with a young woman (Cécile de France). See also Hilary Radner's discussion of *Le Divorce*, a US rom-com/drama hybrid set in Paris which also explores this mode of relationship, Chapter 15 in this volume.

5   This is not to disavow the different guises the rom-com has taken even within the Hollywood mainstream, though space prohibits me from detailing this history here.

6   The ceremony of the Césars (the French equivalent of the Oscars) in late February 2007 offered an interesting illustration of this; the auteur-director Pascale Ferran made a speech after receiving the first of the

five Césars which her film *Lady Chatterley* won (a first for a film made by a woman in France). She criticised the recent changes within French cinema that, in her view (shared by most *cinéphile* critics), favour French popular films (which she also called 'rich' from a budgetary point of view) versus auteur – and in her words 'poor' – cinema. The minister of culture, Renaud Donnadieu de Vabres, present at the ceremony, later wrote an article published in *Libération* (28 February 2007), where he denied the situation and rejected the adjective used: 'je récuse l'opposition introduite par certains entre cinéma commercial et cinéma d'auteur' ['I object to the opposition suggested by some between mainstream commercial cinema and auteur cinema'].

7   Bellon's 'wife' of the title (as *femme* means both woman and wife in French) gradually regains her own identity and name after recovering from the painful departure of her husband. She (re)learns autonomy and subjectivity, a process that eventually leads her to reject her husband when he comes back to her at the end.

8   See Rollet (1998).

9   For a larger discussion of this film, see Rollet (1999), Cairns (1998).

10   If this opening sounds clearly like the first few lines of a Hollywood script, they also directly evoke for a French audience the title of what could be the first ever French rom-com, Claude Lelouch's *Un homme et une femme*, winner of the Palme d'or at the 1966 Cannes film festival as well as the Oscar for the Best Foreign Film the same year.

11   The words in italic are in English in the French version.

12   See, for example, some recent French films made by women such as *Vendredi soir* (2003), *Nadia et les hippopotames* (1999); both films use the massive social 1995 strikes as an important element of their narrative.

~ Chapter 8 ~

1   In order to ensure I compared similarly labelled films, I used the Internet Movie Database, looked at films made since the late 1980s and selected films with either predominantly African-American or Caucasian-American casts.

~ Chapter 9 ~

1   Thanks to my colleagues Steven Peacock, Darren Kerr and Karen Randell for their helpful suggestions and support. Special thanks to Jacqueline Furby for her inspirational comments, unfailing good humour and encouragement.

~ Chapter 10 ~

1   When referring to the 1990s, I do not mean the fixed ten years of the decade, but an approximate period that begins around 1993 or 1994 (as discussions of same-sex marriage became more prominent) and that extends into the initial years of the new century.

2   For more information on the equal marriage rights movement in the 1990s, particularly the development of political, legal and media discourse on the subject, see Cahill (2004), Rauch (2004) and Wardle et al. (2003).

3   The anti-marriage laws that began in the 1990s continue to be passed. In the November 2004 elections, 11 US states ratified such legislation, bringing the total number of states to have approved the addition of anti-same-sex marriage amendments to their Constitutions to nearly 20 (www.now.org).

4   Celestino Deleyto has examined *My Best Friend's Wedding*, along with other recent romantic comedies, as indicative of another related major social shift in the period. He examines how platonic friendship has become increasingly valued above romantic union, both in the genre and elsewhere in popular culture, '[underlining] the crisis of romantic love and heterosexual desire and [presenting] friendship as an increasingly powerful cultural force' (2003: 180).

5   I am not including the spate of television shows that share these concerns, but of particular significance in this context are *Will and Grace* (1998–2006) and *Sex and the City* (1998–2004).

6   Presuming that the romantic comedy's exploration of the difficulty of loving relies solely on tension specific to the battle of the sexes implies that its existence would be endangered by a same-sex couple. The 1990s showed that is not the case.

7   The model/hustler character in *As Good As It Gets* provides one example of a gay character allowed sexuality. However, he is the undeniable villain and catalyst of the tragic events of the story, being the reason Simon is robbed and almost beaten to death.

8   The concern with articulation is highlighted in *As Good As It Gets* and *My Best Friend's Wedding* as Melvin and Julianne are writers by occupation, and both films begin with each character deciding on the right words to express him or herself.

~ Chapter 11 ~

1   As, variously, in *Sleepless in Seattle*, *You've Got Mail*, *Kate and Leopold* (2003) and *Just Like Heaven* (2005).

2   I acknowledge that *The Sweetest Thing* (2002) makes much of onscreen oral sex for comic value, but suggest that this film is a rare instance of

a 'boy rom-com' for girls – a product perhaps of what Ariel Levy calls 'raunch culture' (2005).

3	Except, intriguingly, upon Andy's female boss Paula (Jane Lynch). She had previously confessed to being desperate for some sexual contact, and willing to initiate Andy into the carnal mysteries of which he is ignorant. When the camera pans round his wedding, however, Paula appears to be there without a significant other, a moment that is quite jarring, given the emphasis on partners being conjured for other characters.

~ Chapter 13 ~

1	See Seidman (1981); while the majority of comedians Seidman identifies here are *male* (Mae West being the only notable exception), it is apparent that recent years have seen a proliferation of female comedian comics. Thus, figures such as Lily Tomlin, Whoopi Goldberg, Ellen DeGeneres and, more recently, Jennifer Aniston, may be usefully approached using Seidman's framework. Yet, it remains, as King notes, that 'comedian comedy is, generally, a male-dominated form' (King, 2002: 39). He reasons: 'An explanation for the striking absence of many more [female] performers might simply be that the question of women remaining 'in their place' is of greater sensitivity than that of men, with more at stake' (ibid.: 133).

2	Indeed, if as King notes, 'the term "romantic comedy" implies a . . . *central* and *sustained* focus on the *detail* and *texture* of romance, romantic relationships and character, as both plot material and source of comedy' (2002: 50, my emphasis), then neither of these films are conventional rom-coms.

3	I am grateful to Stacey Abbott and Deborah Jermyn for flagging up the significance of this film to my project.

4	One notable exception is Sandler's *Spanglish* (2004), where the romance plot is paramount and Sandler plays a much more muted, mature version of himself. Significantly, this film pits him as a father of two with a very successful career as a chef, an obvious attempt to suggest this is a much more evolved and relatable Sandler.

5	The tagline of the film asks the very question: 'Would you erase me?'

~ Chapter 14 ~

1	Martin Fradley would like to acknowledge the financial assistance of the Carnegie Institute for the Universities of Scotland that enabled the completion of this essay.

2	'I Do', *Will & Grace*, 6:23.

~ Chapter 15 ~

1   I use the term 'after feminism' to suggest a chronological link to feminism that is not necessarily informed by the philosophical concerns that underlie post-feminism (Holmlund, 2005).

2   For a fuller discussion of the rise of women as a demographic category under the influence of second-wave feminism, see Radner (1995).

3   Not all romantic comedies are similarly implicated. *Bridget Jones' Diary* (2001) and other British romantic comedies place much less emphasis on consumer culture, and in this sense, do not qualify as girly films in the same way as does a film like *13 Going on 30* (2004).

4   The media comments unceasingly on the decline of marriage as a social institution, associated in particular with United States culture. In New Zealand, for example, the *Otago Daily Times* (4 November 2006) reported in its 'World in Focus' section that 'marriage did not figure in . . . 50.2%' of US households, according to the 2005 American Community Survey conducted by the US Census Bureau, leading the newspaper to conclude that 'Americans [are] preferring not to tie the knot'.

5   For a more detailed discussion of *Pretty Woman*'s ambivalences about romance, see Radner (1993).

~ *Filmography*

10 Things I Hate About You (USA, Gil Junger, 1999)
13 Going on 30 (USA, Gary Winick, 2004)
40 Days and 40 Nights (USA, Michael Lehmann, 2002)
The 40-Year-Old Virgin (USA, Judd Apatow, 2005)
A Funny Thing Happened on the Way to the Forum (UK/USA, Richard Lester, 1966)
A Lot Like Love (USA, Nigel Cole, 2004)
A Song is Born (USA, Howard Hawks, 1948)
All Over the Guy (USA, Julie Davis, 2001)
Along Came Polly (USA, John Hamburg, 2004)
America's Sweethearts (USA, Joe Roth, 2001)
American Pie (USA, Paul and Chris Weitz, 1999)
An Affair To Remember (USA, Leo McCarey, 1957)
An Unmarried Woman (USA, Paul Mazursky, 1978)
Anaconda (USA/Brazil/Peru, Luis Llosa, 1997)
Angel Eyes (USA, Luis Mandoki, 2001)
Anger Management (USA, Peter Segal, 2003)
Animal House (USA, John Landis, 1978)
Annie Hall (USA, Woody Allen, 1977)
As Good As It Gets (USA, James L. Brooks, 1997)
At Long Last Love (USA, Peter Bogdanovich, 1971)
L'Auberge espagnole (France, Cédric Klapisch, 2002)
The Awful Truth (USA, Leo McCarey, 1937)
The Bachelor (USA, Gary Sinyor, 1999)
Ball of Fire (USA, Howard Hawks, 1941)
Because I Said So (USA, Michael Lehmann, 2007)
The Best Man (USA, Malcolm D. Lee, 1999)
The Big Chill (USA, Lawrence Kasdan, 1983)
Big Momma's House (USA, Raja Gosnell, 2000)
Big Night (USA, Stanley Tucci and Campbell Scott, 1996)
The Birdcage (USA, Mike Nichols, 1996)
Booty Call (USA, Jeff Pollack, 1997)
Boys Don't Cry (USA, Kimberly Pierce, 1999)

The Break-Up (USA, Peyton Reed, 2006)
The Breakfast Club (USA, John Hughes, 1985)
Bridget Jones' Diary (UK, Sharon Maguire, 2001)
Bridget Jones: The Edge of Reason (UK, Beeban Kidron, 2004)
Brigadoon (USA, Vincente Minnelli, 1954)
Bringing Up Baby (USA, Howard Hawks, 1938)
Broken Flowers (USA, Jim Jarmusch, 2005)
The Brothers McMullen (USA, Edward Burns, 1995)
Bruce Almighty (USA, Tom Shadyac, 2003)
La Bûche (France, Danièle Thompson, 1999)
Carrie (USA, Brian DePalma, 1976)
The Cell (USA, Tarsem Singh, 2000)
Clueless (USA, Amy Heckerling, 1995)
Croupier (UK, Mike Hodges, 1998)
Date Movie (USA, Aaron Seltzer, 2006)
Décalage horaire (France, Danièle Thompson, 2002)
Diner (USA, Barry Levinson, 1982)
Le Divorce (France/USA, James Ivory, 2003)
Dodgeball: A True Underdog Story (USA, Rawson Marshall Thurber, 2004)
Down With Love (USA, Peyton Reed, 2003)
Dumb and Dumber (USA, Farrelly Brothers, 1994)
Duplex (USA, Danny DeVito, 2003)
Enough (USA, Michael Apted, 2002)
Eternal Sunshine of the Spotless Mind (USA, Michel Gondry, 2004)
Le Fabuleux destin d'Amélie Poulain (France, Jean-Pierre Jeunet, 2001)
Fast Times at Ridgemont High (USA, Amy Heckerling, 1982)
La Femme de Jean (France, Yannick Bellon, 1976)
A Fish Called Wanda (USA, Charles Crichton, 1988)
Flirtation Walk (USA, Frank Borzage, 1934)
Forces of Nature (USA, Bronwen Hughes, 1999)
Four Weddings and a Funeral (USA/UK, Mike Newell, 1994)
Frankie and Johnny (USA, Garry Marshall, 1991)
Gazon maudit (France, Josiane Balasko, 1995)
Ghostbusters (USA, Ivan Reitman, 1984)
Gigli (USA, Martin Brest, 2003)
The Goodbye Girl (USA, Herbert Ross, 1977)
The Graduate (USA, Mike Nichols, 1967)
La Grande Vadrouille (France, Gérard Oury, 1966)
The Groomsmen (USA, Edward Burns, 2006)
Grosse Pointe Blank (USA, George Armitage, 1997)
Groundhog Day (USA, Harold Ramis, 1993)
Guess Who? (USA, Kevin Rodney Sullivan, 2005)
Hanging Up (USA, Diane Keaton, 1999)
Hannah and Her Sisters (USA, Woody Allen, 1986)

Heathers (USA, Michael Lehmann, 1989)

His Girl Friday (USA, Howard Hawks, 1940)

Hitch (USA, Andy Tennant, 2005)

The Holiday (USA, Nancy Meyers, 2006)

Hors de prix (France, Pierre Salvadori, 2006)

How to Lose a Guy in 10 Days (USA, Donald Petrie, 2003)

I Capture the Castle (UK, Tim Fywell, 2003)

I Think I Do (USA, Brian Sloane, 1997)

In and Out (USA, Frank Oz, 1997)

The Incredibly True Adventures of Two Girls in Love (USA, Maria Maggenti, 1995)

It Happened One Night (USA, Frank Capra, 1934)

It's a Wonderful Life (USA, Frank Capra, 1946)

Jeffrey (USA, Christopher Ashley, 1995)

Jerry Maguire (USA, Cameron Crowe, 1996)

Jersey Girl (USA, Kevin Smith, 2004)

Just Like Heaven (USA, Mark Waters, 2005)

Kate and Leopold (USA, James Mangold, 2003)

Kissing Jessica Stein (USA, Charles Herman-Wurmfeld, 2001)

Knocked Up (USA, Judd Apatow, 2007)

The Last Kiss (USA, Tony Goldwyn, 2006)

Laws of Attraction (USA, Peter Howitt, 2004)

Legally Blonde (USA, Robert Luketic, 2001)

Little Miss Sunshine (USA, Jonathan Deyton, Valerie Faris, 2006)

Loin du paradis (France, Tonie Marshall, 2001)

Looking for Kitty (USA, Edward Burns, 2006)

Lost in Translation (USA, Sophia Coppola, 2003)

Love Actually (UK, Richard Curtis, 2003)

Love at First Sight (USA, Beeban Kidron, 1996)

The Magnificent Seven (USA, John Sturges, 1960)

Maid in Manhattan (USA, Wayne Wang, 2002)

Mambo Italiano (Canada, Émile Gaudreault, 2003)

Manhattan (US, Woody Allen, 1979)

The Mask (USA, Chuck Russell, 1994)

Me, Myself and Irene (USA, Farrelly Brothers, 2000)

Mean Girls (USA, Mark Waters, 2004)

Mean Streets (USA, Martin Scorsese, 1973)

Miami Rhapsody (USA, David Frankel, 1995)

Mickey Blue Eyes (USA, Kelly Makin, 1999)

Miss Congeniality (USA, Donald Petrie, 2000)

Miss Congeniality 2: Armed and Fabulous (USA, John Pasquin, 2005)

Mr. Deeds (USA, Steven Brill, 2002)

Monster-in-Law (USA/Germany, Robert Luketic, 2005)

Moonstruck (USA, Norman Jewison, 1987)

Muriel's Wedding (Australia/France, P.J. Hogan, 1995)
Music and Lyrics (USA, Marc Lawrence, 2007)
My Beautiful Laundrette (UK, Stephen Frears, 1985)
My Best Friend's Wedding (USA, P.J. Hogan, 1997)
My Fair Lady (USA, George Cukor, 1964)
My Favorite Wife (USA, Garson Kanin, 1940)
Nadia et les hippopotames (France, Dominique Cabrera, 1999)
The Net (USA, Irwin Winkler, 1995)
Never Been Kissed (USA, Raja Gosnell, 1999)
Notting Hill (USA/UK, Roger Michell, 1999)
La Nouvelle Ève (France, Catherine Corsini, 1999)
The Number 23 (USA, Joel Schumacher, 2007)
Nuovomondo (Italy/Germany/France, Emanuele Crialese, 2006)
The Object of My Affection (USA, Nicholas Hytner, 1998)
The Other Sister (USA, Gary Marshall 1999)
Out of Sight (USA, Steven Soderbergh, 1998)
Paper Moon (USA, Peter Bogdanovich, 1973)
Philadelphia (USA, Jonathan Demme, 1993)
The Philadelphia Story (USA, George Cukor, 1940)
Picture Perfect (USA, Glenn Gordon Caron, 1997)
Pillow Talk (USA, Michael Gordon, 1959)
Porky's (Canada, Bob Clark, 1982)
Prête-moi ta main (France, Etienne Lartigau, 2006)
Pretty in Pink (USA, Howard Deutch, 1986)
Pretty Woman (USA, Gary Marshall, 1990)
Punch-Drunk Love (USA, Paul Thomas Anderson, 2002)
Quand j'étais chanteur (France, Xavier Gianolli, 2006)
Raja Hindustani (India, Dharmesh Darshan, 1996)
Romeo Must Die (USA, Andrzej Bartkowiak, 2000)
Romuald et Juliette (France, Coline Serreau, 1989)
Romy and Michelle's High School Reunion (USA, David Mirken, 1997)
The Royal Tenenbaums (USA, Wes Anderson, 2001)
Runaway Bride (USA, Garry Marshall, 1999)
Rushmore (USA, Wes Anderson, 1998)
Sabrina (USA, Billy Wilder, 1954)
Sabrina (Germany/USA, Sydney Pollack, 1995)
Say Anything (USA, Cameron Crowe, 1989)
Semi-Tough (USA, Michael Ritchie, 1977)
Shall We Dance? (USA, Peter Chelsom, 2004)
Shallow Hal (USA, Farrelly Brothers, 2001)
Shampoo (USA, Hal Ashby, 1975)
She's All That (USA, Robert Iscove, 1999)
She's the One (USA, Edward Burns, 1996)
Sidewalks of New York (USA, Edward Burns, 2001)

Sixteen Candles (USA, John Hughes, 1984)
Sleepless in Seattle (USA, Nora Ephron, 1993)
Some Like It Hot (USA, Billy Wilder, 1959)
Something's Gotta Give (USA, Nancy Meyers, 2003)
Speed (USA, Jan de Bont, 1994)
Stranger Than Fiction (USA, Marc Forster, 2006)
The Sure Thing (USA, Rob Reiner, 1985)
Sweet Home Alabama (US, Andy Tennant, 2002)
The Sweetest Thing (USA, Roger Kumble, 2002)
Swingers (USA, Doug Liman, 1996)
The Tao of Steve (USA, Jenniphr Goodman, 2000)
Taxi Driver (US, Martin Scorsese, 1976)
There's Something About Mary (USA, Farrelly Brothers, 1998)
Titanic (USA, James Cameron, 1997)
Toi et moi (France, Julie Lopes-Curval, 2006)
The Truman Show (USA, Peter Weir, 1998)
Two Can Play That Game (USA, Mark Brown, 2001)
Two Tickets to Broadway (USA, James V. Kern, 1951)
Two Weeks Notice (USA/Australia, Marc Lawrence, 2002)
Un divan à New York, (France, Chantal Akerman, 1996)
Un homme et une femme (France, Claude Lelouch, 1966)
Under the Tuscan Sun (USA/Italy, Audrey Wells, 2003)
Up Close and Personal (USA, Jon Avnet, 1996)
Vendredi soir (France, Claire Denis, 2003)
The Wedding Banquet (Taiwan/USA, Ang Lee, 1993)
Wedding Crashers (USA, David Dobkin, 2005)
The Wedding Date (USA, Clare Kilner, 2005)
The Wedding Planner (USA/Germany, Adam Shankman, 2001)
The Wedding Singer (USA, Frank Coraci, 1998)
What Women Want (USA, Nancy Meyers, 2000)
What's Up Doc (USA, Peter Bogdanovich, 1972)
When Harry Met Sally (USA, Rob Reiner, 1989)
While You Were Sleeping (USA, Jon Turteltaub, 1995)
Wimbledon (USA/UK, Richard Loncraine, 2004)
Win a Date with Tad Hamilton! (USA, Robert Luketic, 2004)
The Wood (USA, Rick Famuyiwa, 1999)
You've Got Mail (USA, Nora Ephron, 1998)
Zoolander (USA, Ben Stiller, 2001)

~ *Teleography*

Buffy the Vampire Slayer (WB/UPN, 1997-2003)
Desperate Housewives (ABC, 2004-)
For Your Love (WB, 1998-2002)
The Parkers (UPN, 1999-2004)
Queer Eye for the Straight Guy (NBC, 2003-)
Saturday Night Live (NBC, 1975-)
Sex and the City (HBO, 1998-2004)
The Steve Harvey Show (WB, 1997-2002)
Will and Grace (NBC, 1998-2006)

~ Bibliography

Abramowitz, Rachel (2007) 'Not in the Mood for Love', *Los Angeles Times*, 11 February.

Adorno, Theodor W. (1941) 'On Popular Music', with the assistance of George Simpson, *Studies in Philosophy and Social Science*, New York: Institute of Social Research, 9, 17-48, available at http://www.icce.rug.nl/~soundsscapes/DATABASES/SWA/On_popular_music_1.shtml.

AlSayaad, Nezar (2006) *Cinematic Urbanism: A History of the Modern From Reel to Real*, London and New York: Routledge.

Altman, Rick (1987) *The American Film Musical*, London: BFI.

Anon (2007) *The Time Out Guide to New York*, London: Ebury.

Appleyard, Bryan (2003) 'True Brits? We're All Fakes Actually,' *Sunday Times*, 16 November.

Babington, Bruce and Peter Williams Evans (1989) *Affairs to Remember: The Hollywood Comedy of the Sexes*, Manchester: Manchester University Press.

Barthes, Roland (1977) *Fragments d'un discours amoureux*, Paris: Editions du Seuil.

—— (1988) *Camera Lucida*, trans. Richard Howard, 2nd edn, London: Flamingo.

—— (1990) *A Lover's Discourse: Fragments*, trans. Richard Howard, London: Penguin.

Basinger, Jeanine (1993) *A Woman's View: How Hollywood Spoke to Women, 1930-1960*, London: Chatto and Windus.

Bazin, André (1972) 'De Sica: Metteur en Scène', in *What is Cinema?* (originally published in 1953), trans. Hugh Gray, Berkeley: University of California Press, 2, 61-78.

BBC News (2003) '*Love Actually* Sets UK Film Record', available at http://news.bbc.co.uk/go/pr/fr/-/2/hi/entertainment/3235840.stm.

—— (2004) 'Producers Give Backbone to Industry', available at http://news.bbc.co.uk/go/pr/fr/-/1/hi/entertainment/film/2821801.stm.

Beltran, Mary C. (2002) 'The Hollywood Latina Body as Site of Social Struggle: Media Constructions of Stardom and Jennifer Lopez's "Cross-Over Butt"', *Quarterly Review of Film and Video,* 19:1, 71-86.

—— (2004) 'Más Macha: The New Latina Action Hero', in Yvonne Tasker (ed.) *Action and Adventure Cinema*, London: Routledge, 186-200.

Berg, Charles Ramirez (2002) *Latino Images in Film: Stereotypes, Subversion, Resistance*, Austin: University of Texas Press.

Berry, Jo and Angie Errigo (2004) *Chick Flicks: Movies Women Love*, London: Orion.

Billey, Catherine (2005) 'A Rare Box Office Hat Trick', *New York Times*, 14 February.

Birchall, Claire (2004) '"Feels Like Home": *Dawson's Creek*, Nostalgia and the Young Adult Viewer', in Glyn David and Kay Dickinson (eds) *Teen TV: Genre, Consumption and Identity*, London: BFI, 176-89.

Blau, Georgina (2007) personal interview conducted by Deborah Jermyn with the director of On Location Tours (www.screentours.com), New York, 2 April.

Bogle, Donald (2003) *Toms, Coons, Mulattoes, Mammies & Bucks: An Interpretive History of Blacks in American Films*, New York: Continuum.

Bonila, Paul (2005) 'Is There More to Hollywood Low Brow Than Meets the Eye?', *Quarterly Journal of Film and Video*, 22, 17-24.

Brown, Simon (2003) 'The Greatest Documentary Ever Made: James Cameron's *Titanic*', *Interdisciplinary Literary Studies: A Journal of Criticism and Theory*, 5:1, Fall, 78-88.

Brunovska Karnick, Kristine (1995) 'Commitment and Reaffirmation in Hollywood Romantic Comedy', in Kristine Brunovska Karnick and Henry Jenkins (eds) *Classical Hollywood Comedy*, New York: Routledge, 123-46.

—— and Henry Jenkins (eds) (1995a) *Classical Hollywood Comedy*, London: Routledge.

——, —— (1995b) 'Comedy and the Social World', in Kristine Brunovska Karnick and Henry Jenkins (eds) *Classical Hollywood Comedy*, London: Routledge, 265-81.

Brunsdon, Charlotte (1997) *Screen Tastes: Soap Opera to Satellite Dishes*, London: Routledge.

—— (2004) 'The Poignancy of Place: London and the Cinema', *Visual Culture in Britain*, 5:2, 59-73.

Burch, Noël and Geneviève Sellier (1996) *La Drôle de guerre des sexes du cinéma français*, Paris: Nathan Université.

Burgin, Victor (1996) *In/Different Spaces: Place and Memory in Visual Culture*, Berkeley and Los Angeles: University of California Press.

Burns, Edward (2000) *She's the One*, DVD commentary, 20th Century Fox.

—— (2006) *Looking for Kitty*, DVD commentary, ThinkFilm.

Butler, Judith (2006 [1990]) *Gender Trouble*, London: Routledge.

Byrge, Duane (1987) 'Screwball Comedy', *East-West Film Journal*, 2:1, December, 17-25.

Byron, George Gordon (1958 [1819-24]) *Don Juan*, ed. Leslie A. Marchand, Boston: Houghton Mifflin Co.

Cahill, Sean (2004) *Same-Sex Marriage in the United States: Focus on the Facts*, Lanham: Lexington Books.

Cairns, Lucille (1998) '*Gazon Maudit*, French National and Sexual identities', *French Cultural Studies*, 9:2, 26, 225-37.

Capp, Al (1962) 'The Day Dream', *Show*, December, 72, 136-7.

Case, Jeremy and Natalie Martinez (2002) 'How J.Lo Can You Go?', *Elle Girl*, Autumn, 32-5.

Cavell, Stanley (1981) *Pursuits of Happiness: The Hollywood Comedy of Remarriage*. Cambridge and London: Harvard University Press.

—— (1996) *Contesting Tears: The Hollywood Melodrama of the Unknown Woman*, Chicago: University of Chicago Press.

Charles, Melissa (2004) *Jennifer: The Unofficial and Unauthorised Biography of Jennifer Lopez*, London: Kandour.

Chrisafis, Angelique (2007) 'It's Oui to Rom-Coms and Non to Art House as Cinéphiles Die Out', *Guardian*, 29 January, available at http://film.guardian. co.uk/News_Story/Guardian/0,,2001048,00.html.

Churchill, Winston (1946) 'Sinews of Peace', speech given at Westminster College, Fulton, Missouri, 5 March, available at http://www.nato.int/docu/ speech/1946/s460305a_e.htm.

Cohan, Steven (1999) 'Queering the Deal: On the Road with Hope and Crosby', in Ellis Hanson (ed.) *Out Takes: Essays on Queer Theory and Film*, Durham, NC, and London: Duke University Press, 23-45.

Cox, Alex (2003) 'On Your Marks, Get Set . . . Sell Out!', *Independent*, 6 July, available at http://findarticles.com/p/articles/mi_qn4159/is_20030706/ ai_n12744327.

Creed, Barbara (1995) 'Tribades, Tomboys and Tarts', in Elizabeth Grosz and Elspeth Probyn (eds) *Sexy Bodies: The Strange Carnalities of Feminism*, London: Routledge, 86-103.

Cripps, Thomas (1978) *Black Film as Genre*, Bloomington: Indiana University Press.

—— (1993) *Slow Fade to Black: The Negro in American Film*, 1900-1942, London: Oxford University Press.

Danuta Walters, Suzanna (2001) *All the Rage: The Story of Gay Visibility in America*, Chicago: University of Chicago Press.

Davies, Jude (1995) 'Gender, Ethnicity and Cultural Crisis in Falling Down and Groundhog Day', *Screen*, 36:3, 214-32.

Dawtrey, Adam (1999) 'Working, U Working for Canal Funds', *Daily Variety*, 29 March, available at http://www.variety.com/article/VR1117492760.html.

— (2003) 'Searchlight to Shine for British DNA', *Daily Variety*, 4 September, available at http://www.variety.com/article/VR1117891965.html?categoryid =1236&cs=1&quer=DNA+and+%22Fox+Searchlight%22.

— (2005) 'Hits or Snits?', *Daily Variety*, 1 May, available at http://www.variety. com/article/VR1117921942.html.

Deleyto, Celestino (2003) 'Between Friends: Love and Friendship in Contemporary Romantic Comedy', *Screen*, 44:2, Summer, 167-82.

Dennis, Kevin (2004) 'Very French, Very Charming and Yes . . . They Talk',

IMDb user comments, available at http://www.imdb.com/title/tt0293116/ usercomments.

De Rougemont, Denis (1983) *Love in the Western World*, trans. Montgomery Belgion, Princeton: Princeton University Press.

Doane, Mary Ann (1987) *The Desire to Desire: The Woman's Film of the 1940s*, Bloomington and Indianapolis: Indiana University Press.

Donnadieu de Vabres, Renaud (2007) 'Cinéma, la France joue la qualité', *Libération*, 28 February, 29.

Doty, Alexander (1995) 'There's Something Queer in Here', in Corey Creekmur and Alexander Doty (eds) *Out in Culture: Gay, Lesbian and Queer Essays on Popular Culture*, London: Cassell, 71–90.

—— (2000) *Flaming Classics: Queering the Film Canon*, London: Routledge.

Dowling, Tim (2003) 'Curtis Britain: A Brief Guide', *Guardian*, 13 November, available at http://film.guardian.co.uk/features/featurepages/0,,1084021,00.html.

Drake, Philip (2002) 'Low Blows? Theorizing Performance in Post-Classical Comedian Comedy', in Frank Krutnik (ed.) *Hollywood Comedians: The Film Reader*, London: Routledge, 187–98.

Dyer, Richard (1988) 'White', *Screen*, 29: 4, 44–64.

—— (1999) 'Entertainment and Utopia', in Simon During (ed.) *The Cultural Studies Reader*, London: Routledge, 371–81.

Dyja, Eddie (2001) *BFI Film and Television Handbook 2002*, London: BFI.

Ehrenreich, Barbara, Elizabeth Hess and Gloria Jacobs (1986) *Re-Making Love: The Feminization of Sex*, Garden City: Anchor Press/Doubleday.

Eisenbach, Helen (1999) 'The Clued in Director: An Interview with Amy Heckerling', *Interview,* July, 42.

Elias, Justine (1999) 'Wilted Corsages Are the Least of Their Prom Disasters', *New York Times*, 9 May, Section 13, 63.

Ephron, Nora (2006) 'The Making of WHMS: *How Harry Met Sally*', *When Harry Met Sally*, DVD special feature, MGM.

Errigo, Angie (2002), 'Review: *Punch-Drunk Love*', *Empire*, available at http://www.empireonline.com/reviews/ReviewComplete.asp?FID=13047.

Evans, Peter Williams, and Celestino Deleyto (1998), *Terms of Endearment: Hollywood Romantic Comedy of the 1980s and 1990s*, Edinburgh: Edinburgh University Press.

Feuer, Jane (1987) 'Genre Study and Television', in Robert C. Allen (ed.), *Channels of Discourse Reassembled*, London and New York: Routledge, 138–60.

Fitzgerald, F. Scott (1950 [1926]) *The Great Gatsby*, London: Penguin Books.

Ford, Elizabeth A. and Deborah C. Mitchell (2004) *The Makeover in Movies*, London: McFarland.

Foucault, Michel (1998) *The Will to Knowledge: History of Sexuality, Volume 1*, trans. Robert Hurley, London: Allen Lane, 1979; reprinted London: Penguin Books, 1998.

French, Philip (2004a), 'It'll All Come Out in the Brainwash', *Observer*, 2 May, available at http://film.guardian.co.uk/News_Story/Critic_Review/Observer_Film_of_the_week/0,,1207719,00.html.

—— (2004b) 'Wimbledon', *Observer*, 26 September, available at http://film.guardian.co.uk/News_Story/Critic_Review/Observer_review/0,,1312793,00.html.

Fuchs, Cynthia J. (1993) 'The Buddy Politic', in Steven Cohan and Ina Rae Hark (eds) *Screening the Male: Exploring Masculinities in Hollywood Cinema*, London: Routledge, 194–210.

—— (2001) 'Sidewalks of New York', review, *popmatters.com*, available at http://popmatters.com/film/reviews/s/sidewalks-of-new-york.shtml.

Gardiner, Judith Kegan (ed.) (2002) *Masculinity Studies and Feminist Theory*, New York: Columbia University Press.

Gehring, Wes D. (1986) *Screwball Comedy: A Genre of Madcap Romance*, New York: Greenwood Press.

—— (2002) *Romantic vs. Screwball Comedy: Charting the Difference*, New York: Scarecrow Press.

Gibbons, Fiachra (1999) 'Films Unlock the Troubled Mind', *Guardian*, 3 August, 5.

Giddens, Anthony (1993) *The Transformation of Intimacy: Sexuality, Love and Eroticism in Modern Societies*, Cambridge: Polity.

Gilbey, Ryan (2004) *Groundhog Day*, London: BFI.

Glancy, Mark (1998) 'Hollywood and Britain: MGM and the British "Quota" Legislation', in Jeffery Richards (ed.) *The Unknown 1930s*, London, New York: I.B.Tauris, 57–72.

Glasser, Joyce (2005) 'Amazing Gracie!', *Daily Mail*, 25 March, 62.

Gokulsing, K. Moti and Wimal Dissanayake (1998) *Indian Popular Cinema: A Narrative of Cultural Change*, Stoke-on-Trent: Trentham Books.

Gondry, Michel (2004), *Eternal Sunshine of the Spotless Mind*, DVD commentary, Momentum Pictures.

Gorbman, Claudia (1987) *Unheard Melodies: Narrative Film Music*, London, Bloomington: BFI and Indiana University Press.

Griggers, Cathy (1993) '*Thelma and Louise* and the Cultural Generation of the New Butch-Femme', in Jim Collins, Hilary Radner, and Ava Preacher Collins (eds) *Film Theory Goes to the Movies: Cultural Analysis of Contemporary Film*, London: Routledge, 129–41.

Gross, Edward (2003) 'The Seven Year Slay: *Buffy* Prime Mover Joss Whedon Looks Back on How he Kept his Undead Drama Alive and Kicking Over Its Impressive Run', *Cinefantastique*, 35:4, August/September, 32–38, 75.

Guerrero, Ed (1993) *Framing Blackness: The African American Image in Film*, Philadelphia: Temple University Press.

Halberstam, Judith (1998) *Female Masculinity*, Durham, NC, and London: Duke University Press.

Harvey, James (1987) *Romantic Comedy in Hollywood from Lubitsch to Sturges*, New York: Knopf.

Hayward, Susan (1993) *French National Cinema*, London: Routledge.

Heath, Stephen. (1983) 'Barthes on Love', *SubStance*, 37/38, 100-6.

Henderson, Brian (1978) 'Romantic Comedy Today: *Semi-Tough* or Impossible?', *Film Quarterly*, 31:4, Summer, 11-23.

Henerson, Evan (2005) 'Congenial Bullock Prefers Buddy', *San Diego Union-Tribune*, 25 March, available at http://www.signonsandiego.com/uniontrib/20050325/news_1c25bullock.html.

Higson, Andrew (1995) *Waving the Flag: Constructing a National Cinema in Britain*, New York and Oxford: Oxford University Press.

Holmlund, Chris (2005) 'Postfeminism from A to G', *Cinema Journal*, 44:2, Winter, 116-21.

hooks, bell (1981) *Ain't I A Woman: Black Women and Feminism*, Boston: South End Press.

Iley, Chris (2005) 'I Believe in Love - That's All I'm Guilty Of', *Glamour* (UK), February, 52-6.

Jeffers McDonald, Tamar (2007) *Romantic Comedy: Boy Meets Girls Meets Genre*, London: Wallflower Press.

Jenkins III, Henry (2003) 'Anarchistic Comedy and the Vaudeville Aesthetic', in Frank Krutnik (ed.) *Hollywood Comedians: The Film Reader*, London: Routledge, 91-104.

Jenkins, Henry, and Kristine Brunovska Karnick, (1995), 'Acting Funny', in Kristine Brunovska Karnick and Henry Jenkins (eds) *Classical Hollywood Comedy*, London: Routledge, 149-67.

Jermyn, Deborah (forthcoming 2009) *Sex and the City*, Michigan: Wayne State University Press.

Jha, Priya (2003) 'Lyrical Nationalism: Gender, Friendship and Excess in 1970s Hindi Cinema', in *The Velvet Light Trap*, 51, Spring, 43-53.

Johnson, Diane (1998) *Le Divorce*, London: Vintage.

Johnson, Merri Lisa (2002) 'Fuck You and Your Untouchable Face: Third Wave Feminism and the Problem of Romance', in Merri Lisa Johnson (ed.) *Jane Sexes It Up: True Confessions of Feminine Desire*, New York and London: Four Walls Eight Windows, 13-52.

—— (2004) 'From Relationship Autopsy to Romantic Utopia: The Missing Discourse of Egalitarian Marriage on HBO's *Six Feet Under*', *Discourse*, 26:3, 18-40.

—— (2007) 'Introduction: Ladies Love Your Box: The Rhetoric of Pleasure and Danger in Feminist Television Studies', in Merri Lisa Johnson (ed.) *Third Wave Feminism and Television: Jane Puts It In A Box*, London: I.B.Tauris, 1-27.

Jones, Jacquie (1993) 'The Construction of Black Sexuality: Towards Normalizing the Black Cinematic Experience', in Manthia Diawara (ed.) *Black American Cinema*, New York: Routledge, 247-56.

Katz, Alyssa (1998) 'Kids "R" Us', *The Nation*, 6 April, 35–6.

Kennedy, Colin (2000) 'Uptown Girl', *Empire*, October, 64–71.

King, Geoff (2002), *Film Comedy*, London: Wallflower Press.

Knadler, Steven (2005) 'Blanca from the Block: Whiteness and the Transnational Latina Body', *Genders Online Journal*, 41, available at http://www.genders.org/g41/g41_knadler.html.

Kord, Susanne and Elisabeth Krimmer (2005) 'Running Woman: Sandra Bullock', in Susanne Kord and Elisabeth Krimmer, *Hollywood Divas, Indie Queens and TV Heroines: Contemporary Screen Images of Women*, Oxford: Rowman & Littlefield, 37–55.

Krutnik, Frank (1984), 'The Clown-Prints of Comedy', *Screen*, 25:4–5, July–October, 50–9.

—— (1990) 'The Faint Aroma of Performing Seals: The "Nervous" Romance and the Comedy of the Sexes', *The Velvet Light Trap*, 26, Fall, 57–72.

—— (1994) 'Jerry Lewis: The Deformation of the Comic', *Film Quarterly*, 48:1, 12–26.

—— (1995) 'A Spanner in the Works? Genre, Narrative and the Hollywood Comedian', in Kristine Brunovska Karnick and Henry Jenkins (eds) *Classical Hollywood Comedy*, London: Routledge, 17–38.

—— (1998), 'Love Lies: Romantic Fabrication in Contemporary Romantic Comedy', in Peter William Evans and Celestino Deleyto (eds) *Terms of Endearment: Hollywood Romantic Comedy of the 1980s and 1990s*, Edinburgh: Edinburgh University Press, 15–36.

—— (2002) 'Conforming Passions?: Contemporary Romantic Comedy', in Steve Neale (ed.) *Genre and Contemporary Hollywood*, London: BFI, 130–47.

—— (2003) 'General Introduction', in Frank Krutnik (ed.) *Hollywood Comedians: The Film Reader*, London: Routledge, 1–18.

Lahey, Kathleen A. and Kevin Alderson (2004) *Same-Sex Marriage: The Personal and the Political*, Toronto: Insomniac Press.

Laplanche, Jean (1992) 'Notes on Afterwardsness', trans. Martin Stanton, in John Fletcher and Martin Stanton (eds) *Jean Laplanche: Seduction, Translation, Drives*, London: Institute of Contemporary Arts, 217–23.

—— (1999) *Essays on Otherness*, London and New York: Routledge.

—— and Jean-Bertrand Pontalis (1988) *The Language of Psychoanalysis*, trans. David Nicholson-Smith, London: Karnac and the Institute of Psychoanalysis.

Lapsley, Robert and Michael Westlake (1993) 'From *Casablanca* to *Pretty Woman*: The Politics of Romance', in Anthony Easthope (ed.) *Contemporary Film Theory*, London: Longman, 179–203.

LaSalle, Mick (2001), 'N.Y. Tale is Warmed-Over Woody: "Sidewalks" a Trite Manhattan Sex Story', review, *San Francisco Chronicle*, 21 November, available at http://www.sfgate.com/cgi-bin/article.cgi?f=/c/a/2001/11/21/DD155990.DTL.

Leitch, Thomas (1992) 'The World According to Teenpix', *Literature Film Quarterly*, 20:1, 43–8.

Lent, Tina Olsin (1995) 'Romantic Love and Friendship: The Redefinition of Gender Relations in Screwball Comedy', in Kristine Brunovska Karnick and Henry Jenkins (eds) *Classical Hollywood Comedy*, London and New York: Routledge, 314-31.

Levy, Ariel (2005) *Female Chauvinist Pigs: Women and The Rise Of Raunch Culture*, New York: Simon & Schuster.

McGale, Lesley (2003) 'The Comedy of Steve Martin', unpublished PhD thesis, Aberbeen: University of Aberdeen.

McGuire, William (ed.) (1979) *The Freud/Jung Letters*, London: Picador.

McWilliam, Kelly (forthcoming 2008) *When Carrie Met Sally*, London: I.B.Tauris.

Meyer, Moe (ed.) (1994) *The Politics and Poetics of Camp*, London: Routledge.

Michael, Charlie (2005) 'Why the French Love . . . Adam Sandler?: *Punch-Drunk Love* and the Poetics of Comedian Comedy', conference paper, London: Society for Cinema and Media Studies.

Millar, Stuart (1997) 'Magic of the Movies', *Guardian*, 24 June, 14-15.

Mishra, Vijay (2002), *Bollywood Cinema: Temples of Desire*, London: Routledge.

—— (2006) 'Bollywood Cinema: "A Critical Genealogy"', *Working Paper 20*, Asian Studies Institute, Victoria University of Wellington, 1-34.

Mitchell, Elvis (2004) 'Washing that Girl Out of his Head', *New York Times*, 19 March, available at http://movies2.nytimes.com/mem/movies/review.html?titlel=Eternal%20Sunshine%20of%20the%20Spotless%20Mind%20(Movie).

Mizejewski, Linda (2004) *Hardboiled and High Heeled: The Woman Detective in Popular Culture*, New York: Routledge.

Modleski, Tania (1991) *Feminism without Women: Culture and Criticism in a 'Postfeminist' Age*, London and New York: Routledge.

—— (1994) *Loving With a Vengeance: Mass-Produced Fantasies for Women*, London and New York: Routledge.

—— (1999) *Old Wives' Tales: Feminist Re-Visions of Film and Other Fictions*, London: I.B.Tauris.

Murphy, Robert (1986) 'Under the Shadow of Hollywood', in Charles Barr (ed.) *All Our Yesterdays*, London: BFI, 47-71.

—— (2000) 'A Path Through the Moral Maze', in Robert Murphy (ed.) *British Cinema of the 90s*, London: BFI, 1-16.

National Park Foundation (2006-7) Official Guide to Ellis Island and Statue of Liberty, 24th edn, available from Ellis Island administration.

Nayar, Sheila J. (2004) 'Invisible Representation: The Oral Contours of a National Popular Cinema', *Film Quarterly*, 57:3, 13-23.

Neale, Steve (1992) 'The Big Romance or Something Wild?: Romantic Comedy Today', *Screen*, 33:3, Autumn, 284-99.

Negra, Diane (2006) 'Where the Boys Are: Postfeminism and the New Single Man', *Flow TV*, 4:3, available at http://flowtv.org/?p=223.

O'Day, Marc (2004) 'Beauty in Motion: Gender, Spectacle and Action Babe Cinema', in Yvonne Tasker (ed.) *Action and Adventure Cinema*, London: Routledge, 201-18.

Orenstein, Arbie (1967) 'Maurice Ravel's Creative Process', *Musical Quarterly*, 53, 467-91.

Parker, Alan (2002) 'Building a Sustainable UK Film Industry', speech given to BAFTA, 5 November, available at http://ukfc.artlogic.net/usr/ukfcdownloads/102/BaSFI.pdf.

Patnaik, Priyadarshi (2004) *Rasa in Aesthetics: An Application of Rasa Theory to Modern Western Literature*, reprint, New Delhi: D.K. Printworld.

Paul, William (1994) *Laughing Screaming: Modern Hollywood Horror and Comedy*, New York: Columbia University Press.

—— (2002) 'The Impossibility of Romance: Hollywood Comedy 1978-1999', in Steve Neale (ed.) *Genre and Contemporary Hollywood*, London: BFI, 117-29.

Phillips, Adam (1993) *On Kissing, Tickling and Being Bored*, London: Faber and Faber.

Phillips, Adam (1994) *On Flirtation*, London: Faber and Faber.

Pinel, Vincent (2000) *Ecoles, genres et mouvements au cinéma*, Paris: Larousse Bordas.

Pomerance, Murray (2007) *City That Never Sleeps: New York and the Filmic Imagination*, New Brunswick, NJ, and London: Rutgers University Press.

Potter, Cherry (2002) *I Love You But . . .: Romance, Comedy and the Movies*, London: Methuen.

Projansky, Sarah (2001) *Watching Rape: Film and Television in Postfeminist Culture*, New York: New York University Press.

Radner, Hilary (1993) '"Pretty Is as Pretty Does": Free Enterprise and the Marriage Plot', in Jim Collins, Hilary Radner and Ava Preacher Collins (eds) *Film Theory Goes to the Movies*, New York: Routledge, 56-76.

—— (1995) *Shopping Around: Feminine Culture and the Pursuit of Pleasure*, New York: Routledge.

Radway, Janice A. (1984) *Reading the Romance: Women, Patriarchy and Popular Literature*, Chapel Hill and London: University of North Carolina Press and Verso.

Rajadhyaksha, Ashish (2003) 'The Bollywoodization of the Indian Cinema: Cultural Nationalism in a Global Arena', *Inter-Asia Cultural Studies*, 4:1, 25-39.

Rauch, Jonathan (2004) *Gay Marriage*, New York: Times Books, Henry Holt and Co.

Redmond, Sean (2006) 'Intimate Fame Everywhere', in Su Holmes and Sean Redmond (eds) *Framing Celebrity: New Directions in Celebrity Culture*, London: Routledge, 27-43.

Reid, Mark (2003) 'The Black Gangster Film', in Barry Keith Grant (ed.) *Film Genre Reader III*, Austin: University of Texas Press, 472-89.

Reiner, Rob (2006) voiceover commentary and 'The Making of WHMS: *How Harry Met Sally*', *When Harry Met Sally* DVD special feature, MGM.

Reitano, Joanne (2006) *The Restless City: A Short History of New York From Colonial Times to the Present*, London and New York: Routledge.

Rich, Adrienne (1986) 'Compulsory Heterosexuality and Lesbian Existence', in *Blood, Bread, and Poetry*, New York: Norton Paperback.

Rich, Frank (1972) 'Woody Allen Wipes the Smile off his Face', *Esquire*, May, 72-6, 148-9.

Riviere, Joan (1986 [1929]) 'Womanliness as Masquerade', in Victor Burgin, James Donald and Cora Kaplan (eds) *Formations of Fantasy*, London: Routledge, 35-44.

Roeper, Richard (2006) *'Looking for Kitty'*, audio review, available at http://www.rottentomatoes.com/source-395/?letter=l&sortby=movie&page=2.

Rollet, Brigitte (1998) *Coline Serreau*, Manchester: Manchester University Press.

—— (1999) 'Unruly Woman?: Josiane Baslasko and French Comedy', in Phil Powrie (ed.) *Contemporary French Cinema: Continuity and Difference*, Oxford: Oxford University Press, 127-36.

Romney, Jonathan (1997) *Short Orders: Film Writing*, London: Serpent's Tail.

Rowe, Kathleen (1995a) 'Comedy, Melodrama and Gender: Theorizing the Genres of Laughter', in Kristine Brunovska Karnick and Henry Jenkins (eds), *Classical Hollywood Comedy*, New York: Routledge, 39-59.

—— (1995b) *The Unruly Woman: Gender and The Genres of Laughter*, Texas: University of Texas Press.

Rubinfeld, Mark D. (2001) *Bound to Bond: Gender, Genre, and the Hollywood Romantic Comedy*, Westport, CT: Praeger.

Said, Edward (1993) *Culture and Imperialism*, London: Chatto and Windus.

Salholz, Eloise (1990) 'The Future of Gay America', *Newsweek*, 12 March, 20-5.

Samuel, Katie (2006) 'J-Lo's Baby Secret's Out!', *Closer*, 9-15 September, 14.

Sanders, James (2004) 'Sex and the Mythic Movie Dream of New York City', *New York Times*, 22 February, 2, 17.

Schatz, Thomas (1981) *Hollywood Genres: Formulas, Filmmaking, and the Studio System*, New York: Random House.

Schruers, Fred (2003) 'Isn't He Romantic', *Premiere*, October, 82-6.

Scott, A.O. (2001) 'A Green Light for Love at the Frazzled Corners of Life', review, *New York Times*, 21 November, available at http://movies2.nytimes.com/mem/movies/review.html?_r=1&res=9805EEDF1F3BF932A15752C1A9679C8B63&oref=slogin.

Seidman, Steve (1981) *Comedian Comedy: A Tradition in Hollywood Film*, Michigan: UMI Research Press.

Sellier, Geneviève (2004a) 'Le cinéma d'auteur-e français, ou l'intime comme évitement du social', in Geneviève Sellier and Eliane Viennot (eds) *Culture d'élite, culture de masse et différence des sexes*, Paris: L'Harmattan, 105-21.

—— (2004b) 'Cinéma commercial, cinéma d'élite: vers un dépassement?', in Jean-Pierre Esquenazi (ed.) *Cinéma contemporain, état des lieux*, Paris: L'Harmattan, 167-79.

Shary, Timothy (2002) *Generation Multiplex: The Image of Youth in Contemporary American Cinema*, Austin: University of Texas Press.

—— (2005) *Teen Movies: American Youth on Screen*, London: Wallflower Press.

Smith, Anna (2005) '*Miss Congeniality 2: Armed and Fabulous*', *Sight and Sound*, 15:5, May, 65-6.

Smith, Paul Julian (2004) 'Tokyo Drifters', *Sight and Sound*, 14:1, January, 12-16.

Spargo, Tamsin (1999) *Foucault and Queer Theory*, Cambridge: Icon Books.

Spector Person, Ethel (1989) *Dreams of Love and Fateful Encounters: The Power of Romantic Passion*, London: Penguin.

—— (1995) *By Force of Fantasy*, London: Penguin.

Speed, Lesley (1995) 'Good Fun and Bad Hair Days: Girls in Teen Film', *Metro*, 101, 24-30.

—— (2000) 'Together in Electric Dreams: Films Revisiting 1980s Youth', *Journal of Popular Film and Television*, 28:1, Spring, 22-9.

Stacey, Jackie (1990) 'Romance', in Susannah Radstone and Annette Kuhn (eds) *The Women's Companion to International Film*, London: Virago, 345-6.

Steinherr, Alessandra (2004) 'Meeting Jennifer Lopez', *Cosmopolitan* (UK), February, 152-4.

Stewart, Susan (1993) *On Longing: Narratives of the Miniature, the Gigantic, the Souvenir, the Collection*, Durham, NC, and London, Duke University Press.

Street, Sarah (2002) *Transatlantic Crossings: British Feature Films in the USA*, New York: Continuum.

Sullivan, Andrew (1997) *Same-Sex Marriage: Pro and Con*, New York: Vintage Books.

Sullivan, Nikki (2003) *A Critical Introduction to Queer Theory*, Edinburgh: Edinburgh University Press.

Sutton, Paul (2004) 'Afterwardsness in Film', *Journal for Cultural Research*, 8:3, 385-405.

Tasker, Yvonne (1998) *Working Girls: Gender and Sexuality in Popular Cinema*, London: Routledge.

—— (2004) 'Family/Romance: Reading the Post-Feminist Action Heroine', 31 January, available at http://www.uta.fi/laitokset/tiedotus/ Mediatutkimuspaivat/PAPERIT/MTP04YvonneTasker.pdf.

—— (2006) 'Fantasizing Race and Gender in Contemporary US Action Cinema', in Linda Ruth Williams and Michael Hammond (eds) *Contemporary American Cinema*, Maidenhead: Open University Press, 410-28.

Theweleit, Klaus (1994) *Object-Choice: All You Need is Love . . .*, trans. Malcolm R. Green, London: Verso.

Thompson, Kristin (1985) *Exporting Entertainment*, London: BFI.

—— (1999) *Storytelling in the New Hollywood: Understanding Classical Narrative Technique*, Cambridge, MA: Harvard University Press.

Tobias, Scott (2002) '*Sidewalks of New York*', review, A.V. Club, available at http://www.avclub.com/content/node/6056.

Tookey, Christopher (2001) '*Miss Congeniality*', *Daily Mail*, 23 March, 53.

Toynbee, Polly (2003) 'It's Only a Movie, But it Could Teach Blair A Lot,

Actually', *Guardian*, 3 December, available at http://www.guardian.co.uk/print/0,3858,4810754-103677,00.html.

Toumarkine, Doris (2005) '*Miss Congeniality 2: Armed and Fabulous*', *Film Journal International*, May, 40-1.

Tracy, Kathleen (2000) *Jennifer Lopez*, Toronto: ECW Press.

Tran, Mark (2006) 'The Not-So-Special Relationship', *Guardian*, 30 November, available at http://www.guardian.co.uk/international/story/0,,1960873,00.html.

Travers, James (2004) '*Décalage horaire*', review, available at http://www.filmsdefrance.com/FDF_Decalage_horaire_rev.html.

UK Film Council (2005-6) *Statistical Yearbook 2005-2006*, online, available at http://rsu.ukfilmcouncil.org.uk/?y=2005&c=3.

Variety (2006) *Box Office Film Search Results*, available at http://www.variety.com/index.asp?layout=filmsearch_exact&dept=Film&movieID19373.

Vincendeau, Ginette (1989) 'Daddy's Girl, Oedipal Narratives in 1930s French Films', *Iris*, 5:8, January, 71-81.

—— (1995) *Encyclopaedia of European Cinema*, London: Cassel and BFI.

—— (1996) *The Companion to French Cinema*, London: Cassel and BFI.

Walker, Alexander (1968 [1966]) *Sex in The Movies* (originally published as *The Celluloid Sacrifice*), London: Pelican Books.

Wardle, Lynn D., Mark Strasser, William C. Duncan and David Orgon Coolidge (eds) (2003) *Marriage and Same-Sex Unions: A Debate*, Westport, CT: Praeger.

Watson, Neil (2000) 'Hollywood UK', in Robert Murphy (ed.) *British Cinema of the 90s*, London: BFI, 80-7.

Wiegman, Robyn (2002) 'Unmaking: Men and Masculinity in Feminist Theory', in Judith Kegan Gardiner (ed.) *Masculinity Studies and Feminist Theory*, New York: Columbia University Press, 31-59.

Whedonesque (2007) 'Buffy March Madness', *whedonesque.com*, available at http://whedonesque.com/comments/12621.

Williams, Linda (1991) 'Film Bodies: Gender, Genre, and Excess', *Film Quarterly*, 44:4, Summer, 2-13.

Winter, Jessica (2001) 'Imitations of Life: *Bangkok Dangerous; Sidewalks of New York*', review, *The Village Voice*, available in the USA at http://www.villagevoice.com/film/0147,winter,30088,20.html.

Wizard Staff (2007) 'Slay Ride: Joss Whedon Assembles a Squad of All-Star Slayers to Stake his Claim on *Buffy*'s "Season 8" Comic Series', *Wizarduniverse.com*, available at http://www.wizarduniverse.com/magazine/wizard/003709924.cfm, accessed 17 April 2007.

Working Title Films (2003) *Laundrettes and Lovers: From Storyboard to Billboard*, London: Boxtree.

Zacharek, Stephanie (1999) 'Is This As Good As It Gets?', *Salon*, 9 June, available at http://www.salon.com/ent/feature/1999/06/09/romantic/index.html.

~ Index